CW00920059

MICROSOFT®
ACCESS 2002
VISUAL BASIC®
FOR APPLICATIONS
STEP BY STEP

Evan Callahan

PUBLISHED BY
Microsoft Press
A Division of Microsoft Corporation
One Microsoft Way
Redmond, Washington 98052-6399

Library of Congress Cataloging-in-Publication Data
Callahan, Evan, 1966-
    Microsoft Access 2002 Visual Basic for Applications Step by Step / Evan Callahan.
        p. cm.
    Includes index.
    ISBN 0-7356-1358-3
    1. Microsoft Access. 2. Microsoft Visual Basic. 3. Database management. I. Title.

  QA76.9.D3 C3627 2001
  005.75'65--dc21   2001042551

Printed and bound in the United States of America.

1 2 3 4 5 6 7 8 9   QWT   6 5 4 3 2 1

Distributed in Canada by Penguin Books Canada Limited.

A CIP catalogue record for this book is available from the British Library.

Microsoft Press books are available through booksellers and distributors worldwide. For further informa-
tion about international editions, contact your local Microsoft Corporation office or contact Microsoft
Press International directly at fax (425) 706-7329. Visit our Web site at www.microsoft.com/mspress.
Send comments to *mspinput@microsoft.com*.

Acquisitions Editor: Kong Cheung
Project Editor: Jean Cockburn
Technical Editor: Brian Johnson

Body Part No. X08-04875

Contents

Part 1 Automating Database Tasks

Contents

Part 2 Programming in Visual Basic

Part 3 Creating a Custom Application

Acknowledgments

Writing a book, like learning a new computer program, is an exciting and daunting experience. Looking back on the hours I spend tapping away at the keyboard, I like to recall the many people I've had the good fortune to work with, and those who make my life outside of work so fulfilling.

Special thanks go to Casey Doyle, who approached me about writing for Microsoft Press and helped me develop a vision for this book, and to Pm Weizenbaum, whose editor's pen added so much to my first edition. And for their efforts shaping this fourth edition, thanks to Kong Cheung and Jean Cockburn. Thanks also to the editorial and production team at Microsoft Press: Cheryl Penner, Becky Wendling, Brian Johnson, Gina Cassill, Kerri DeVault, Rob Nance, and Bill Teel.

Most importantly, I'm happy to thank my wonderful wife, Margaret Delp; my parents, Jim and Judy Callahan; and my sister, Melissa Callahan for all their love and support. Any inspiration you find hidden in these pages comes from their influence in my life.

Introduction

This book teaches you how to create database applications in Microsoft Access 2002. If you're using Access and are ready to move on to Microsoft Visual Basic programming, this is the book for you.

Access has taken the database world by storm with its ease of use for storing and retrieving information. As you'll see, it's also quite possibly the most productive tool available for creating database applications. Access uses a powerful programming language, Visual Basic—the same language you'll find in other Microsoft Office applications, or that you may have used to develop applications for Microsoft Windows or the Web. Using the programming techniques you'll learn in this book, you'll be able to take advantage of Access in new ways, creating your own custom solutions quickly. What's more, if you're working on databases for others to use, you'll learn to create a foolproof user interface to help them get their work done easily.

Microsoft Access 2002 Visual Basic Step by Step walks you through tasks one at a time, keeping you on track with clear instructions and frequent illustrations of what you should see on the screen. In each chapter, you'll solve a new puzzle and become familiar with another important area of Access or Visual Basic.

The book is divided into four parts:

Part 1: Automating Database Tasks The book starts you off with practical, straightforward solutions for customizing your Access databases. It also introduces Visual Basic for Applications—the programming language in Access—and teaches the basic concepts you'll need along the way. In this part, you'll use Access wizards and simple programming code to create and customize a contact management database.

Part 2: Programming in Visual Basic This part teaches you to use the programming tools built into Access to write and debug Visual Basic code. You'll continue using the contact management database, creating additional features as you go.

Part 3: Creating a Custom Application This part walks you through the process of creating a custom user interface for a database application. You'll work with a new database that manages subscriptions to a journal, preparing it to be delivered to users. Along the way, you'll create a dialog box, make forms and reports work together seamlessly, and add custom menus and toolbars.

Part 4: Working with Data and Objects The last part of the book takes you further into the underlying structure of Access. It teaches you how to take direct control of objects such as forms, reports, and databases—and how to manipulate objects in another application, such as Microsoft Word. In this part, you'll use advanced programming techniques to add features to an issue-tracking application.

Important

This book is designed for use with Microsoft Access 2002 (version 10) or Microsoft Office XP Professional, Professional Special Edition, or Developer for the Windows 98, Windows NT 4.0, Windows 2000, Windows Me, or Windows XP operating systems. To find out what software you're running, you can check the product package or you can start the software, click the Help menu, and then click About Microsoft Access. If your software is not compatible with this book, a *Step by Step* or *Fundamentals* book for your software is probably available. Please visit our World Wide Web site at *http://www.microsoft.com/mspress* or call 1-800-MSPRESS for more information.

For more information about Microsoft Access, see *http://www.microsoft.com/office/access.*

Getting Help

This book is designed for Access users who are starting to write macros and for programmers familiar with another programming system (such as Microsoft Visual Basic or COBOL) who want to use Access as a platform for developing applications. You'll get the most out of this book if you're already familiar with the basic capabilities of Microsoft Excel, such as entering values and formulas into worksheets.

Learning about Visual Basic for Applications (VBA) and about how Access works with VBA can seem overwhelming. That's why you need this book. It starts with simple, practical tasks and then takes you on to advanced concepts and powerful applications.

Every effort has been made to ensure the accuracy of this book and the contents of its CD-ROM. If you do run into problems, please contact the appropriate source for help and assistance.

Getting Help with This Book and Its CD-ROM

If your question or issue concerns the content of this book or its companion CD-ROM, please first search the online Microsoft Knowledge Base, which provides support information for known errors in or corrections to this book, at the following Web site:

http://www.microsoft.com/mspress/support/search.asp

If you do not find your answer in the online Knowledge Base, send your comments or questions to Microsoft Press Technical Support at

mspinput@microsoft.com

Getting Help with Microsoft Access 2002

If your question is about a Microsoft software product, including Access, and not about the content of this book, please search the Microsoft Knowledge Base at

http://support.microsoft.com/directory/

In the United States, Microsoft software product support issues not covered by the Microsoft Knowledge Base are addressed by Microsoft Product Support Services. The Microsoft software support options available from Microsoft Product Support Services are listed at

http://support.microsoft.com/directory/

Outside the United States, for support information specific to your location, please refer to the Worldwide Support menu on the Microsoft Product Support Services Web site for the site specific to your country at

http://support.microsoft.com/directory/

Help with Access and Visual Basic

Access has a vast online Help system that you can use to learn new topics or get answers to your individual questions. You'll find Help especially valuable as you learn to create applications with Access.

There isn't only reference information in Help—it also includes how-to information for nearly every task and graphical introductions to features of Access. Additionally, there is a complete reference topic on every function, method, property, and other element that you can use in Access. And as you'll see, Help has several innovative ways for you to locate the topics you need.

The Office Assistant, a friendly animated "character" that sits on top of your work, lets you find Help topics by typing in a question or phrase in your own words—you don't have to guess the exact words that are in the online index. This capability makes the Office Assistant the most useful method for getting help if you have a question while you work. For example, if you wanted to know about displaying a list of values, you could simply type *looking up values*. The Office Assistant will interpret your text and display a list of topics.

Microsoft
Access Help

[?]

To display the Office Assistant, click the Microsoft Access Help button on the toolbar. Anytime you want to ask a question, just click the Office Assistant, type the text of your question, and then click Search. If you're working on Visual Basic code in the Visual Basic window, the Office Assistant detects this and searches for programming topics instead of general topics.

Tip

While the animated Office Assistant is a lot of fun, you can access the same Help topics using the Contents and Answer Wizard tabs in the Help window—tools that are more powerful, because they allow you to browse through more results than the Office Assistant can show in its small window. For this reason, many advanced users and programmers prefer to turn off the Office Assistant altogether and navigate through Help topics using the Answer Wizard. To turn off the Office Assistant, click the Office Assistant, click Options, clear the Use The Office Assistant check box, and then click OK. After you've done this, clicking the Microsoft Access Help button (or the Help button in any Office application) bypasses the Office Assistant and goes straight to the Office Help window. If you miss having the company of the Office Assistant, you can always turn it back on—just click the Help menu, and then click Show The Office Assistant.

Using the Book's CD-ROM

The CD-ROM inside the back cover of this book contains all the practice files you'll use as you work through the exercises. For example, when you're learning how to use Visual Basic code in Access, you'll open one of the practice files—a database containing several tables, forms, and reports created for use with this book—and then customize one of the existing forms it contains. By using practice files, you won't waste time creating the samples used in the chapters—instead, you can jump right in and concentrate on learning how to use Access 2002.

Important

The CD-ROM does not contain the Access 2002 software. You should purchase and install that program before using this book.

System Requirements

To use this book, you will need

- Microsoft Windows 98, Windows NT 4, Windows Millennium Edition, Windows 2000, or Windows XP
- Microsoft Access 2002
- Microsoft Word 2002 and Outlook 2002 (required for Chapter 14)

Installing the Practice Files

You need to install the practice files on your hard disk before you use them in the chapters' exercises. Follow these steps to prepare the CD's files for your use:

1   Insert the CD-ROM into the CD-ROM drive of your computer.

A starting menu appears.

Important

If the menu does not appear, start Windows Explorer. In the left pane, locate the icon for your CD-ROM and click the icon. In the right pane, double-click the file StartCd.exe.

2   On the starting menu, click Install Practice Files to launch the installation program.

3   Complete the installation program.

A folder named C:\Access VBA Practice Files will be installed on your hard disk.

Using the Practice Files

Each chapter's introduction lists the files that are needed for that chapter and explains any file preparation that you need to take care of before you start working through the chapter.

Each chapter explains how and when to use any practice files. The file or files that you'll need are indicated in the margin at the beginning of the chapter above the CD icon:

FileName

The following table lists each chapter's practice files.

Chapter	File Name
Chapter 1: Get Started Quickly with Wizards	Ch01 Client Data.txt
Chapter 2: Customize an Application with Visual Basic	Ch02 Contacts.mdb
Chapter 3: Find and Filter Records in a Form	Ch03 Contacts.mdb
Chapter 4: Respond to Data Entry Events	Ch04 Contacts.mdb
Chapter 5: Write Your Own Functions	Ch05 Contacts.mdb
Chapter 6: Monitor and debug Your Code	Ch06 Contacts.mdb
Chapter 7: Respond to Errors and Unexpected Conditions	Ch07 Contacts.mdb
Chapter 8: Gather Information in a Dialog Box	Ch08 Subscription.mdb
Chapter 9: Navigate Through Your Application	Ch09 Subscription.mdb
Chapter 10: Display Custom Menus and Toolbars	Ch10 Subscription.mdb
Chapter 11: Put Final Touches on an Application	Ch11 Subscription.mdb
Chapter 12: Explore Objects and Collections	Ch12 Issues.mdb
Chapter 13: Customize Reports with Visual Basic	Ch13 Issues.mdb
Chapter 14: Share Data with Other Applications	Ch14 Issues.mdb Ch14 Memo.dot
Chapter 15: Connect to the Web	Ch15 Issues.mdb Reassign.htm Reassign_files subfolder

Uninstalling the Practice Files

After you finish working through this book, you can uninstall the practice files to free up hard disk space.

Tip

If you saved any files outside the Access folder, they will not be deleted by the following uninstall process. You'll have to manually delete them.

To uninstall the practice files, follow these steps:

1 On the Windows task bar, click the Start button, point to Settings, and then click Control Panel.

2 Double-click the Add/Remove Programs icon.

3 Click Microsoft Access 2002 VBA SBS Files, and click Add/Remove. (If you're using Windows 2000 Professional, click the Remove or Change/Remove button.)

4 Click Yes when the confirmation dialog box appears.

Important

If you need additional help installing or uninstalling the practice files, please see the section "Getting Help" earlier in this book. Microsoft's product support does not provide support for this book or its CD-ROM.

Conventions and Features

You can save time when you use this book by understanding how the Step by Step series shows special instructions, keys to press, buttons to click, and so on.

Convention	Meaning
1 2	Numbered steps guide you through hands-on exercises in each topic.
●	A round bullet indicates an exercise that has only one step.
Filename.doc 	This icon at the beginning of a chapter lists the files that the lesson will use and explains any file preparation that needs to take place before starting the lesson. Practice files that you'll need to use in a topic's procedure are shown above the CD icon.
Tip	This section provides a helpful hint or shortcut that makes working through a task easier.
Important	This section points out information that you need to complete the procedure.
Troubleshooting	This section shows you how to fix a common problem.
Save 	When a button is referenced in a topic, a picture of the button appears in the margin area with a label.
Alt+Tab	A plus sign (+) between two key names means that you must press those keys at the same time. For example, "Press Alt+Tab" means that you hold down the Alt key while you press Tab.
Blue boldface type	Text that you are supposed to type appears in **blue boldface type** in the procedures.

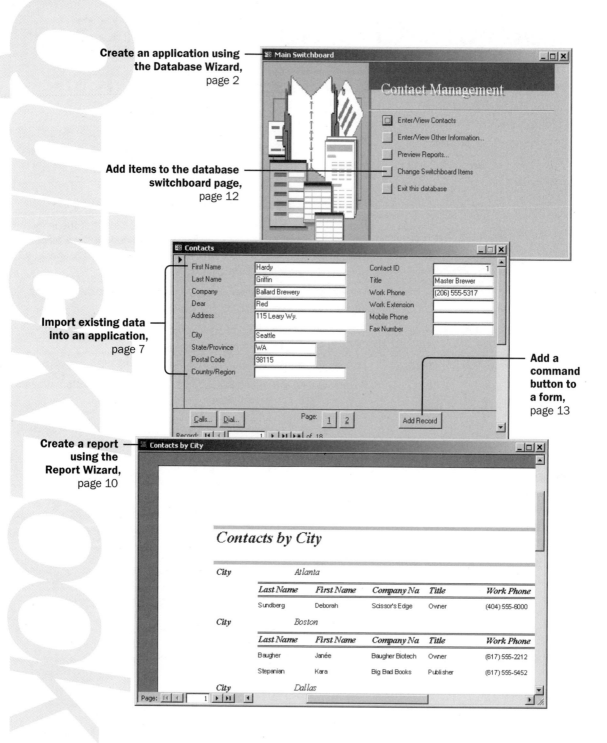

Create an application using the Database Wizard, page 2

Main Switchboard

Contact Management

- Enter/View Contacts
- Enter/View Other Information...
- Preview Reports...
- Change Switchboard Items
- Exit this database

Add items to the database switchboard page, page 12

Contacts

First Name	Hardy	
Last Name	Griffin	
Company	Ballard Brewery	
Dear	Red	
Address	115 Leary Wy.	
City	Seattle	
State/Province	WA	
Postal Code	98115	
Country/Region		

Contact ID	1
Title	Master Brewer
Work Phone	(206) 555-5317
Work Extension	
Mobile Phone	
Fax Number	

Import existing data into an application, page 7

Calls... Dial...   Page: 1 2   Add Record

Record: 1 of 18

Add a command button to a form, page 13

Create a report using the Report Wizard, page 10

Contacts by City

Contacts by City

City				
	Atlanta			
Last Name	**First Name**	**Company Na**	**Title**	**Work Phone**
Sundberg	Deborah	Scissor's Edge	Owner	(404) 555-6000
City	Boston			
Last Name	**First Name**	**Company Na**	**Title**	**Work Phone**
Baugher	Janée	Baugher Biotech	Owner	(617) 555-2212
Stepanian	Kara	Big Bad Books	Publisher	(617) 555-5452
City	Dallas			

Page: 1

Chapter 1
Get Started Quickly with Wizards

After completing this chapter, you will be able to:
- ✔ Create a database with the Database Wizard.
- ✔ Add an additional object to a wizard-created database.
- ✔ Create a command button with a wizard.

Ever try to write a letter or a report, but you just can't get the first word down on the page? A blank page is a big obstacle to progress. This is why we often seek help from others, and why brainstorming is such a good technique—ideas good or bad help you come up with other ideas, and next thing you know, you have a good start.

Like working from a blank page, creating a database application from scratch is a difficult task. In fact, before you can do any customizing or programming, you have to get most of your database in place and working! Fortunately, Microsoft Access includes several *wizards* that can help you get started quickly. Wizards ask you questions about the databases or objects you want to create and then create them for you. For example, the Database Wizard can create all the basic elements of a database application—tables, forms, reports, and other objects. After the wizard does its work, you can start using the application right away, or modify the user interface it creates, add new objects, even delete some of the objects it creates and replace them with your own.

In this chapter, you'll create an entire database application from scratch using the Database Wizard and customize the application in various ways.

Ch01 Client Data.txt

This chapter uses the practice file Ch01 Client Data.txt that you installed from the book's CD-ROM. For details about installing the practice files, see "Using the Book's CD-ROM" at the beginning of this book.

Getting Started
- ● Start Microsoft Access 2002. Click the Start button on the taskbar, point to Programs, and then click Microsoft Access.

Using Wizards for Application Development

It seems like wizards are popping up all over the place these days—usually to help users perform difficult tasks without needing to know all the ins and outs of the software. But there are several wizards included in Access that help make your job as an application developer much easier as well. You might want to try out the following wizards:

- Database Wizard
- Import Text Wizard
- Command Button Wizard
- Combo Box Wizard
- Option Group Wizard
- Database Splitter Wizard

These wizards will not only help you get work done faster, they'll also help you learn more about application development as you work. Even so, it's important to remember that anything you accomplish with a wizard you could do on your own in Access. In fact, the wizards themselves are written in the Visual Basic programming language and use ordinary Access forms for their interface, just like the applications you'll create.

As you learn to program Access using Visual Basic, you'll go much further than wizards can take you. But there's no sense turning down the help wizards have to offer.

Creating a Database Using the Database Wizard

The Database Wizard can create several common types of databases for business and personal use, including the following:

- Asset tracking
- Contact management
- Event management
- Expenses
- Inventory control
- Ledger
- Order entry
- Resource scheduling
- Service call management
- Time and billing

Tip

Even if the Database Wizard doesn't have just the database you need, the databases it creates may provide you with ideas for your own applications. Additionally, all the techniques you'll use to modify the wizard-created database apply equally to tables and forms you create on your own.

Create the Contacts Database

New

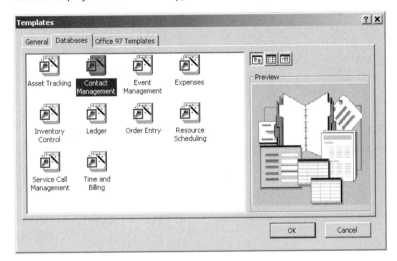

1   If the New File pane isn't already open at the right side of the Access window, click the New button.

2   In the New File pane, click General Templates.

Access displays the Templates dialog box.

3   Click the Databases tab.

Access displays icons for each type of database the Database Wizard can create for you.

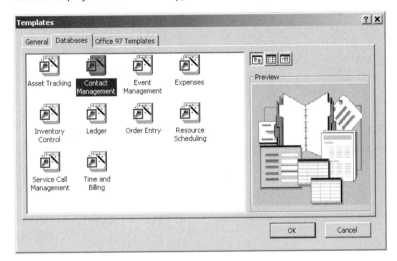

4   Double-click the Contact Management icon.

Access asks you to provide a file name and location for the new database file.

5   Move to the folder where you installed the practice files (probably C:\Access VB Practice Files).

6   In the File Name box, type **Ch01 Contacts**, and then click Create.

The Database Wizard starts up and lists the types of information that the Contact Management database will include.

7   Click Next.

The Database Wizard asks if you want to include any optional fields in your database. You won't need any optional fields, so you needn't make any changes.

8   Click Next.

The Database Wizard asks what style you want it to use when creating forms for the application.

9   Click Standard, and then click Finish.

The Database Wizard gets busy creating the Contacts database, which may take a minute or two. It then opens the *Switchboard* form, which shows up each time the database opens and guides users through the database. A *Switchboard* form provides buttons and text that open other forms and reports in an application—a sort of control center for users.

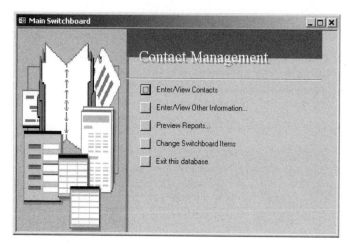

Tip

If the Access property sheet appears on top of the *Switchboard* form (because you left it open in another database), close it now so that it won't be in the way.

What Is a Database Application?

The Contacts database you've created is more than an ordinary Access database: with its *Switchboard* form and the other forms and reports it contains, the Contacts database is an *application*. This term refers to the fact that the database has its own custom-built user interface, designed especially to help users of the database navigate through its forms and reports and get work done with the database. Database applications range from those as simple as the Contacts database, which has a very specific job, to complete business solutions that contain many objects and large amounts of Visual Basic code.

Developing custom applications is the central purpose of programming Access with Visual Basic. Access databases can be tailored to solve specific user problems and make information easier to get into and out of the computer. Because its simple interface leaves plenty of room for customization, the Contacts database is a great place to start.

View the *Contacts* Form

The first item on the *Switchboard* form allows users to open the *Contacts* form, the main form in the application, where they can view and enter contact information in the database.

1   On the *Switchboard* form, click Enter/View Contacts.

The *Contacts* form opens, ready to accept new records. In addition to text boxes and other controls for all the information stored in the *Contacts* table, the form includes a footer with command buttons that users can click to perform common actions.

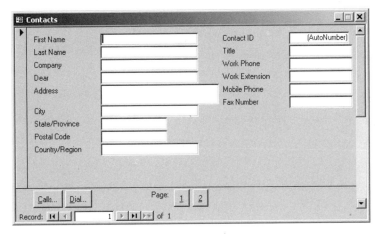

2 Close the *Contacts* form.

What Else Does the Wizard Create?

The Database Wizard creates all the bare essentials of a database application, along with a few goodies to help users navigate in the application. Here's a list of everything the Contacts database includes.

- Tables that store information about contacts, contact types, and phone calls (The wizard automatically sets table properties and creates relationships between the tables.)

- Forms for entering contact information and phone call information

- Reports that summarize information about contacts and phone calls

- The *Switchboard* form and the *Switchboard Items* table, which make up the application switchboard that you see when you open the Contacts database

Important

The *Switchboard* form that the wizard creates is a special form that you shouldn't try to change directly. It contains Visual Basic code that, along with the *Switchboard Items* table, displays the text you see on the form and makes the buttons work. Although you can't easily modify the way the *Switchboard* form works, you can add or remove buttons, as you'll see later in the chapter.

View the Objects in the Contacts Database

A quick look at the Database window shows all the objects the Database Wizard creates for the application. This should help you see that there's nothing magical about the database the wizard creates—it's just a few objects pulled together with a nice cover sheet.

Database Window

1 Click the Database Window button.

2 Click each of the Tables, Forms, and Reports shortcuts to view the four tables, seven forms, and two reports the wizard created.

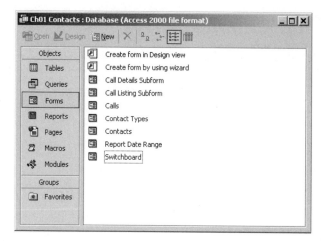

For many Access users, the tables, forms, and reports created by the Database Wizard are fine just the way they are. But as a database developer, you'll want to customize these objects and add new objects. Now that the Database Wizard has done its work, you can choose to keep all or part of the wizard-created database, adding or modifying objects to meet the needs of your users.

3 Minimize the Database window.

Click the Minimize button
to minimize the window.

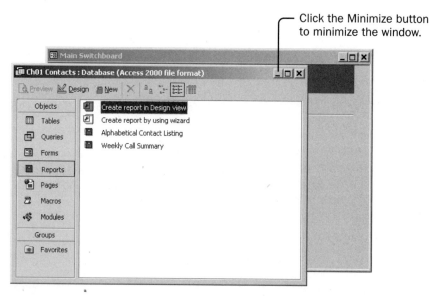

Tip

You might have noticed that the title bar of the database window says that the database is in Access 2000 format. In order to allow compatibility with the previous version, Access 2002 creates databases in the older format by default.

Entering Information into the Database

The first thing you need to do after creating a database is get some data into it. The Contact Management application lets you keep a list of the types of contacts you have so that you can categorize each contact you enter in the database. Before going any further, it makes sense to enter this preliminary information.

Enter Contact Types

You can use the *Switchboard* form to open a form for entering contact types.

1 On the *Switchboard* form, click Enter/View Other Information.

2 Click Enter/View Contact Types.

The *Contact Types* form opens, ready for a new record.

3 Type **Client**.

4 Click the New Record button.

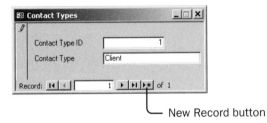

New Record button

Access saves the record and moves to a new record.

5 Type **Contractor**.

6 Click the New Record button, and then type **Personal**.

7 Close the *Contact Types* form. (Click the Close button in the upper right corner of the Form window.)

8 Click Return To Main Switchboard.

This returns you to the initial switchboard menu.

Now when you enter contacts, you'll be able to select one of these three types for each contact record.

Using Existing Data with a New Database

As you've seen, the *Contacts* form is empty—it doesn't display any records. But suppose you already have some contact information that you've been storing in another program, and you don't want to retype it into your Access application. One of the sample files included on the companion CD is Ch01 Client Data, a comma-delimited text file containing names, addresses, and phone numbers that you can add to the *Contacts* table. This file could easily have been exported from another spreadsheet or database system in order to move it into Access.

Before you import data into an existing table, you should make sure it's in a format that Access can accept. For example, you can import a Microsoft Excel worksheet, a dBASE file, or a text file. Additionally, the data in the file you want to import must be compatible with the structure of the table you're adding it to. If it isn't, you may need to edit the file before importing it, to get it ready for Access. For example, the Ch01 Client Data text file already has the correct field names for the *Contacts* table in the first row of the file, so Access can determine which fields to store data in.

Import Data into the *Contacts* Table

1 On the File menu, point to Get External Data and then click Import.

Access displays the Import dialog box, where you can select from a variety of data formats to import.

2 In the Files Of Type box, click Text Files.

The Import dialog box shows the Ch01 Client Data text file, which is provided with the practice files you installed.

3 Click Ch01 Client Data, and then click Import.

Access starts the Import Text Wizard, which helps you select options for importing delimited or fixed-width text files. The wizard automatically detects that the Ch01 Client Data text file is in Delimited format.

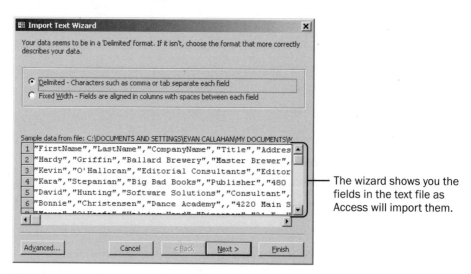

The wizard shows you the fields in the text file as Access will import them.

4 Click Next.

5 Click the First Row Contains Field Names option, and then click Next.

6 Click the In An Existing Table option, click the *Contacts* table in the drop-down list, and then click Finish.

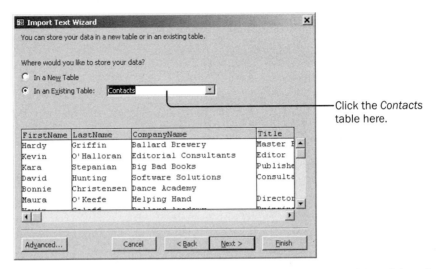

Click the *Contacts* table here.

Access appends records from the text file to the existing *Contacts* table and then displays a message indicating that it's finished successfully.

7   Click OK.

View New Records in the *Contacts* Form

Now, when users open the *Contacts* form, they'll see the client records you've added, and they'll be all set to start logging calls or adding additional contacts. You can also check to see that the contact types you added to the database are available on the form.

1   On the *Switchboard* form, click Enter/View Contacts.

The form displays the first record you imported into the *Contacts* table. Because the text file includes only a subset of the fields in the table, many of the text boxes are blank.

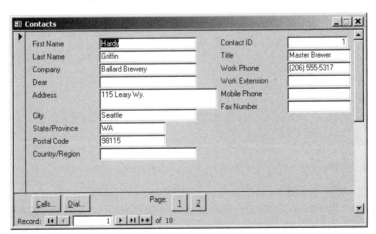

Database
Window

2 Click the Page 2 button in the form footer.

3 Click the down arrow next to the Contact Type box, and then click Client.

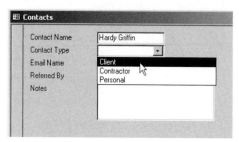

As you can see, the three types of contacts you added are available in the list.

4 Close the *Contacts* form.

Adding an Object to Your Application

Although the Database Wizard creates several useful forms and reports for the Contacts database, you're sure to need additional ones in your application. Suppose users need to print an up-to-date phone list for current contacts, organized by the city they're located in. You can create this form easily by using the Report Wizard.

Create a Contact List Report Organized by City

1 Click the Database Window button.

2 Click the Reports shortcut.

3 Double-click Create Report By Using Wizard.

The Report Wizard starts and asks you which fields you want on the report.

4 Click the down arrow next to the Tables/Queries box, and then click Table: Contacts.

5 In the Available Fields box, double-click the City field, followed by the LastName, FirstName, CompanyName, Title, and WorkPhone fields.

The Report Wizard adds the fields to the Selected Fields list.

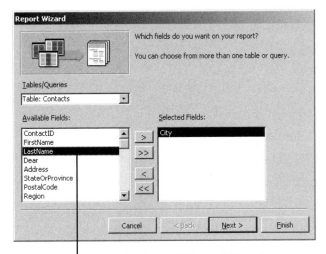

Double-click a field to add it to the report.

6 Click Next.

The wizard asks which fields you want to use for grouping data in the report.

7 Double-click the City field in the list, and then click Next.

8 The wizard asks which fields you want to sort in the report.

9 Click the LastName field in the first sorting box, click the FirstName field in the second sorting box, and then click Next.

The wizard asks how you want to lay out your report.

10 In the layout box, click Outline 1, and then click Next.

11 Choose a style for your report (or accept the default style), and then click Next.

The wizard asks what title you'd like for the report.

12 Type **Contacts By City**, and then click Finish.

The Report Wizard creates the Contacts By City report and displays it in Print Preview.

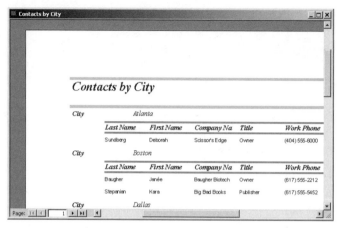

13 Close the report.

14 Minimize the Database window.

Add the New Report to the *Switchboard* Form

After you create new objects, you can add them to the *Switchboard* form that the Database Wizard created.

1 On the *Switchboard* form, click Change Switchboard Items.

Access starts the Switchboard Manager, which helps you modify the items available on the *Switchboard* form.

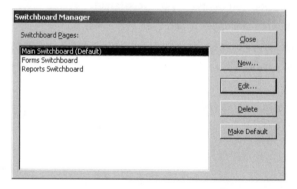

2 Click Reports Switchboard, and then click Edit.

3 Click New to display the Edit Switchboard Item dialog box.

4 In the Text box, type **Preview the Contacts By City Report**.

5 In the Command box, click Open Report.

6 In the Report box, click Contacts By City, and then click OK.

7 Click Preview The Contacts By City Report, and then click Move Up.

8 Click Close.

9 Click Close again.

The Switchboard Manager updates the *Switchboard Items* table so that your new item appears in the *Switchboard* form.

Try the New Switchboard Button

1 On the *Switchboard* form, click Preview Reports.

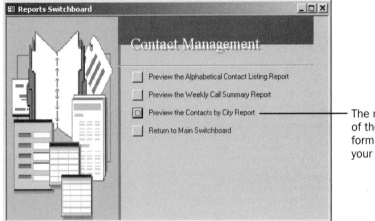

The reports page of the *Switchboard* form now shows your new option.

2 Click Preview The Contacts By City Report.

The button opens your report.

3 Close the report window.

4 On the *Switchboard* form, click Return To Main Switchboard.

Adding a Command Button to a Form

You've seen how the buttons on the *Switchboard* form help users open the forms and reports they need to use. In this way, buttons can help users navigate, tying objects together into a powerful application.

Once users get to the forms in your application, they'll want to find common tasks at their fingertips so that the forms are easy to use. One way to ensure this is by creating command buttons to automate tasks on your application forms. As you may have noticed, the Database Wizard already created some useful command buttons on the *Contacts* form.

Open the *Contacts* Form and Try a Command Button

1 On the *Switchboard* form, click Enter/View Contacts.

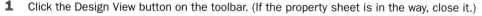

These buttons open other forms or perform common actions.

2 Click the Calls button.

The *Calls* form appears. When you click the button, it runs a few lines of Visual Basic code programmed by the Database Wizard. Next you'll add your own button to the *Contacts* form, which will work in much the same way.

3 Close the *Calls* form.

Create a Command Button to Move to a New Record

New Record

When you open the *Contacts* form, it displays the first existing contact record. If you want to enter a new contact, you can move to the new record at the end of the recordset by clicking the New Record button at the bottom of the form window. Or, you can use the Insert menu's New Record command with the same effect.

But suppose you want to make this command more accessible to other users so that they won't have to find it on the menu or know about the navigation buttons—after all, new users won't be as familiar with Access as you are. To bring this command to the forefront, go into the form's Design view and place another button in the form footer that performs this action whenever you click it. The Command Button Wizard makes the button work automatically by writing Visual Basic code for you.

Design View

1 Click the Design View button on the toolbar. (If the property sheet is in the way, close it.)

2 Scroll down in the form to display the Form Footer section.

3 If the toolbox isn't displayed, click the Toolbox button on the toolbar.

Toolbox

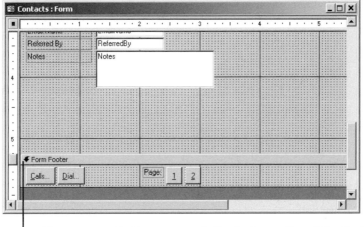

4 In the toolbox, make sure the Control Wizards tool is selected, and then click the Command Button tool.

The command buttons appear in the footer section of the *Contacts* form.

Control Wizards
tool (selected)

5 In the form footer, click just to the right of the Page 2 button.

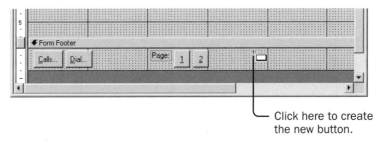

Click here to create
the new button.

The Command Button Wizard starts, asking what actions you want the new button to perform.

6 In the Categories list, click Record Operations.

15

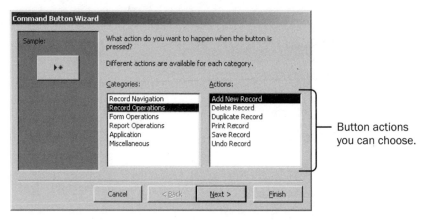

Button actions
you can choose.

7   In the Actions list, click Add New Record, and then click Next.

The wizard asks whether you want a picture or text on your button.

8   Click the Text option, and then click Next.

When you create your own buttons, you may want to use the pictures that the wizard provides for them—there's an extensive library of icons available to choose from. The wizard
even shows you a preview of the picture for the button you've chosen. In this case, however, the existing buttons on the *Contacts* form have text on them, so for the sake of consistency it makes sense to use text on the Add Record button as well.

9   Type **AddRecord** as the button name, and then click Finish.

Tip

Although the button's caption (Add Record) includes a space, you don't want to include a
space in the button's name. Throughout this book, you'll give objects names without spaces,
because this makes them easier to refer to in Visual Basic code.

The wizard finishes creating the button and places it on your form. Behind the scenes, it
also writes several lines of Visual Basic code and attaches them to the button for you.

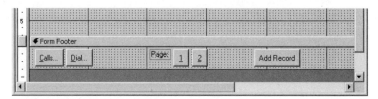

Try the New Command Button

Let's make sure the Add Record button does what you intended.

Form View

1   Click the Form View button on the toolbar.

2   Click the Add Record button.

Access moves to the new record in the *Contacts* table, displaying a fresh form for you to enter data into.

How Does the Button Work?

If you create a button without using the Command Button Wizard, the button won't do anything when you click it. What did the wizard do to make the button perform as you asked?

Here's how it works: Whenever you perform any action in a form—click a button or change a field's value, for example—an *event* occurs. Every event is a chance for your application to perform some action, such as running a macro or a Visual Basic procedure. When the Command Button Wizard created the button, it attached an *event procedure* to the button's Click event. This way, every time the button is clicked, the Visual Basic code in the event procedure runs, causing Access to perform the desired action—in this case, moving to the new record.

Creating Other Command Buttons

You can see how easy it is to customize your forms by adding command buttons. And, as you saw when using the Command Button Wizard, adding a record is just one type of operation you can create a button for—the Command Button Wizard can create buttons for all kinds of other tasks as well. Here are some other common operations you can create buttons for:

- Navigating between records
- Finding and filtering data
- Opening forms and reports
- Printing and other miscellaneous tasks

Using the Command Button Wizard is like "programming without programming"—even after programming with Access becomes second nature, you still may want to rely on the Command Button Wizard to give you a head start.

Close the *Contacts* Form

1 Close the form window.

2 When Access asks if you want to save changes to the *Contacts* form, click Yes.

Tip

When you save the form, Access saves not only the new button, but also the Visual Basic code that the wizard created for it. Because a form's module is stored along with the form, you don't have to save the Visual Basic code separately.

Moving from Macros to Visual Basic

You can learn to perform many database tasks using Visual Basic code. Some of these tasks can also be accomplished with Access macros. However, macros are much less flexible and powerful than Visual Basic—and because there are Visual Basic equivalents for just about every macro action, you can do nearly all the same things in Visual Basic that you can in macros. Because of Visual Basic's power and flexibility, the Database Wizard and the Command Button Wizard create Visual Basic event procedures, not macros.

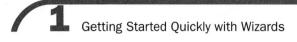

If you have existing macros in your databases, it will soon be time to convert them to Visual Basic—this way, you'll have a consistent strategy for customization in your applications. Access makes the move to Visual Basic easy by including commands that replace your macros with Visual Basic procedures. To convert an individual macro, click the macro in the Database window, click Save As/Export on the File menu, and then click Save As Visual Basic Module. To convert all the macros used with a form, open the form in Design view, point to Macro on the Tools menu, and then click Convert Form's Macros To Visual Basic. Access not only creates procedures for all the macros, it attaches them to the same events so that your application works just as before.

Chapter Wrap-Up

1 On the *Switchboard* form, click Exit This Database.

2 On the File menu, click Exit.

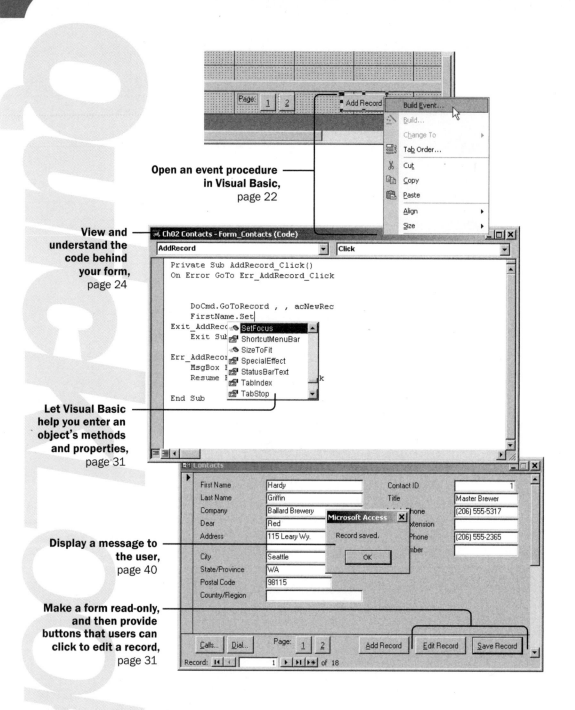

Open an event procedure in Visual Basic, page 22

View and understand the code behind your form, page 24

Let Visual Basic help you enter an object's methods and properties, page 31

Display a message to the user, page 40

Make a form read-only, and then provide buttons that users can click to edit a record, page 31

Page: 1 2 Add Record

Build Event...
Build...
Change To ▸
Tab Order...
Cut
Copy
Paste
Align ▸
Size ▸

Ch02 Contacts - Form_Contacts (Code)

AddRecord   Click

```
Private Sub AddRecord_Click()
On Error GoTo Err_AddRecord_Click


    DoCmd.GoToRecord , , acNewRec
    FirstName.Set
Exit_AddRecor  SetFocus
    Exit Su     ShortcutMenuBar
                SizeToFit
                SpecialEffect
Err_AddRecor    StatusBarText
    MsgBox      TabIndex
    Resume      TabStop           k

End Sub
```

Contacts

First Name   Hardy   Contact ID   1
Last Name   Griffin   Title   Master Brewer
Company   Ballard Brewery   hone (206) 555-5317
Dear   Red   xtension
Address   115 Leary Wy.   Phone (206) 555-2365
                                 mber

Microsoft Access ✕
Record saved.
OK

City   Seattle
State/Province WA
Postal Code   98115
Country/Region

Calls... Dial... Page: 1 2   Add Record   Edit Record   Save Record
Record: ◄◄ ◄ 1 ► ►◄ ►* of 18

Chapter 2
Customize an Application with Visual Basic

After completing this chapter, you will be able to:

✔ View and understand the Visual Basic code created by the Command Button Wizard.

✔ Edit code in the Visual Basic window.

✔ Set form and control properties using Visual Basic code.

✔ Display a message box.

When you take the city bus around town, trip planning is of the utmost importance. Where does the bus stop? How close does it get you to your destination? Like it or not, the bus follows a predetermined route. But wouldn't it be nice if you had complete control of the bus route? You could just sit near the bus driver and say, "Take a left at the next light, then head that way for half a mile or so—I'll get off at the second building on the right."

We all love to be in control of our situation—a characteristic especially true of computer users and programmers. If there's one type of complaint you'll hear from computer users, it's along the lines of, "This machine doesn't let me do what I want it to," or "I sure wish I could make the software work a different way." Working with Microsoft Access is no exception. Sure, you can get lots of work done without too much extra effort, and you can even customize the way your application looks and behaves. But if you want it to work a specific way, or if you're developing an application for others who have specific needs, it's time to get into Microsoft Visual Basic. It takes more work to customize an application, but there are unlimited possibilities when you make the effort to program your own solutions in Visual Basic.

In this chapter, you'll start taking control—telling the application how to work, rather than following the rules built into Access.

Ch02
Contacts.mdb

This chapter uses the practice file Ch02 Contacts.mdb that you installed from the book's CD-ROM. For details about installing the practice files, see "Using the Book's CD-ROM" at the beginning of this book.

Getting Started

● Start Access and open the Ch02 Contacts database in the practice files folder.

Customizing a Command Button

Usually when you create a button using the Command Button Wizard, the button works as planned. But what if you create a button with a wizard and it doesn't work quite right? Or what if the wizard doesn't offer a button that does what you want? You've probably guessed by now: the answer lies in the Visual Basic code that makes the button work.

In this section, you'll open the Visual Basic event procedure for the Add Record button. When you do, you'll get your first look at the Visual Basic window, which contains all the tools and commands for creating Visual Basic code in Access or other Microsoft Office applications. After exploring the Visual Basic code for the Add Record button, you'll write your first line of code, making a small improvement to the code the wizard created.

Open the *Contacts* Form

● On the main *Switchboard* form, click Enter/View Contacts.

The *Contacts* form displays the first record in the recordset.

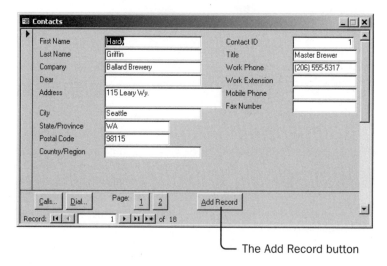

The Add Record button

Open an Event Procedure in Visual Basic

Next you'll take a look at the event procedure that makes the Add Record button work.

Design View
1 Click the Design View button.

Now you'll tell Access to open the button's event procedure in Visual Basic.

2 Scroll down in the form to display the form footer.

3 With the right mouse button, click the Add Record button.

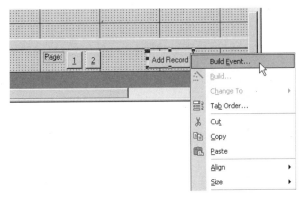

4 Click Build Event.

The Build Event command tells Access to open the Visual Basic window and display the default event procedure for the selected object. For a command button, the default event procedure is the *Click* event procedure, so the Visual Basic code window shows the *AddRecord_Click* procedure.

The Visual Basic window appears whenever
you ask to view your application's code.

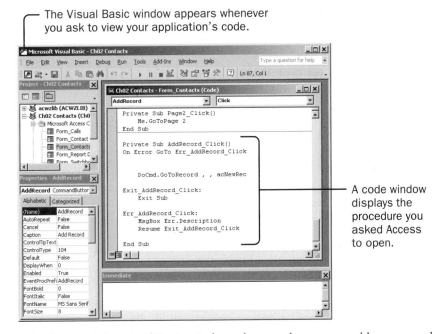

A code window
displays the
procedure you
asked Access
to open.

Take a look around the Visual Basic window—browse the menus and hover over the toolbar buttons to view their ScreenTips. This is where you'll be spending a lot of your time as you learn more about programming with Access.

Viewing the Visual Basic Code Behind Your Application

Every Access database application has a Visual Basic *project* that stores all its Visual Basic code. When you first view or run code in a database, Visual Basic opens its associated project. Projects in turn contain *modules*, each storing code for a different purpose. The Project window, displayed by default in the upper left corner of the Visual Basic window, provides a table of contents for the modules in your application.

The project window displays a list of all the modules that can contain Visual Basic code for your application.

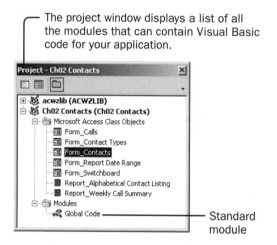

Standard module

Each form and report in a database has its own attached form module or report module for storing Visual Basic code—for example, the code that the wizard created for your button is stored in the form module for the *Contacts* form. Most Visual Basic code you'll write will belong to an individual form or report; however, if you write code that applies to more than one form or report, you can store it in one or more standard modules, using separate modules to group code for different purposes.

Tip

When you view form or report modules or read about them in the Access documentation, you may see them referred to as *class modules*. For the purposes of this book, you needn't concern yourself with the meaning of this phrase (it's borrowed from object-oriented computer science); just remember that form and report modules are in the larger category of class modules, while standard modules are not.

Within your application's modules, Visual Basic code comes in units called *procedures*, each performing a single task—for example, the code that responds to the clicking of the Add Record button is one procedure. A module can contain many procedures, one for each event you want to respond to or each task you want to perform.

Take a Closer Look at the Button's *Click* Event Procedure

Let's focus on the event procedure that the Command Button Wizard created for the Add Record button. When you first open a module, Visual Basic displays all procedures in the module; if you scroll up and down in the Code window, you'll see several other Visual

Basic procedures that the Database Wizard created for the *Contacts* form. To simplify the display, you can switch from Full Module view to Procedure view so that the Code window displays only one procedure at a time.

● Click the Procedure View button (at the lower left corner of the Code window).

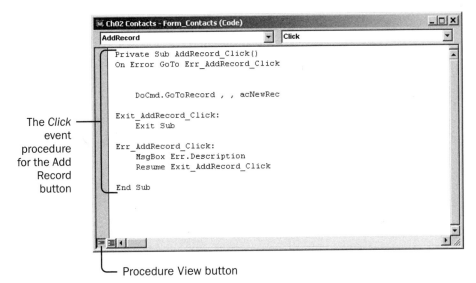

The *Click* event procedure for the Add Record button

Procedure View button

Now the window displays only one event procedure, the *AddRecord_Click* procedure.

The Visual Basic code in this procedure runs each time you click the Add Record button. The main attraction in the procedure is the following line of Visual Basic code, which tells Access to move to the new record:

```
DoCmd.GoToRecord , , acNewRec
```

Let's take apart this line piece by piece to understand how it works. Along the way, you'll learn a few important terms.

■ · Each word that Visual Basic recognizes as part of its programming language is called a *keyword*. There's a keyword for every statement, function, method, object, and property you use to program Access.

■ The first keyword in the line is *DoCmd* (read as "DO-command"), which you'll be seeing quite a bit when programming Access. *DoCmd* is an *object*—it shares this honorable position with other objects you're already familiar with, such as forms, reports, and controls. You use the *DoCmd* object to perform common actions in the Access interface, such as opening a form, printing a report, and choosing a menu command.

■ The second keyword is *GoToRecord*, which is a *method* of the *DoCmd* object. Each object that Access recognizes has its own set of methods that you use with that object. The methods of the *DoCmd* object are all the actions it allows you to perform—in fact, if you've created macros in Access, you'll recognize the things you can do with the *DoCmd* object as the actions available in the Macro window. The *GoToRecord* method, as its name suggests, tells Access to move to a specified record in the current recordset.

- To execute a method on an object, such as the *DoCmd* object, you type the object immediately followed by its method, separating the keywords with a period.

- What follows the *GoToRecord* method are its *arguments*, which provide any information that's necessary to carry out the method. The arguments for the *GoToRecord* method, for example, allow you to specify critical options such as which record you want to go to. You specify arguments by typing a space after the method and then typing the argument values separated by commas. If you don't need to specify one or more of the argument values, you can leave them out by simply typing a comma for each—for example, the line of code on the previous page skips the first two arguments, supplying only the third argument.

- Some methods, such as *GoToRecord*, have specially-defined *constant* values that you can enter as arguments. The argument *acNewRec* is a constant that tells the *GoToRecord* method to move to the new record at the end of the recordset. (Other options include moving to the next record or the first record in the recordset.) The constant *acNewRec* actually stands for the number 5—but the constant name is much easier to remember and makes your code easier to understand.

To sum up, this line of code uses the *GoToRecord* method of the *DoCmd* object to move to the specified record—in this case, to the new record.

What Else Did the Wizard Create?

Although the *DoCmd* line we dissected and discussed is what really does the job in the *AddRecord_Click* procedure, you may be wondering about the rest of the code the Command Button Wizard created. Here's the complete procedure:

```
Private Sub AddRecord_Click()
On Error GoTo Err_AddRecord_Click

    DoCmd.GoToRecord , , acNewRec

Exit_AddRecord_Click:
    Exit Sub
Err_AddRecord_Click:
    MsgBox Err.Description
    Resume Exit_AddRecord_Click
End Sub
```

The *Private Sub* and *End Sub* lines designate the beginning and end of the procedure. You'll see similar lines at the beginning and end of every event procedure—but because Visual Basic adds them to event procedures automatically, you won't usually have to think about them.

The remaining lines in the procedure—other than the *DoCmd* line—provide error handling for the procedure. The Command Button Wizard includes these error handling lines so that in case an error occurs, your application won't come to a halt. In Chapter 7, you'll learn how to add your own error-handling code to procedures; for now, rest assured that the wizard took care of it for you.

Modifying a Command Button Created Using the Wizard

The Command Button Wizard is a great tool for customizing your applications, but it isn't perfect. Although it creates buttons for a variety of tasks, it can't anticipate everything you'll want your buttons to do. Fortunately, if the wizard doesn't get it quite right, you can modify the buttons it creates to suit your application's needs. That's just what you'll do with the Add Record button in this section.

There's nothing really *wrong* with the Add Record button—when you click it, you jump to the new record in the recordset—but it could use some polishing. To get it just right, you'll first change a property and then add a line of Visual Basic code to the button's event procedure.

Add an Access Key for the Command Button

The Add Record button is missing a handy feature that the other buttons on the *Contacts* form already possess. The other buttons have *access keys*—underlined characters that let you "press" the buttons using the keyboard. Because many users like to have the option of using the keyboard instead of the mouse, it's always wise to make your applications work as well with the keyboard as with the mouse. For the Add Record button, you'll make the "A" into an access key.

To provide an access key for a button, all you have to do is edit the Caption property of the button—which determines the actual text shown on the button—to include the ampersand (&) symbol. This symbol in a button's caption tells Access that the next character in the caption is the access key for the button.

In order to make changes to the form, you'll first need to switch back from Visual Basic to Access. Visual Basic provides a toolbar button that brings Access to the front.

View Microsoft
Access

1 Click the View Microsoft Access button on the toolbar.

The *Contacts* form, still in Design view, comes to the front. Note that you don't have to close the form module in the Visual Basic window to continue working on the form in Access. Visual Basic stays open in the background, and you can switch back to it whenever you like.

2 With the right mouse button, click the Add Record button, and then click Properties on the shortcut menu.

Access displays the property sheet for the Add Record button.

3 Click the All tab in the property sheet.

4 In the Caption property box, click the left edge of the Add Record text (before the "A"), and then type **&**.

Adding the ampersand symbol tells the wizard to make the "A" in Add Record the access key for the button. This way, the user can press Alt+A to achieve the same effect as clicking the Add Record button. The button won't actually show the ampersand, but the "A" will appear underlined on the button.

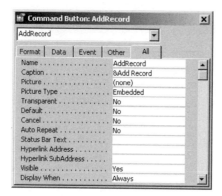

5   Close the property sheet.

Use the Access Key to Press the Command Button

Form View

1   Click the Form View button on the toolbar.

2   Press Alt+A.

Access moves to the new record in the *Contacts* table just as if you'd clicked the button using the mouse.

Add a Line to Your Event Procedure to Change the Focus

The Add Record button needs one other modification. Notice that after you press the button, the *focus* is still on the Add Record button—there's no current field or insertion point for typing data. In order to begin entering data, the user must first click the First Name field on the form. Ideally, you'd like the focus to move automatically to the first field in the record. To make it do this, you'll write a single line of Visual Basic code.

After you click the Add Record button...

...you want the focus to be on the first field so the user can begin entering data.

1 Switch back to Visual Basic. (On the Windows taskbar, click the Microsoft Visual Basic - Ch02 Contacts button.)

Visual Basic still displays the *AddRecord_Click* event procedure.

2 Click the blank line underneath the *DoCmd* line in the event procedure, press Tab, and then type **FirstName**.

FirstName is the name of a control object on your form. (Be sure not to insert a space into the name *FirstName*—the underlying control name doesn't contain a space.) Next, you'll specify a method that you want to use with the *FirstName* object: the *SetFocus* method. As you saw earlier in the chapter, you separate a method from its object with a period.

3 Type a period, and then type **Set**.

When you type a period after an object name, Visual Basic assumes that you want to follow the period with a method or property of that object. To help you enter a valid method or property, Visual Basic displays a list underneath the line you're typing. As you continue typing, the list automatically scrolls down to display entries that begin with the characters you type.

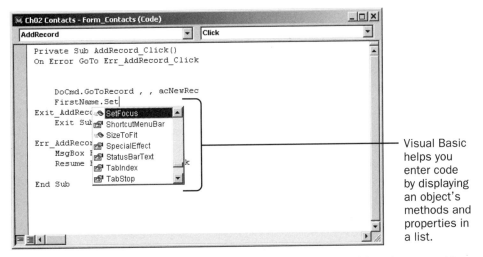

Visual Basic helps you enter code by displaying an object's methods and properties in a list.

Typing **Set** was enough to move to the *SetFocus* method in the list. Although you could continue typing code or double-click any method or property in the list, pressing the Spacebar is the easiest way to enter the selected item in the list.

4 Press the Spacebar, and then press Enter.

Now the line of Visual Basic code is complete:

```
FirstName.SetFocus
```

This line tells Access to set the focus to the specified form or control object—in this case, the *FirstName* control.

Here's the procedure with the new line of code:

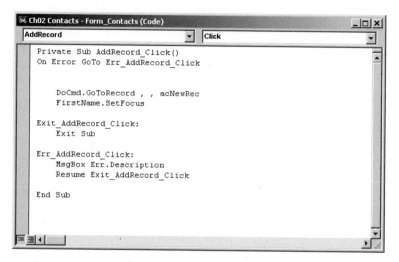

```
Ch02 Contacts - Form_Contacts (Code)                          _ □ ×
AddRecord                           ▼    Click                       ▼
    Private Sub AddRecord_Click()
    On Error GoTo Err_AddRecord_Click


        DoCmd.GoToRecord , , acNewRec
        FirstName.SetFocus

    Exit_AddRecord_Click:
        Exit Sub

    Err_AddRecord_Click:
        MsgBox Err.Description
        Resume Exit_AddRecord_Click

    End Sub
```

Test the Command Button

View Microsoft
Access

1 Switch to Access. (Click the View Microsoft Access button on the toolbar.)

2 Click the Add Record button.

Access moves to the new record in the *Contacts* form. This time, however, you'll notice that the insertion point is flashing in the First Name field, ready for the user to enter data.

As you continue to polish your application, you'll want to use the *SetFocus* method whenever you can anticipate what users will want to do next. Moving to a form or control with *SetFocus* is a great way to save extra clicks, making your application easier to use.

Editing a Form's Module While in Form View

You may have noticed that you were able to make your addition to the *Click* event procedure while the *Contacts* form was in Form view—in a sense, you changed the underlying design of the form without switching to Design view. This is a unique feature of Visual Basic as compared to many programming languages: you can edit a code module "on the fly" while the code in the module is potentially being used by the form. You'll soon discover how useful this can be, because you won't usually have to restart a complex application in order to make minor changes.

You'll discover as you work with Visual Basic that you can even edit code in a Visual Basic procedure while it's running. In cases where you make a significant change, Visual Basic might need to reset your code and start over. For now, however, you can appreciate the fact that you don't have to constantly switch between Form and Design views to examine and edit code.

Save Your Changes to the Add Record Button

Now that you've finished modifying the button, save your changes.

Save

● Click the Save button on the toolbar.

Access saves your changes to the form and its form module.

Making a Form Read-Only by Default

If you type in any of the fields in the *Contacts* form, you begin editing the recordset. This is one of the great advantages of Access over many other database systems: data is almost always available for both viewing and updating. However, business users are commonly worried about "messing up" the information in a database—their data is important, and they don't want it to be too easy to make changes to it.

In this section, you'll modify the *Contacts* form to provide a solution to this common data-entry request. The idea is to make the default mode for a form *read-only* so that users can't make changes unless they specifically ask to. This way, users can open the form and look at contact information without worrying about accidentally making a change.

The first step is easy: to make a form read-only, you simply set the AllowEdits property for the form to *No*. But you also need a way for users to tell you when they *do* want to make changes. What you want is an additional two buttons on your form: one for indicating that a user wants to edit data, one for saving the record they've edited. For one of these buttons, you won't use the Command Button Wizard at all—instead, you'll create the button on your own and then write a custom Visual Basic event procedure to make the button work.

┌─ You'll make the form read-only by default...

Contacts					
First Name	Hardy		Contact ID	1	
Last Name	Griffin		Title	Master Brewer	
Company	Ballard Brewery		Work Phone	(206) 555-5317	
Dear	Red		Work Extension		
Address	115 Leary Wy.		Mobile Phone	(206) 555-2365	
			Fax Number		
City	Seattle				
State/Province	WA				
Postal Code	98115				
Country/Region					

Calls.. | Dial.. | Page: 1 2 | Add Record | Edit Record | Save Record

Record: |◄| |◄| 1 |►| |►I| |►*| of 18

... and then provide buttons that users can ─┘
click to begin and finish editing a record.

Make Existing Records Read-Only in the *Contacts* Form

Design View

1 Click the Design View button on the toolbar.

2 Double-click the form selection box at the upper left corner of the form window (at the intersection of the rulers).

Double-click here to select the
form and display its properties.

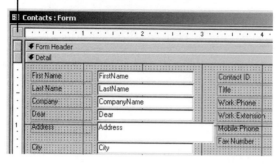

Access displays the form's properties in the property sheet.

3 Click the AllowEdits property, and then set the property to *No*.

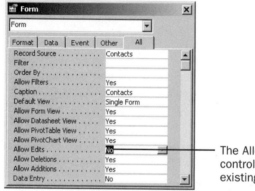

The AllowEdits property
controls whether you change
existing records in the form.

That's all it takes to solve the problem of accidentally editing data; now when you open the form to an existing record, you won't be able to change data. Note that we're leaving the other two "Allow" properties—AllowDeletions and AllowAdditions—set to *Yes* so that users can still delete or add records. Accidental deletions shouldn't be a problem because Access warns users before deleting records.

4 Close the property sheet.

Form View

5 Click the Form View button on the toolbar.

6 Try to type a few letters in the First Name field.

Nothing happens, because the record is read-only—so the existing data is safe.

Important

As you can see in the previous illustration, the property sheet displays spaces between words in property names to make them easier to read. When you use properties in Access or Visual Basic, however, you don't type spaces between words. On this form, for example, the actual property name is AllowEdits, not Allow Edits as shown in the property sheet.

Creating a Command Button Without a Wizard

Now that the form is read-only, you need a command button that sets the AllowEdits property back to *Yes*. But the Command Button Wizard doesn't offer a button that changes the value of a property. It's time to up the ante and push beyond where the wizard goes!

First you'll create the button and set its properties. Then you'll use the Build Event command to create your own event procedure for the button's *Click* event.

Create the Edit Record Command Button

Design View

1 Click the Design View button on the toolbar.

2 Scroll down in the form to display the form footer.

3 If the toolbox isn't displayed, click the Toolbox button on the toolbar.

Command Button

4 In the toolbox, click the Control Wizards tool to deselect it, and then click the Command Button tool.

Deselecting the Control Wizard tool tells Access that you don't want to use a wizard to create this control—you'll set its properties on your own.

5 In the form footer, click just to the right of the Add Record button.

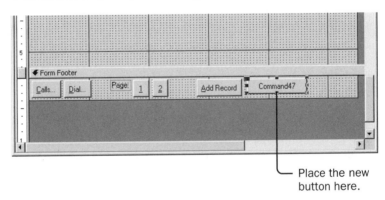

└─ Place the new button here.

Without the Control Wizards tool selected, the button appears immediately, but with a default name (such as *Command47*) and no associated event procedure.

Properties

6 Click the Properties button on the toolbar.

7 In the Name property box, type **EditRecord**.

8 Press Enter, and then in the Caption property box type **&Edit Record**.

The ampersand character in the button's caption tells Access to make the "E" in Edit Record the access key for the command button.

Important

Be sure to include a space in the button's caption, but *not* in the underlying control name. None of the fields or controls on the *Contacts* form contain spaces in their names because spaces make fields and controls more difficult to work with. (Every time you type the name, you have to enclose it in brackets.)

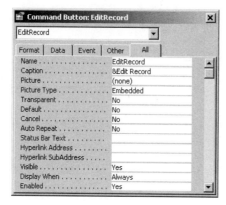

9 Close the property sheet.

Create the Button's *Click* Event Procedure

As it stands, the new button won't *do* anything when you click it. You need to write a Visual Basic event procedure to make it work.

1 With the right mouse button, click the Edit Record button, and then click Build Event on the shortcut menu.

Access displays the Choose Builder dialog box. (If you wanted to create an expression or a macro rather than Visual Basic code, you could choose Expression Builder or Macro Builder.)

2 Click Code Builder, and then click OK.

Access tells Visual Basic to open the form module for the *Contacts* form and create an event procedure for the button's *Click* event.

The procedure that Visual Basic creates is called *EditRecord_Click*. The name of an event procedure has two parts, separated by an underscore character: the name of an object, and the name of the event that the procedure responds to. You can think of the name *EditRecord_Click* as meaning "the code that runs when you click the *EditRecord* control."

3   Press Enter, press the Tab key, and then type the following line of Visual Basic code:

```
Me.AllowEdits = True
```

Tip

As you enter this line, you'll notice that Visual Basic again helps you by displaying a list of options under the code you're typing—first when you type the period and again when you type the equal sign. In this case, just continue typing the entire command.

The equal sign (=) in Visual Basic code means "assign the value of the expression on the right to the thing identified on the left." The thing on the left here is the expression *Me.AllowEdits*, which refers to the AllowEdits property of the form—to refer to a property of the current form in the form's module, you use the *Me* keyword, followed by a period, followed by the property name. This code tells Visual Basic to assign *True* to the expression on the left. It's as if the form is telling Visual Basic, "Set my AllowEdits property to *True*."

Setting a property to *True* in Visual Basic code is the same as setting the property to *Yes* in the form's property sheet. (To set a property to *No* in code, you assign it the value *False*.)

4   Press Enter, and then type the following line so that the focus will move back to the first control on the form—just as in the *AddRecord_Click* event procedure:

```
FirstName.SetFocus
```

Press Enter. Your event procedure should look like this:

Try the Edit Record Button

Form View

The *Contacts* form is still in Design view. To test the code, you'll switch to Form view.

1   Click the Form View button.

2   Click the Dear field, and then try to type in it.

35

You can't type anything—the record is still read-only.

3 Click the Edit Record button you just created.

Although it happened so fast you couldn't have seen it, Access ran your event procedure when you clicked the button. The AllowEdits property should now be set to Yes. Also, you'll notice that the focus is on the First Name field as you specified using the *SetFocus* method in the event procedure. But you want to edit the Dear field to add this contact's nickname to the record.

4 Click the Dear field, and then type **Red**.

You can now edit data, which means that the button's event procedure successfully changed the AllowEdits property to *True*.

Important

If you typed anything incorrectly when creating your event procedure, clicking the button will most likely cause an error message to appear. If this happens, don't worry—Visual Basic displays your code so that you can check what you entered against the creation steps. After making corrections to the procedure, click the Continue button on the toolbar and then switch back to Access.

Add Comments to Your Event Procedure

When you first look at any Visual Basic procedure—even if you wrote it yourself—it's sometimes really tough to figure out what the procedure does and why it's there. To help make your applications easier to understand, it's extremely important to include *comments* embedded in your code. Comments are like notes to yourself, helping to explain what you were thinking of when you wrote the code.

To add a comment to Visual Basic code, simply precede the text of your comment with an apostrophe (').

1 Switch to Visual Basic.

2 Click the blank line underneath the *Private Sub* statement in the Code window, and then type the following line:

```
' Make the Contacts form editable.
```

Now when you look at this event procedure later on, you won't need to figure out what it does or why you wrote it.

3 Press Enter. You'll notice that Visual Basic displays the comment text in green.

4 Click the far right side of the line that includes the *SetFocus* method, press Tab twice, and then type the following text:

```
' Move to the FirstName field.
```

As you can see, a comment can either begin on a new line or explain the line of code to the left. A comment on a line by itself often gives information about several lines of code or a whole procedure, while a comment to the right of a line of code usually explains what that one line does.

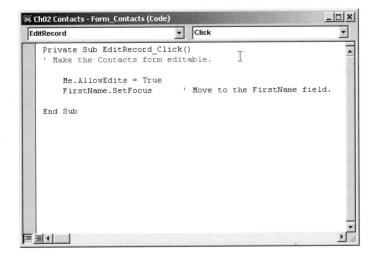

Create a Command Button to Save the Current Record

With the two buttons you've created, users can either add new records or edit existing ones. But there's one more button you need to add.

When entering or editing data for a contact, you can save the data by either moving to a new record or closing the form. Or you can use the Save Record command (on the Records menu) to explicitly save the current record. But you want to make this command more accessible to users so that they won't have to find it on the menu. Because the Command Button Wizard creates such a button, you may as well use it.

View Microsoft
Access

1 Switch to Access.

2 Click the Design View button on the toolbar.

3 Scroll down in the form to display the form footer.

Control
Wizards

4 In the toolbox, click the Control Wizards tool, and then click the Command Button tool.

5 In the form footer, click just to the right of the Edit Record button.

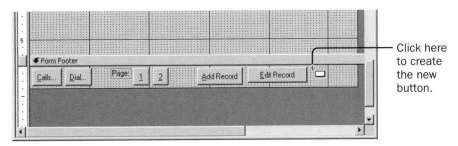

Click here to create the new button.

The Command Button Wizard starts, asking what actions you want the new button to perform.

6 In the Categories list, click Record Operations.

7 In the Actions list, click Save Record, and then click Next.

The wizard asks whether you want a picture or text on your button.

8 Click the Text option.

9 In the Text box, click the left edge of the Save Record text, and then type **&**.

Adding the ampersand symbol tells the wizard to make the "S" in Save Record the access key for the button.

10 Click Next.

11 Type **SaveRecord** as the button name, and then click Finish.

The wizard finishes creating the button and its event procedure and places it on your form.

12 If necessary, resize and align the buttons in the footer so that they're uniform. (When you create buttons by different methods, it's easy for them to end up with different shapes or sizes.)

Tip

When you make final adjustments to controls on a form or report, you may find it difficult to line them up just right and make them all the same size. To align or size a group of controls easily, click the controls and then choose one of several Size or Align commands from the Format menu.

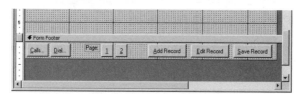

Save

13 Click the Save button on the toolbar.

Access saves both the form and its module.

Creating Event Procedures for Form Events

Up to this point, you've worked only with procedures for the Click event—code that runs when you click a button. But there are many other events you can respond to. In this section, you'll work with event procedures for two form events.

When a user clicks the Edit Record button you created, your code makes the form editable. When the user moves to another record or saves the current record, you need to return the form to its read-only state so that records won't be vulnerable to accidental changes until the Edit Record button is clicked again.

Much of the trick in programming with Access is figuring out which event to attach code to. You could have added code to the Save Record button that would set the form's AllowEdits property back to *False*. But there are other ways the user could save an edited record—using a menu command, for example—and your application needs to anticipate all these possibilities. Additionally, the user could move to another record without saving the record at all, in which case you also want to return the AllowEdits property to *False*.

The two cases you need to catch are:

■ Whenever the user moves to another existing record

■ Whenever the user saves the current record using any method

For the first case, you'll create your own event procedure for the form's Current event, which occurs whenever Access displays an existing record in a form. For the second case, you'll create an event procedure for the form's AfterUpdate event, which occurs whenever a record is saved in a form. Between the two, you'll be sure to return the form to its read-only state at the appropriate times.

Create a Procedure for the Form's *Current* Event

Earlier in this chapter you used the Build Event command on the shortcut menu to create or open the *Click* event procedure for a button. But the Build Event command always opens the default event for the object you choose. Because the Current event isn't the default event for a form, you'll have to use a more general method to open the event procedure—you'll create the procedure by setting an event property in the property sheet.

1   Double-click the form selection box at the upper left corner of the form window (at the intersection of the rulers).

   Access displays the form's properties in the property sheet.

2   Click the Event tab in the property sheet.

3   Click the OnCurrent property, and then click the Build button to the right of the property box.

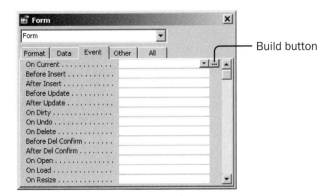

4   Click Code Builder, and then click OK.

   Access tells Visual Basic to create the *Form_Current* event procedure and display it in a Code window.

5 Press Enter and then Tab, and then type the following line of Visual Basic code:

```
Me.AllowEdits = False    ' Return the form to its read-only state.
```

By setting the form's AllowEdits property to *False*, this line of code returns the form to its read-only state each time you move to an existing record in the form.

6 Press Enter.

Copy the Procedure to the Form's *AfterUpdate* Event

You need the same code to run when the *AfterUpdate* event occurs. Rather than retype the *Form_Current* code, you can just copy the code from one procedure to another.

1 In the Code window, click the line of code you added. (Click to the left of the line of code—but to the right of the gray margin—so that the whole line is highlighted.)

2 On the Edit menu, click Copy.

View Microsoft Access

3 Switch to Access.

4 Click the AfterUpdate property, and then click the Build button to the right of the property box.

5 Click Code Builder, and then click OK.

Visual Basic displays the *Form_AfterUpdate* event procedure.

6 Press Enter

7 On the Edit menu, click Paste.

Displaying a Message to the User

It's important to communicate with users of your application. One way to do this is by using a message box. Using the *MsgBox* statement, you can give some feedback in response to events in your application.

The same users who worry about accidentally changing data are equally concerned that their changes get registered when they finish editing a record. For these users, you can display a message in response to the *AfterUpdate* event, confirming that the record was saved.

Add Code That Displays a Message Box

1 Press Tab, type **MsgBox**, and then press the Spacebar.

A box appears underneath the line you're typing, displaying the names of the arguments available with *MsgBox*. This is another way that Visual Basic helps you as you enter code—just when you need to know the syntax for a Visual Basic statement or function, there it is.

Syntax information for the *MsgBox* statement

2 Type **"Record Saved."**, and then press Enter.

This completes the *MsgBox* line, passing as an argument the message that you want to display to the user. Because it's a string argument, you enclose the message in quotation marks. (In Visual Basic, any text data or combination of text and numbers is referred to as a *string*.)

Here's the complete code for the *Form_AfterUpdate* event procedure:

Tip

If the syntax that pops up for a function or statement doesn't provide enough information, you can always turn to online Help. To display a Help topic with complete information about any Visual Basic keyword in the Code window, just click the keyword and then press the F1 key.

Save Your Changes to the *Contacts* Form

Now that you've finished adding all the buttons to the form and editing their event procedures, save your changes to the form.

1 Close Visual Basic.

Access returns to the front.

2 Close the property sheet.

Save

3 Click the Save button on the toolbar.

Access saves your changes to the form and its form module.

Try the Buttons with Your Changes

Let's make sure the Edit Record and Save Record buttons work together as you intended. Suppose you find out the mobile phone number of the first contact and want to enter it in the *Contacts* form.

Form View

1 Click the Form View button on the toolbar.

2 Click the Edit Record button.

3 Click the Mobile Phone field, and then type **(206) 555-2365**.

When you change data in a record and haven't yet saved the new information, the record selector (at the left side of the form) displays a pencil icon.

The pencil icon indicates that your changes haven't been saved.

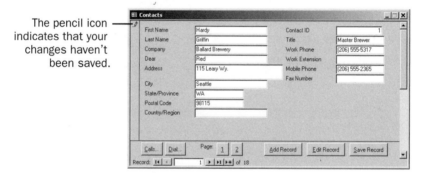

4 Click the Save Record button.

Access saves the record in the *Contacts* table and changes the pencil back to the current record indicator. Having saved the record, it fires the form's *AfterUpdate* event, which in turn runs your event procedure and displays your message.

5 Click OK.

6 Click the First Name field, and then try to type a few letters.

Because the form's *AfterUpdate* event procedure set the AllowEdits property back to *False*, you can't edit data any longer. Everything's working as planned!

7 Close the *Contacts* form.

Chapter Wrap-Up

1   On the *Switchboard* form, click Exit This Database.

2   On the File menu, click Exit.

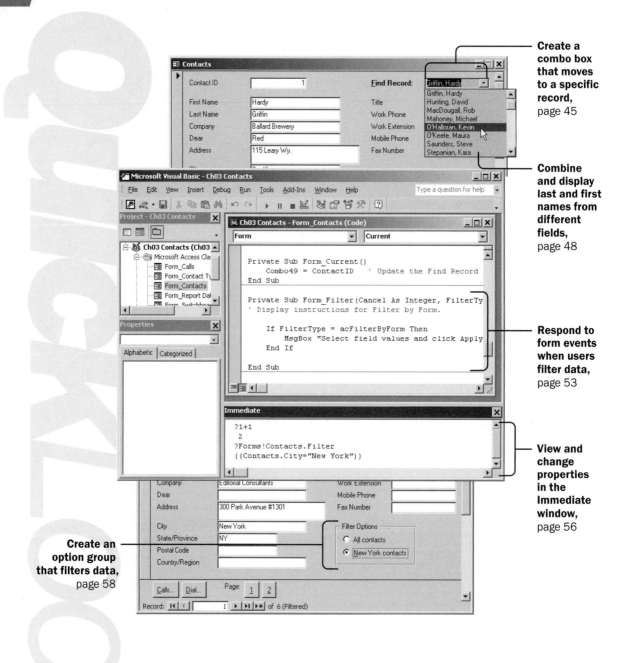

Create a combo box that moves to a specific record, page 45

Combine and display last and first names from different fields, page 48

Respond to form events when users filter data, page 53

View and change properties in the Immediate window, page 56

Create an option group that filters data, page 58

Chapter 3
Find and Filter Records in a Form

After completing this chapter, you will be able to:

✔ **Create a combo box that moves to a specific record in a form.**

✔ **Filter data to show a subset of records.**

✔ **Use the Immediate window to view and change properties.**

✔ **Respond to filtering events.**

✔ **Create an option group.**

"Where did I put that phone number? I know it's in here somewhere...." How many times have you filed some important information away, only to spend precious time looking for it later? And while this routine is especially commonplace in the world of the "paper" office, it isn't altogether solved when you put information in your computer—you can still spend plenty of time wading through files and records trying to find what you need.

In the 19th century, scientists discovered the laws of thermodynamics, which govern all physical systems in nature. The second law, they said, is that every system tends toward entropy—everything is becoming more and more disorderly. Sound familiar? These scientists didn't intend the law to apply directly to our daily lives, but nonetheless, the premise seems to hold true. The more information we have, the more difficult it is to find what we want—and the more important it is that we locate the details we need quickly.

Not surprisingly, the key to a useful database is being able to find information quickly. As an application developer, you need to consider what information users will need, and help them get to it as quickly as possible. In this chapter we'll concentrate on retrieving data from a database.

Ch03
Contacts.mdb

This chapter uses the practice file Ch03 Contacts.mdb that you installed from the book's CD-ROM. For details about installing the practice files, see "Using the Book's CD-ROM" at the beginning of this book.

Getting Started

● Start Microsoft Access, and open the Ch03 Contacts database in the practice files folder.

Creating a Combo Box to Find Records

Perhaps the most common task you'll perform in any database application is to look up an existing record. In the Contacts database, when you need someone's phone number or address, you want to jump to the person's record quickly. The standard way to find a specific record in a form is by using the Find command. To locate a record by last name, for example, you first click the Last Name field, then you click the Find button, and then you type the name you're looking for and click OK. Not only does this method require several actions for a common task, it assumes that you know the exact last name and can spell it correctly.

You can provide better methods for users to find records in your applications. One way is to create a combo box on the form where users can select a contact name from a list. This type of combo box requires setting quite a few properties, as well as writing a macro or event procedure that moves to the record. Fortunately, the Combo Box Wizard can do most of this for you—you need only put on the final touches to make it work just right.

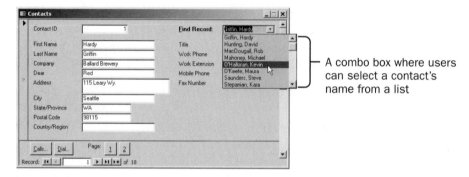

A combo box where users can select a contact's name from a list

Open the *Contacts* Form and Switch to Design View

1 On the main *Switchboard* form, click Enter/View Contacts.

Design View

2 Click the Design View button on the toolbar.

Create a Combo Box That Finds Records

Control Wizards

To create the Find Record combo box, you'll use the Combo Box Wizard.

1 In the toolbox, make sure the Control Wizards tool is selected, and then click the Combo Box tool.

Combo Box

2 Click the top of the form above the left side of the *Title* field.

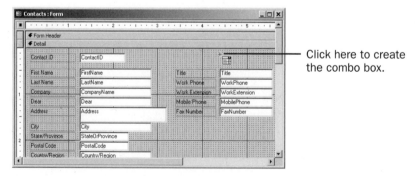

Click here to create the combo box.

3 The Combo Box Wizard starts, asking how you want the combo box to get the values it will display in the list.

4 Select the third option, Find A Record On My Form Based On The Value I Selected In My Combo Box, and then click Next.

The wizard asks which fields you want to include in the combo box.

5 Double-click the LastName field to add it to the Selected Fields list.

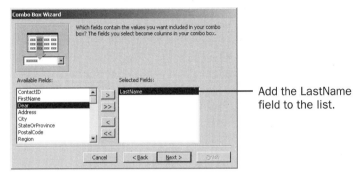

Add the LastName field to the list.

6 Click Next.

The wizard displays the list of last names.

7 Drag the right side of the field selector in the LastName column to make it about half again as wide, and then click Next.

The wizard asks what label you want for your combo box.

8 Type **&Find Record:** and then click Finish.

The wizard creates the combo box and places it on your form. Behind the scenes, the wizard has set properties and added a Microsoft Visual Basic event procedure so that the combo box can find records in the form.

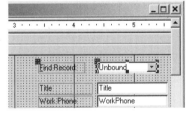

Change the Appearance of the Combo Box

Before you try out the combo box, you'll want to modify its appearance just a bit. For starters, the wizard might not have created the control in just the right size or position. Additionally, because this is a special control on the form—it's a helpful tool, but users don't have to enter any data in it—you'll want it to stand out in appearance.

1 If the combo box isn't lined up with the boxes below it, click and drag it to the correct position.

2 Click the right edge of the combo box and drag to make it the same width as the controls below it.

Fill/Back Color

3 On the toolbar, click the arrow next to the Fill/Back Color button, and then click the light gray box.

Bold

B

4 Click the label to the left of the control, and then click the Bold button on the toolbar. (If the label box is too small to fit the text, move the mouse pointer to the right edge of the label until you see the sizing cursor, and then double-click to resize the label.)

Try Out the Combo Box

Now the Find Record combo box is ready to use.

Form View

1 Click the Form View button on the toolbar.

2 Click the arrow next to the Find Record combo box.

Access displays the list of contacts' last names.

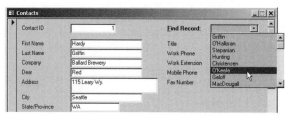

3 Click O'Keefe.

Access moves to the record for Maura O'Keefe in the *Contacts* form.

Modify the Combo Box List

The Find Record combo box works as planned, but the list it displays isn't quite right. First of all, the list isn't alphabetized. Secondly, the list includes only last names. Ideally, you'd like it to display "last name comma first name"—such as Geloff, Kevin—so that you can more easily find the record you want.

Design View

1 Click the Design View button on the toolbar.

2 With the right mouse button, click the Find Record combo box, and then click Properties on the shortcut menu.

Access displays the property sheet for the combo box.

3 Click the All tab in the property sheet.

4 Click the RowSource property, and then click the Build button to the right of the property box.

Access displays the Query Builder window. It shows the query that provides values for the combo box drop-down list. You want to modify this query so that it displays last names combined with first names.

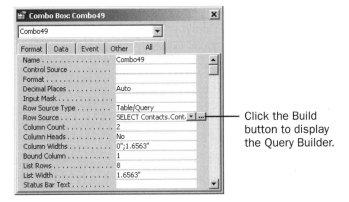

Click the Build
button to display
the Query Builder.

5 In the Query By Example (QBE) grid in the lower part of the window, click the box displaying the LastName field, and change the text to the following expression: **LastName & ", "
& FirstName.** (Inside the quotation marks, be sure to include a space after the comma.)

This expression combines three string values with the ampersand (&) operator. When you
want to put more than one string of text together in expressions or in Visual Basic code,
you combine them with an ampersand. This is known as *concatenating* the strings. In this
case, the expression concatenates each contact's last name and first name, separated
by a comma and a space.

Note that when you click outside the expression, Access automatically adds a label
(*Expr1:*) for the expression and encloses the field names in brackets. If you want to see
the whole expression, you can make the column wider by dragging the right edge of its column selector to the right.

6 Click the Sort box underneath the expression you just entered, click the drop-down arrow,
and then click Ascending.

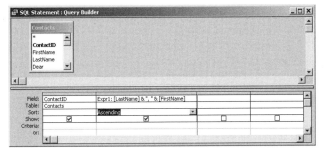

7 Close the Query Builder window, clicking Yes when prompted to choose whether you want
to save changes to the query.

8 Close the property sheet.

Try Out the New List

Now the Find Record combo box should display complete names in alphabetical order.

Form View

1 Click the Form View button on the toolbar.

2 Click the arrow next to the Find Record combo box.

Sure enough, Access displays the list of names in order, last names followed by first names.

3 Click Geloff, Kevin. (You may need to scroll up in the list.)

Add Code to Keep the Combo Box Synchronized

There's one last idiosyncrasy with the Find Record combo box: although it finds records well enough, it doesn't always display the name of the current contact. If you change records with some other method than using the combo box, the combo box doesn't stay synchronized—it continues to show the name you last selected there. Because this could be misleading, you'll add a line of code to the form's module to fix the problem.

1 Click the Next Record button at the bottom of the form window.

As you can see, while the form changes to the next record, the Find Record combo box doesn't update to display the current name—it still shows Geloff, Kevin.

When you move among records, the Find Record combo box doesn't stay synchronized.

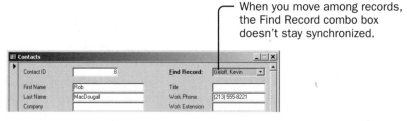

This happens because this combo box, unlike all other controls on the form, is an *unbound* control. Unbound controls can be very useful in an application, because users can change them without changing any data and the application can respond accordingly. The flip side, however, is that if you want an unbound control to display data, you have to set its value in code yourself.

Design View

2 Click the Design View button on the toolbar.

3 Double-click the Find Record combo box.

The property sheet displays the properties of the combo box. Note the name of the combo box in the title bar of the property sheet—something like *Combo49*—which is a default name given to the control when the wizard creates it. You'll need to know this name for the code you'll write.

4 Click the Form Selection box at the upper left corner of the form window. (You may need to move or close the toolbox.)

The property sheet displays the properties of the form.

5 Click the Event tab in the property sheet.

6 Click the OnCurrent property, and then click the Build button to the right of the property box.

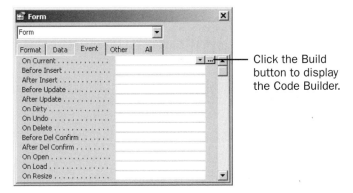

Click the Build button to display the Code Builder.

7 Select Code Builder, and then click OK.

Visual Basic displays the form module for the *Contacts* form and automatically inserts the *Form_Current* event procedure. The module opens in Full Module view, so other procedures are displayed in the window before and after the *Form_Current* procedure.

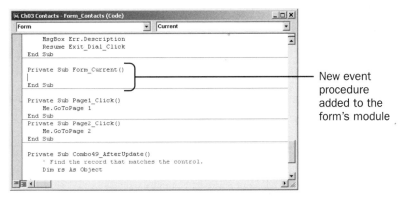

New event procedure added to the form's module

8 Press the Tab key, and then add the following line of Visual Basic code to the procedure (substituting the actual number of the combo box on your own form):

```
Combo49 = ContactID     ' Update the Find Record combo box.
```

This code sets the value of the combo box control to the value of the *ContactID* control. This way, each time you move to a new contact, the combo box will change along with the rest of the form. As when you set a property, all you do to set the value of a control is type the control name followed by the equal sign (=) and the value you want to set it to.

View Microsoft Access

9 Switch to Access.

10 Close the property sheet.

11 Click the Form View button on the toolbar.

12 Click the arrow next to the Find Record combo box, and then click Geloff, Kevin.

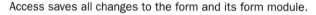

13 Click the Next Record button at the bottom of the form window.

While the form changes to the record for Rob MacDougall, the *Form_Current* event procedure runs, and your code synchronizes the Find Record combo box: it displays *MacDougall, Rob*.

Save Your Changes to the *Contacts* Form

It took a bit of work, but now the *Contacts* form has a highly visible, easy-to-use tool for jumping to a contact's record. Now save your changes to the form.

Save

● Click the Save button on the toolbar.

Access saves all changes to the form and its form module.

Filtering Data

The combo box you created jumps to an individual record in the recordset. However, all the rest of the records are still available—you can move to other records by clicking the record navigation buttons at the bottom of the form window. But when you're trying to locate certain contacts, you may not want all the records to be available. For example, suppose your company is located in New York City, and you want to place calls to local customers. To browse through contacts located in New York City, excluding all contacts in other cities, you use a *filter*.

Apply Filter

You can think of a filter as a funnel for data that lets through the specific records you ask for, but keeps all the rest out of view. In fact, the Filter icon in Access is a funnel—you can see it on the Apply Filter button on the toolbar.

There are three Access filtering commands available to the user.

■ **Filter By Selection** Limits data to records that have the currently selected value. For example, if you're viewing a contact in New York, you can click the City field and then the Filter By Selection button, and contacts from all other cities will be filtered out of the recordset.

■ **Filter By Form** Displays a blank version of the current form, where you can select from existing field values and then apply the filter to view records that match the selected criteria. For example, you can click the Filter By Form button, select New York in the list of City values, and then click the Apply Filter button to show only contacts in New York. Using Filter By Form, you can specify criteria for more than one field at a time.

■ **Advanced Filter/Sort** Displays a query window, where you can drag fields to the QBE grid and specify criteria for sorting. This type of filter is the most flexible, but requires an understanding of the Access query window.

Unless you disable them, these standard filtering commands are available to users. Even if your application doesn't do any filtering of its own, these commands allow users to browse through a subset of data in a table or form.

Filter Records in the *Contacts* Form Using Filter By Form

Suppose you want to view contacts in New York City.

Filter By Form

1 Click the Filter By Form button on the toolbar.

The form changes to display the Filter By Form view, where users can specify criteria for the records they want to see.

2 Click the City field, and then click the arrow next to the text box.

Access displays all the cities where contacts are located.

3 Click New York.

Apply Filter

4 Click the Apply Filter button.

The form displays only contacts in New York City. Note that the text at the bottom of the form window indicates that the recordset in the form is filtered.

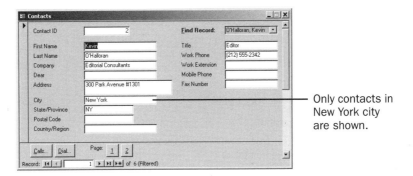

Only contacts in New York city are shown.

Responding to Filtering Events

Although the filtering interface in Access is very flexible, there's always room for improvement. If you want to control or customize filtering in your application, you can write Visual Basic event procedures that respond to one of two filtering events. The first of these events is the Filter event, which is triggered whenever a user chooses the Filter By Form or Advanced Filter/Sort command. You can respond to the Filter event to customize these commands.

The other filtering event is the ApplyFilter event, which occurs when the user finishes specifying a filter and clicks the Apply Filter button, or when the user clicks the Filter By Selection button, which applies a filter immediately. This event also occurs when the user removes a filter—basically, whenever the set of records displayed is about to be changed. You can respond to the ApplyFilter event to change filtering behavior when the user chooses these buttons or commands.

To start, you'll provide a simple customization of the Filter By Form command by responding to the Filter event with an event procedure.

Display a Message When the User Filters

For beginning users, the Filter By Form interface can be confusing—when a user clicks this button, the form changes slightly in appearance and goes blank, and a user might not know what to do next. It would be helpful to display a simple message, providing the user with a hint explaining what to do.

1 Switch to Visual Basic by clicking the Microsoft Visual Basic – Ch03 Contacts button on the Windows task bar.

Visual Basic still shows the *Form_Current* event procedure. Because you're already viewing an event procedure for the form, the easiest way to create the procedure is by using the Code window's Procedure box, which lists all the procedures and events for a given object and allows you to switch between procedures.

2 In the Procedure box at the top of the Code window, select Filter from the list of events.

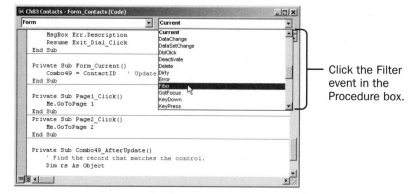

Click the Filter event in the Procedure box.

Visual Basic creates the *Form_Filter* procedure for you—you don't have to go back to the property sheet. Behind the scenes, Visual Basic also automatically attaches the procedure to the control's Filter event. It does this by setting the control's OnFilter property (the one that corresponds to the Filter event) to *[Event Procedure]*.

3 Type the following Visual Basic code for the procedure:

```
' Display instructions for Filter by Form.

    MsgBox "Select field values and click Apply Filter button."
```

This code displays the message whenever the user chooses a filtering command.

Using the *If...Then* Statement to Check a Condition

There's just one problem with the *Form_Filter* event procedure: there's more than one filtering command that can trigger the Filter event. Because your message is applicable only if the user chose the Filter By Form command, you want your code to check and make sure this was the command. Fortunately, it's easy to find out which command the user chose—Access provides this information using the *FilterType* argument of the event procedure.

Check Whether the User Chose Filter By Form

To perform steps in code only when a condition is met, you use the Visual Basic *If...Then* statement. In this case, the condition you want to check is whether the *FilterType* argument of the event procedure is equal to the value of the constant *acFilterByForm*. If it is, that's when you want to display your message.

● Add lines of code before and after the existing line in the procedure so that it reads as follows (you'll also want to add a tab before each line to indent it properly):

```
If FilterType = acFilterByForm Then
    MsgBox "Select field values and click Apply Filter button."
End If
```

The code between the *If...Then* and *End If* statements runs only if the condition is true—in this case, if the *FilterType* argument is equal to the value of the constant *acFilterBy-Form*. In plain English, you can read these three lines of code as saying, "If the filter type the user chose is Filter By Form, then please display this message; otherwise, please do nothing." (In reality, you don't need to say "please" to your computer.)

Try the Event Procedure

Now that it's fixed, let's make sure the event procedure works as planned.

View Microsoft
Access

1 Switch to Access.

Filter By Form

2 Click the Filter By Form button on the toolbar.

The Filter event occurs, triggering your event procedure. Because you chose the Filter By Form button, the condition in the *If...Then* statement is true, and the *MsgBox* statement runs and displays your message.

3 Click OK.

After your procedure finishes, the form appears in Filter By Form view.

4 Click the Close button on the toolbar.

Using conditional code as you've done here makes your application "smart"—it provides logic to your procedures, and is the first step toward powerful Visual Basic programming. This simple use of the *If...Then* statement performs just one action. But that's only the beginning of what you can do using conditional statements in Visual Basic. Soon, you'll use the *If...Then* statement to execute several lines of code depending on the value of a condition.

Understanding Filtering Properties

Whenever the user filters data using any of the standard filtering commands, Access sets two form properties that reflect the filtering status of the form: the Filter property and the FilterOn property. The Filter property describes the criteria for the current filter—for example, the criterion for contacts in New York can be expressed as

```
City = "New York"
```

The FilterOn property setting determines whether the filter is currently applied. When there's no filter, the FilterOn property is set to *False*; when the user applies a filter, it gets set to *True*.

In Visual Basic code, you can use the Filter and FilterOn properties to determine what the current filter is and whether it's in effect. More importantly, you can set these properties to affect the current filter on a form—actually changing the records that are displayed. This allows you to provide a custom filtering interface, setting the filtering status behind the scenes whenever you want. In this section, you'll see how these properties work on the *Contacts* form, and then provide a custom method for changing the filter on the form.

Using the Immediate Window to View and Set Properties

In programming lingo, a "bug" is an error or mistake in programming code. Visual Basic has several tools that help you find bugs, or problems. The most basic of these tools is the Immediate window. In later chapters, you'll learn many techniques for debugging Visual Basic code with the Immediate window and other tools. But there are also simple uses for the Immediate window—one of which you'll try out in this section as you learn more about filtering data.

Usually, you place Visual Basic code in a module, and the code runs later on—for example, in response to an event. But in the Immediate window, when you type Visual Basic code it runs right away, as soon as you press the Enter key.

Try Out the Immediate Window

Because it's so convenient, the Immediate window is a great place to try things out. It's also a good place to find out the current value of a property or expression. If you want to know the value of any Visual Basic expression, you can display it in the Immediate window by typing a question mark (?) followed by the expression.

1 Switch to Visual Basic.

2 On the View menu, click Immediate Window.

The Immediate window appears at the bottom of the Visual Basic window, ready for you to enter Visual Basic commands.

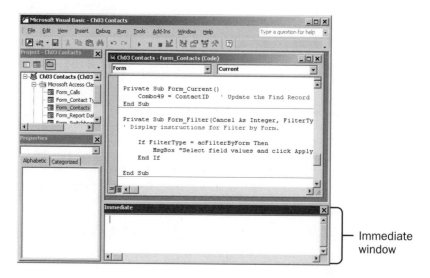

Immediate window

3   Type **Beep**, press Enter, and listen closely.

Your computer beeps—*Beep* is a Visual Basic statement, and when you type it in the Immediate window, it runs immediately.

4   Type **?1+1** and press Enter.

Typing this statement asks Visual Basic a question: "What is the value of 1+1?" Visual Basic displays the answer directly underneath your statement in the Immediate window—it's *2*. Bet you didn't know that Access comes equipped with such a fancy calculator!

Use the Immediate Window to Set Filtering Properties

Making your computer beep (or add) is hardly a powerful use of the Immediate window. But now that we've established what it does, let's put the Immediate window to work. First you'll use the Immediate window to find out the value of the filtering properties for the *Contacts* form. Then you'll actually change the value of these properties from the Immediate window—in just the same way you've set properties in your event procedures.

1   Type **?Forms!Contacts.Filter**

This statement asks Visual Basic to tell you the value of the expression to the right of the question mark—an expression that refers to the Filter property of the *Contacts* form. This expression is like an address to someone's house, describing to Visual Basic exactly what property you're talking about. Here's how the expression works: the keyword *Forms* refers to the collection of forms in the current database; you follow it with an exclamation point (!) and the name of a form, such as *Contacts*. Then, to indicate a property of the form, you follow the form reference with a period and the name of the property.

In short, this statement asks the question, "What is the value of the Filter property for the *Contacts* form?"

2   Press Enter.

Visual Basic displays the value of the expression—the filter you applied earlier to see only contacts in New York.

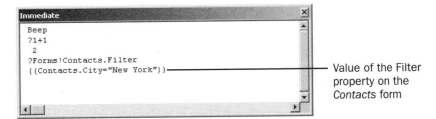

Value of the Filter property on the *Contacts* form

3   Type **?Forms!Contacts.FilterOn** and press Enter.

The window displays the value of the FilterOn property for the *Contacts* form. Because the filter is currently applied on the *Contacts* form, the value of the FilterOn property is *True*.

4   Type **Forms!Contacts.FilterOn = False** and press Enter.

This statement sets the FilterOn property of the *Contacts* form to *False*, effectively removing the filter from the form—just as if the user had clicked the Remove Filter button.

5 Close the Immediate window by clicking the Close button at the right side of the title bar.

6 Switch to Access.

As you can see, the form now displays all contact records—you successfully removed the filter using the Immediate window.

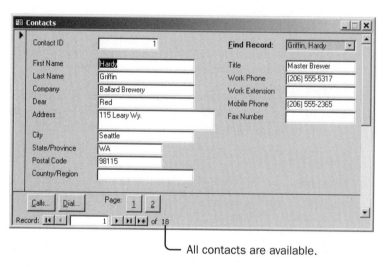

All contacts are available.

By viewing and setting the Filter and FilterOn properties in code, you can monitor or change the filter of any form. Now that you've seen how these properties work in the Immediate window, it's time to use them to customize the *Contacts* form.

Creating an Option Group to Filter Data

Suppose the filter you've set—to view contacts in New York—is very common in your application. You should make it easy for users to filter records, even if they don't know how to use Filter By Form. A good way to do this is by adding an *option group* to the form: a group of buttons from which users can choose the records they want to see.

In this section, you'll add an option group to the *Contacts* form with two options for viewing records: viewing all contacts, or viewing just New York contacts. Whenever the user clicks a different option in the group, an event procedure that you write will respond by changing filtering properties to affect which records are displayed in the form.

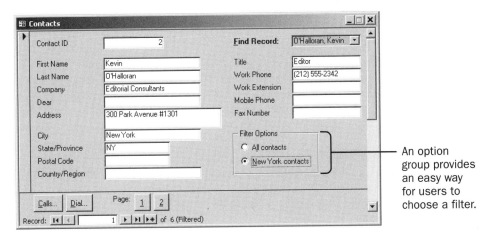

An option group provides an easy way for users to choose a filter.

Create the Option Group

An option group has many parts—but you can create them all at once using the Option Group Wizard. The wizard lets you specify all the options in the group, and it takes care of the details.

Design View

1 Click the Design View button on the toolbar.

2 If the toolbox isn't displayed, click the Toolbox button on the toolbar.

Option Group

3 In the toolbox, click the Option Group tool.

4 Scroll down a bit in the form window, and click the open space below the Fax Number field.

The Option Group Wizard starts, asking what option buttons you want in the option group.

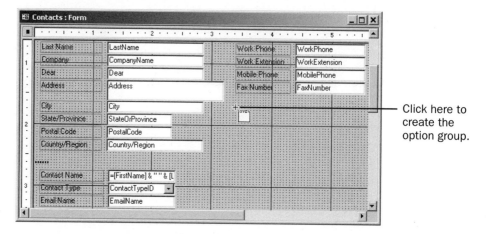

Click here to
create the
option group.

Important

If you haven't installed all available wizards (not all are installed with Office 2002 by default), Access will need to install the Option Group Wizard from the Office CD-ROM or a network location when you try to create the option group in this procedure. Install the wizard if you're prompted to do so, and proceed to the next step.

5 Type **A&ll contacts** and then press Tab.

6 Type **&New York contacts** and then click Next.

The wizard asks if you want a default button to be selected automatically when you open the form, suggesting the All Contacts button. Leave All Contacts selected.

7 Click Next.

The wizard shows you the values that each of the options will have. The All Contacts option corresponds to the number 1, the New York Contacts option to the number 2.

8 Click Next.

The wizard asks whether you want to use the value later or store the value in a field—that is, whether you want your option group to be an unbound or a bound control. You want the default option—Save The Value For Later Use—making the option group an unbound control.

9 Click Next.

The wizard asks about the style you want for your option group and buttons. Change it if you want to be fancy—the wizard shows you an example of what your choice will look like—or just accept the default style.

10 Click Next.

The wizard asks what label you want for the option group.

11 Type **Filter Options** and then click Finish.

The wizard creates the option group and its two buttons, and then places it on your form. Unfortunately, the wizard doesn't give the option group a very sensible name (it's something like *Frame74*). Because you want to refer to the option group in Visual Basic code, you should rename it in the property sheet.

Properties

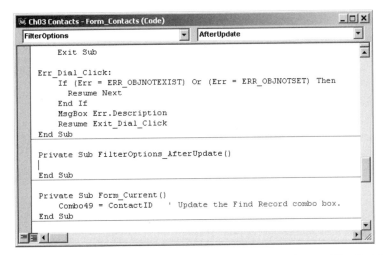

12 Click the Properties button on the toolbar, and then click the Other tab in the property sheet.

13 In the Name property box, type **FilterOptions**.

Add an Event Procedure to Run the Option Group

The option group you've created is an unbound control, like the Find Record combo box you created earlier. To make it work, you need to write an event procedure that sets the filter properties for the *Contacts* form. Each time you click an option in an option group, its AfterUpdate event occurs, so you can respond accordingly. In the event procedure, you'll perform a different action depending on which option button the user clicks.

1 Click the Event tab in the property sheet.

2 Click the AfterUpdate property, and then click the Build button to the right of the property box.

3 Select Code Builder, and then click OK.

Access switches to Visual Basic and creates the *AfterUpdate* event procedure for the option group.

```
Exit Sub

Err_Dial_Click:
    If (Err = ERR_OBJNOTEXIST) Or (Err = ERR_OBJNOTSET) Then
        Resume Next
    End If
    MsgBox Err.Description
    Resume Exit_Dial_Click
End Sub


Private Sub FilterOptions_AfterUpdate()
|
End Sub


Private Sub Form_Current()
    Combo49 = ContactID    ' Update the Find Record combo box.
End Sub
```

4 Enter the following code for the procedure (except the *Sub* and *End Sub* lines, which are already there):

```
Private Sub FilterOptions_AfterUpdate()
' Apply or remove the filter for the option the user chose.
```

(continued)

continued

```
If FilterOptions = 2 Then
    Me.Filter = "City = 'New York'"
    Me.FilterOn = True       ' Apply the filter.
Else
    Me.FilterOn = False      ' Remove the filter.
End If
End Sub
```

Let's walk through this code line by line:

■ As you've seen, the *If…Then* structure lets you perform an action only if a certain condition is true. But before, you added only one line of code between the *If…Then* and *End If* statements. This code uses *If…Then* in a powerful new way—if the condition is true, Visual Basic runs all the indented lines under the *If…Then* statement. This is known as a *block* of code, which is indented to show that it all belongs within the same *If…Then…End If* structure.

The condition here tests whether the value of the option group is *2*, the number of the New York Contacts option. If the user clicks the second option in the group, the condition is true, and Visual Basic will run the code in the block.

■ The first statement in this block of code sets the Filter property for the form. The Filter property accepts a string setting, which means you surround the setting in quotation marks. This setting says that you only want the form to show records for which the City field is equal to the value *'New York'*—which you surround with single quotation marks because it's also a string value.

■ The second statement in the block sets the form's FilterOn property to *True*, applying the filter. When Visual Basic runs this statement, it will cause Access to requery the records in the form, displaying only those that meet the filter criteria.

■ The *If…Then* structure in this procedure uses another new feature: the *Else* keyword, which allows you to add a line or block of code that runs if the condition is false. You can think of this *If…Then* statement as saying, "If the option group value is 2, do this block of code; otherwise do this other block of code."

■ The other block in this case is a single line that sets the FilterOn property to *False*. This way, if the user clicks the All Contacts option, your event procedure will remove the filter.

■ The *End If* statement marks the end of the *Else* code block. Any lines after this one would run regardless of whether the condition is true. Every *If…Then* statement must have a corresponding *End If* statement.

Try the Option Group

It's time to test the code by clicking values in the option group.

View Microsoft
Access

1 Switch to Access.

2 Close the property sheet.

Form View

3 Click the Form View button on the toolbar.

The option group shows its default value—the All Contacts option—and all records are available in the form.

4 Click the New York Contacts button in the option group.

The AfterUpdate event occurs for the option group, and your event procedure runs. Because the option you selected is option number 2, your code sets the Filter property to show only New York contacts and applies the filter.

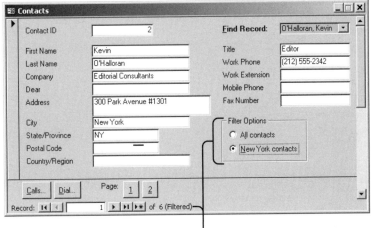

> The code in your event procedure applies the filter to show only contacts in New York.

5 Click the All Contacts button in the option group.

This time, your event procedure removes the filter.

Add an Event Procedure That Runs When the User Filters Data

The option group works great, but there's still one problem with this strategy—it doesn't take into account the fact that other standard filtering commands are still available. What if the user changes the filter in another way? Will the option group update automatically?

As you customize your applications, it's important to anticipate conflicts like this. Let's take a look at this problem, and add another event procedure to solve it.

1 Click the City field.

For this contact, the value of the City field is Seattle.

Filter By Selection

2 Click the Filter By Selection button on the toolbar.

The form now displays only contacts in Seattle. But the option group still shows All Records—which is no longer true! To avoid misleading users, you should update the option group control whenever users filter data.

The easiest way to indicate that the user's filter is in effect is for the option group to show neither option in the group as selected. To do this, you want to set the value of the option group control to *Null* any time the user applies a filter. (*Null* is a special value in Access that means "no value at all.")

If the user removes the filter, on the other hand, you might as well set the option group value to *1* (the All Contacts option), because removing the filter is the same as clicking the All Contacts option.

Design View

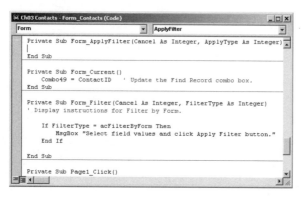

3 Click the Design View button on the toolbar.

4 Switch to Visual Basic.

5 In the Object box at the top of the Code window, click Form in the list of objects.

6 In the Procedure box, click ApplyFilter in the list of events.

```
Ch03 Contacts - Form_Contacts (Code)                                _ □ ×
Form                              ▼  ApplyFilter                        ▼
  Private Sub Form_ApplyFilter(Cancel As Integer, ApplyType As Integer)
  |
  End Sub

  Private Sub Form_Current()
      Combo49 = ContactID    ' Update the Find Record combo box.
  End Sub

  Private Sub Form_Filter(Cancel As Integer, FilterType As Integer)
  ' Display instructions for Filter by Form.

      If FilterType = acFilterByForm Then
          MsgBox "Select field values and click Apply Filter button."
      End If

  End Sub

  Private Sub Page1_Click()
```

7 Type the following code for the procedure:

```
Private Sub Form_ApplyFilter(Cancel As Integer, ApplyType As Integer)
' Set the option group value to match the user's filtering action.

    If ApplyType = acShowAllRecords Then
        FilterOptions = 1      ' Set the All Contacts option.
    ElseIf Filter <> "City = 'New York'" Then
        FilterOptions = Null   ' Don't set any option value.
    End If


End Sub
```

Here's what this code does:

■ The *If...Then* statement checks to see whether the *ApplyType* argument to the event procedure is equal to the constant value *acShowAllRecords*. This *ApplyType* value would indicate that the user removed the filter to show all contact records.

■ If the condition is true—the user did remove the filter—the line of code after the *If...Then* statement sets the *FilterOptions* control value to 1, automatically selecting the All Contacts button in the option group.

■ If the condition is false, it probably means that the user selected a filtering command other than your option group, so you'll want to set the option group control to *Null*. However, the ApplyFilter event might have been triggered when your own option group code set the filter for New York contacts—in which case you don't want to change the option group setting at all. To determine which of these is the case, the *ElseIf* line checks to make sure the Filter property is not equal (<>) to the string for New York contacts.

■ Assuming this second condition is true—the user applied a filter to see a set of records other than New York contacts—the line of code after the *ElseIf* statement sets the value of the *FilterOptions* control to *Null*, causing the control to show neither option as selected.

8 Switch to Access.

Form View

9 Click the Form View button on the toolbar.

10 Select the New York Contacts option.

The form displays only those records for which the city is New York.

Remove Filter

11 Click the Remove Filter button on the toolbar.

When you remove the filter, the *ApplyFilter* event procedure runs, automatically returning the option group to the All Records option.

Filter By
Selection

12 Click the City field, and then click the Filter By Selection button on the toolbar.

The form now displays only contacts in Seattle, just as you requested. Even better, because of your event procedure, the option group now appears without either option selected, indicating that you have applied your own filter.

As you can see, filtering is a powerful feature—but you'll need to consider carefully how the various filtering commands interact. Fortunately, with the Filter and ApplyFilter events and the Filter and FilterOn properties, Access provides all the tools you need to control filtering in your Visual Basic code.

Chapter Wrap-Up

1 Close the *Contacts* form, clicking Yes when Access asks if you want to save changes.

2 On the *Switchboard* form, click Exit This Database.

3 On the File menu, click Exit.

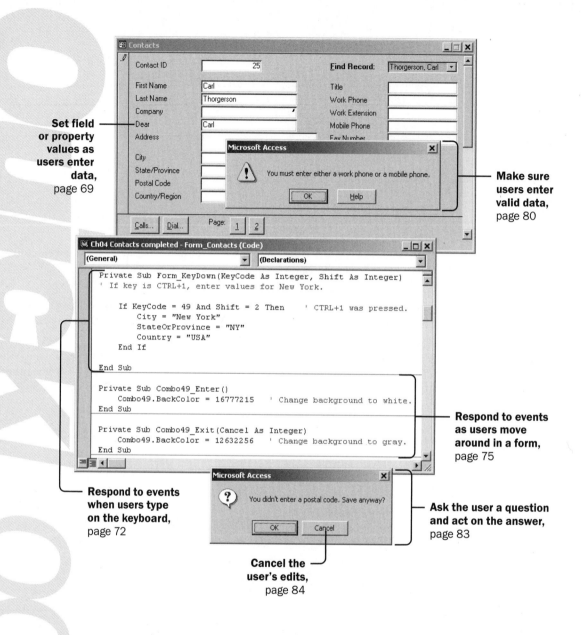

Set field or property values as users enter data, page 69

Make sure users enter valid data, page 80

Respond to events as users move around in a form, page 75

Respond to events when users type on the keyboard, page 72

Ask the user a question and act on the answer, page 83

Cancel the user's edits, page 84

Text visible in the figure:

Contacts window:
- Contact ID: 25
- First Name: Carl
- Last Name: Thorgerson
- Company:
- Dear: Carl
- Address:
- City:
- State/Province:
- Postal Code:
- Country/Region:
- Find Record: Thorgerson, Carl
- Title:
- Work Phone:
- Work Extension:
- Mobile Phone:
- Fax Number:
- Calls... Dial... Page: 1 2

Microsoft Access dialog:
You must enter either a work phone or a mobile phone.
OK   Help

Code window: Ch04 Contacts completed - Form_Contacts (Code)
(General)   (Declarations)

```
Private Sub Form_KeyDown(KeyCode As Integer, Shift As Integer)
' If key is CTRL+1, enter values for New York.

    If KeyCode = 49 And Shift = 2 Then    ' CTRL+1 was pressed.
        City = "New York"
        StateOrProvince = "NY"
        Country = "USA"
    End If

End Sub


Private Sub Combo49_Enter()
    Combo49.BackColor = 16777215    ' Change background to white.
End Sub

Private Sub Combo49_Exit(Cancel As Integer)
    Combo49.BackColor = 12632256    ' Change background to gray.
End Sub
```

Microsoft Access dialog:
You didn't enter a postal code. Save anyway?
OK   Cancel

Chapter 4
Respond to Data Entry Events

After completing this chapter, you will be able to:

✔ Set the value of a control in code.

✔ Respond to users' actions as they move around in a form.

✔ Make sure that the data a user enters is valid.

✔ Ask a question and perform different actions based on a user's choice.

Data entry can be time-consuming and monotonous, especially with a database system that's poorly designed. But data entry is also an art—when you get on a roll, you can surprise yourself with how quickly you enter information. The key to a successful data entry system lies in anticipating what information gets entered; providing shortcuts; and avoiding unnecessary clicking, typing, and moving around. With an efficient data entry form, there's time to concentrate on getting the information right, rather than just getting the job done.

As a database developer, one of your primary concerns is to facilitate this job of getting information into the database—after all, a database is not worth much more than the data you can put into and get out of it. Your goal is to make data entry as easy and fast as possible. At the same time, you want to ensure that the data that's entered is complete and accurate. It's a big challenge. In this chapter, you'll learn how to enhance a data entry form by anticipating the way users will enter data and by writing Microsoft Visual Basic code to respond to events.

Ch04
Contacts.mdb

This chapter uses the practice file Ch04 Contacts.mdb that you installed from the book's CD-ROM. For details about installing the practice files, see "Using the Book's CD-ROM" at the beginning of this book.

Getting Started

● Start Microsoft Access, and open the Ch04 Contacts database in the practice files folder.

Understanding Form and Control Events

Events are happening on your forms and controls all the time. Every time you press a key, use the mouse, or change data, an event occurs. Click the mouse—event! Change a field—event! And each event gives you a chance to make something happen in your application by attaching code to the event procedure.

Open the *Contacts* Form

● On the main *Switchboard* form, click Enter/View Contacts.

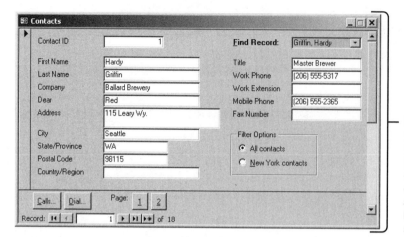

Every time the user clicks the mouse, presses a key, or changes data, events are occuring behind the scenes.

From the point of view of your application, the events on a form occur randomly. The application has no way of knowing *why*, for example, the user enters a certain control, or what the user will do next—it has to take each event as it comes. In some ways, events are like little fires popping up here and there, and your application is the fire department, running in to put them out. And like the fire department, your application must be prepared for anything.

The trick to programming events is figuring out which events to respond to and how. After you set up the responses, your application works automatically. Table 4-1 provides a list of the most common things users do on a data entry form, along with the events that an application can respond to.

Events for Common Actions on Data Entry Forms

User actions	Associated events
Opening and closing the form	Open, Close, Load, Unload
Moving to and from the form	Activate, Deactivate
Moving from control to control	Enter, Exit, GotFocus, LostFocus
Moving from record to record	Current
Pressing keys	KeyDown, KeyUp, KeyPress
Clicking the mouse	Click, DblClick, MouseDown, MouseUp, MouseWheel
Changing data and saving records	Dirty, BeforeUpdate, AfterUpdate, Undo
Adding records	BeforeInsert, AfterInsert
Deleting records	Delete, BeforeDelConfirm, AfterDelConfirm
Filtering records	Filter, ApplyFilter

These are only the most common events you might want to respond to in code—there are still others. In this chapter, you'll write Visual Basic code to respond to just a few of these events.

Performing Actions as the User Moves in a Form

Access provides some cues to the user moving through a form: the title bar changes color when a form is active, the blinking insertion point indicates the current field, and the record indicator shows the current record, just to name a few. But you may want to customize this behavior or add additional cues for the user. You do this by responding to certain events. For example, when the user switches to a form, the *Activate* event occurs. To change something about the form or the Access interface when a form becomes the active window, you write an event procedure for the *Activate* event. To return the interface to its previous state when the user moves to another form, you write code for the Deactivate event to reverse the effect.

You can also respond as the user moves within a form. As you saw in Chapters 2 and 3, each time the user moves from one record to another, the *Current* event occurs for the new record. In addition, several events occur each time the user moves between controls on a form. When the user moves from one control to another, the *Exit* and *LostFocus* events occur for the control the user leaves, and the Enter and GotFocus events occur for the control the user moves to.

Suppose you want to change the color of a control whenever it is the active control on a form. You can do this by creating event procedures for the control's *Enter* and *Exit* events.

Tip

The Enter and Exit events occur when the user moves into or out of a control, but not when the user switches between windows in Access (staying in the same control in each window). If you only care which control is current on the form, you can use *Enter* and *Exit*; if you also want to run the same code each time a control gets the focus from another window, use *GotFocus* and *LostFocus* instead.

Change the Background Color of a Combo Box

You'll notice that the Find Record combo box has its background color set to light gray to show that entering data in the control isn't required. But you'll want to make this control appear white again whenever it's the active control—after all, it seems a bit strange to select data from a control that's gray, as if it were disabled. To do this, you'll write a simple procedure for the control's *Enter* event.

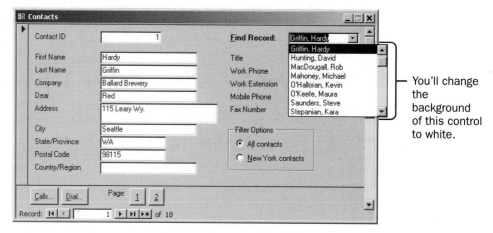

You'll change the background of this control to white.

1 Click the Design View button.

2 With the right mouse button, click the Find Record combo box, and then click Properties on the shortcut menu.

3 Click the Event tab in the property sheet.

4 Click the OnEnter property, and then click the Build button next to the property box.

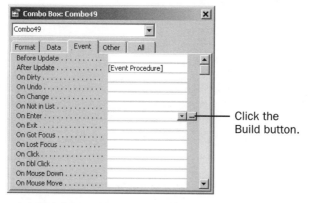

Click the Build button.

5 Click Code Builder, and then click OK.

Access tells Visual Basic to open the form module for the *Contacts* form and create the event procedure for the combo box.

Remember, the name of the combo box is actually a default name—something like *Combo49*—that the Combo Box Wizard assigned when you created the control. You can see the name assigned by the wizard by looking at the event procedure's name (in the Sub statement at the top of the window).

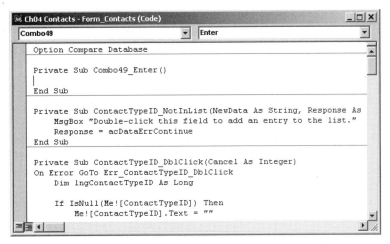

6 Press the Tab key and type the following line of Visual Basic code for the procedure (substituting the actual number of your combo box for "49").

```
Combo49.BackColor = 16777215    ' Change background to white.
```

This code sets the BackColor property to color 16777215, the code for the color white. Just as when you set a property of a form, you set a control property by typing the property name followed by the equal sign and the value you want to set it to. With a control property, however, you also have to let Visual Basic know which control you have in mind. To do this, you type the control name and a period before the property name.

Add a Procedure to Change the Color Back

The combo box will now change to white when you enter it—but you want to leave it the way you found it. To change the color back to gray when you leave, you'll write another procedure for the control's *Exit* event.

1 In the Procedure box at the top of the Code window, select Exit from the list of events.

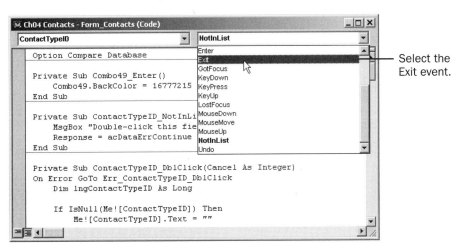

Select the Exit event.

Visual Basic creates the *Exit* event procedure for you—and also sets the control's OnExit property to [Event Procedure] so that the procedure will run when you exit the control.

2 Press Tab and type the following Visual Basic code for the procedure (again substituting the number of your combo box):

```
Combo49.BackColor = 12632256    ' Change background to gray.
```

This code sets the BackColor property of the combo box to the code for gray.

Tip

Want to use other colors? You can find out the code for another color easily by setting a color using the palette in Form Design view, and then looking in the property sheet to see the corresponding code for the color you chose.

View Microsoft Access

Form View

Try Out the New Event Procedures

1 Switch to Access.

2 Close the property sheet.

3 Click the Form View button.

4 Click the down arrow next to the Find Record combo box.

The *Enter* event for the combo box occurs, and your code changes the control's background to white.

5 Click the First Name field again.

Back to an inconspicuous gray!

Performing Actions as the User Changes Data

Each time you change the value of a control, several events occur. Most of the events have to do with pressing keys and changing the focus, but three events deal specifically with changes to data: *Dirty*, *BeforeUpdate*, and *AfterUpdate*. *Dirty* occurs when the user first tries to make a change to data in the current record; *BeforeUpdate* occurs when the user tries to move out of a changed control or save a changed record; *AfterUpdate* occurs when the change to a control or record is successfully completed.

In this section, you'll respond to the *AfterUpdate* event to perform an action after the user changes a control. Later in the chapter, you'll respond to the *BeforeUpdate* event to perform an action when the user tries to save a record.

Setting the Value of a Control "Auto-magically"

When entering data, there's nothing better than having the database enter information for you wherever it can. One way you can achieve this is to set the DefaultValue property for fields in your tables so that when you add a new record, Access fills in the field's value automatically. But this strategy doesn't work well if you want to fill in a field "on the fly" in response to an entry in another field. In this case, you can use an event procedure to respond to the user updating the one field, and provide Visual Basic code that updates the other field.

For example, the *Contacts* form has a Dear field that stores an informal name or nickname to be used in the salutation of a letter. For a person named Thomas, the user might want to set this value to Tom so that a letter can use the familiar name in its greeting. The thing is, users will want to address most people by their first name—so during data entry, you'd like the Dear field to get filled in automatically with the value the user enters in the First Name field. Then, if necessary, they can always change the Dear field to something else.

Add an Event Procedure to Set the *Dear* Control's Value

The event that occurs when the user moves out of a field after changing its value is the *AfterUpdate* event. You'll place code in the *AfterUpdate* event procedure for this event to copy the *FirstName* value to the Dear field.

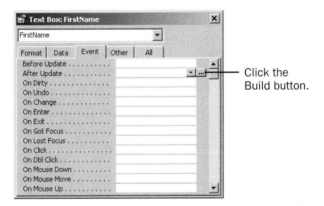

You want this field to be filled in automatically.

Design view

1 Click the Design View button.

2 With the right mouse button, click the *FirstName* control, and then click Properties on the shortcut menu.

The property sheet shows event properties for the *FirstName* control.

3 Click the *AfterUpdate* event, and then click the Build button.

4 Select Code Builder, and then click OK.

Visual Basic displays the *FirstName_AfterUpdate* event procedure.

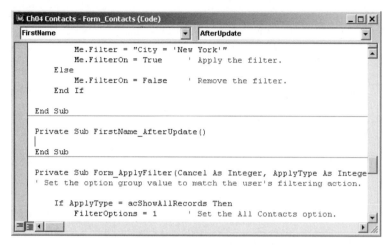

```
Ch04 Contacts - Form_Contacts (Code)                          _ □ ×
FirstName                          ▼    AfterUpdate                 ▼
            Me.Filter = "City = 'New York'"
            Me.FilterOn = True        ' Apply the filter.
        Else
            Me.FilterOn = False       ' Remove the filter.
        End If

    End Sub

    Private Sub FirstName_AfterUpdate()

    End Sub

    Private Sub Form_ApplyFilter(Cancel As Integer, ApplyType As Intege
    ' Set the option group value to match the user's filtering action.

        If ApplyType = acShowAllRecords Then
            FilterOptions = 1         ' Set the All Contacts option.
```

5   Type the following Visual Basic code for the procedure:

```
' Copy the FirstName value to the Dear control.

    Dear = FirstName
```

This line of code sets the value of the *Dear* control to the same value as the *FirstName* control.

Try Out the Event Procedure

1   Switch to Access.

2   Close the property sheet.

3   Click the Form View button.

4   Click the New Record button.

5   In the First Name field, type **John**, and then press Tab.

When you move out of the field, the AfterUpdate event occurs. Your code runs, setting the value of the Dear field. At this point, you could continue entering the record, either skipping the Dear field or manually changing its value if necessary. Instead, now that you know it works, clear the new record without saving it.

6   Press the Esc key.

Add Code to Check Whether the Dear Field is Blank

There's a minor glitch with our plan for the Dear field. Imagine this scenario: you enter a record for a Thomas Blanque, the first name *Thomas* gets copied to the Dear field, but you then change the Dear field to *Tom*. Then you realize you misspelled Thomas, so you go back and spell it correctly. Can you guess what happens? Your event procedure copies over the Dear field containing Tom— which really isn't what you want. Instead, you want the *Contacts* form to be smarter: you want it to copy the first name to the Dear field only when the Dear field is blank.

1 Switch to Visual Basic.

2 Add two lines of code before and after the existing line in the procedure so that it reads as follows. (You'll also want to add a tab before the word *Dear* to indent the line.)

```
If IsNull(Dear) Then
    Dear = FirstName
End If
```

The *IsNull* function in Visual Basic returns *True* if the item in parentheses is null (contains no value), *False* if it contains a value—so in this line, the code after the Then keyword gets run only if the Dear field is blank.

View Microsoft
Access

3 Switch to Access.

4 In the First Name field, type **Tomas**, and then press Tab.

Your event procedure runs. Because the Dear field is null, the event procedure copies the first name value to the Dear field just as it did before.

5 In the Last Name field, type **Blanque**.

6 Press Tab twice, and then in the Dear field, type **Tom**.

7 In the First Name field, click between the "T" and the "o" and type the **h** in Thomas.

8 Press Tab.

Your event procedure runs. This time, however, it doesn't copy the first name value to the Dear field because you've already filled it in—which means the expression *IsNull(Dear)* is false.

Responding to Keyboard Events

One way to provide shortcuts for users of your application is by giving them special keys that perform common actions. Keyboard shortcuts aren't as visible as command buttons—but you can have only so many command buttons on a form. In this section, you'll write an event procedure that responds to keyboard events and sets the value of several controls on the *Contacts* form.

Every time you press a key on a form, three events occur: *KeyDown*, *KeyPress*, and *KeyUp*. You use *KeyPress* to respond to normal characters—such as letters and numbers—as the user types them. You use the *KeyDown* and *KeyUp* events to handle the exact keys that are being pressed on the keyboard, including combinations that use special keys like Shift, Alt, and Ctrl.

Add a *KeyDown* Event Procedure to Set Control Values

Most of your contacts are in New York City, so you want a quick way to enter values for New York City in a contact's record. To do this, you'll create a *KeyDown* procedure for the City field that detects when a user presses the Ctrl key and the number 1 key at the same time.

Design View

1 Click the Design View button.

2 With the right mouse button, click the City field, and then click Properties on the shortcut menu.

The property sheet displays the Event properties for the City field.

3 Click the OnKeyDown property, and then click the Build button.

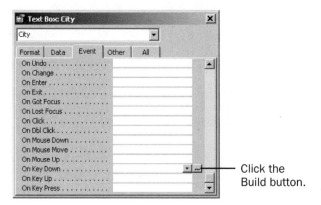

Click the
Build button.

4 Select Code Builder, and then click OK.

Visual Basic displays the *City_KeyDown* event procedure.

5 Enter the following Visual Basic code for the procedure (the *Sub* and *End Sub* lines are already present).

```
Private Sub City_KeyDown(KeyCode As Integer, Shift As Integer)
' If key is CTRL+1, enter values for New York.

    If KeyCode = 49 And Shift = 2 Then    ' CTRL+1 was pressed.
        City = "New York"
        StateOrProvince = "NY"
        Country = "USA"
    End If
End Sub
```

The code in this procedure runs whenever a key or combination of keys is pressed. Using the *KeyCode* and *Shift* arguments, which contain numbers representing the key that was pressed and the status of the Shift, Ctrl, and Alt keys at the time it was pressed, the procedure determines whether the key combination was in fact the number 1 key along with the Ctrl key. (The *KeyCode* value for the number 1 key is *49*, and the Shift code of 2 indicates that the Ctrl key was pressed.) If the key combination is Ctrl+1, the three statements in the block assign values for New York City to the three controls on the *Contacts* form.

View Microsoft
Access

Form View

New Record

1 Switch to Access.

2 Close the property sheet.

3 Click the Form View button on the toolbar.

4 Click the New Record button on the toolbar.

5 Click in the City field, and then press Ctrl+1.

Your event procedure runs, filling in the three fields.

6 Press Esc.

Apply the Keyboard Handler Anywhere on the Form

As it stands, your keyboard shortcut works only if the focus is on the City field. If you want it to apply anywhere on the form, you'll have to modify the code to respond to the

KeyDown event for the form instead of just for the *City* control. There's also another step you'll need to know about. Normally, keyboard events all occur for the control that has the focus, but they don't occur for the form. If you want all key events to be available to the form's event procedures, you can set the KeyPreview property for the form.

Design View

1 Click the Design View button.

2 Double-click the form selection box. (It's in the upper left corner of the window, at the intersection of the rulers.)

The property sheet displays Form properties.

3 Set the KeyPreview property to *Yes*.

Now all key events, regardless of which control they belong to, will fire the form's keyboard-handling procedures first, followed by those for the control that has the focus.

4 Close the property sheet.

5 Switch to Visual Basic.

6 In the header for the *City_KeyDown* procedure (the *Private Sub* statement), select the word *City*, type **Form**, and then click on another line of code in the procedure to register the change.

Change the name from *City_KeyDown* to *Form_KeyDown*.

```
Ch04 Contacts - Form_Contacts (Code)                              _ □ X

City                              ▼   KeyDown                          ▼

    Option Compare Database

    Private Sub Form_KeyDown(KeyCode As Integer, Shift As Integer)
    ' If key is CTRL+1, enter values for New York.

        If KeyCode = 49 And Shift = 2 Then     ' CTRL+1 was pressed.
            City = "New York"
            StateOrProvince = "NY"
            Country = "USA"
        End If

    End Sub

    Private Sub Combo49_Enter()
        Combo49.BackColor = 16777215     ' Change background to white.
    End Sub
```

View Microsoft Access

Now the code you originally wrote for the control responds to the form's *KeyDown* event, so it will apply from anywhere on the form.

7 Switch to Access.

Form View

8 Click the Form View button on the toolbar.

9 Click the New Record button on the toolbar.

New Record

10 Press Ctrl+1.

Your event procedure runs, filling in the three fields.

11 Press Esc.

Save

12 Click the Save button on the toolbar.

Access saves your changes to the form.

The *Contacts* form is coming along very nicely—with code to set control values automatically, it's getting easier to use all the time. But we're not finished yet!

Validating Data

When entering data, it's easy to make mistakes or leave out important information. Errors or omissions in your data make your database less valuable and harder to use. One advantage of a database system is that it can check the data you enter, sometimes even refusing to save data that doesn't follow the rules. This process is referred to as *validation*, because it involves checking data to make sure it is valid.

There are several ways Access checks data, most of which don't involve any programming. For a complex data-entry form, you'll typically use one or more of the following validation features.

Data types This is the most simple form of validation, used in every database. Quite simply, Access doesn't allow you to store data in a field if the data is inappropriate for the field's data type. For example, Access makes sure a Date field always stores only a date.

InputMask property This property helps users enter data in fields that have formatting characters, such as the hyphens and parentheses in postal codes or phone numbers. Access allows only values that fit the input mask.

Required property By setting this property for fields in a table, you can make sure they aren't left blank. If a user tries to blank a required field or save a record without entering a value for a required field, Access displays a message.

ValidationRule property By setting this property for fields, tables, or controls on forms, you can make sure data follows rules that you set. When the user updates a field or saves a record, Access checks the data to make sure it fits with any validation expressions you've entered, and displays a message if it doesn't. You can specify the message that Access displays by setting the ValidationText property.

BeforeUpdate event procedure If you want to provide complex field validation that you can't write a validation expression for, you can write an event procedure that checks the data. Unlike other forms of validation in which Access automatically displays a message, your *BeforeUpdate* event procedure must display a message and cancel the update.

The *Contacts* form already uses input masks. In this section, you'll add other validation expressions, first setting properties in the *Contacts* table, and then creating a *BeforeUpdate* event procedure that checks data each time a user saves a record.

Require That Each Record Have a Complete Name

To ensure that a field always has a value, you set the Required property in the table.

1 Close the *Contacts* form.

You have to close the *Contacts* form because you can't modify the design of a table when the form is open.

Database
Window

2 Click the Database Window button on the toolbar.

3 In the Database window, click the Tables shortcut, select the *Contacts* table, and then click Design.

Access opens the table in Design view.

4 Click the FirstName field.

5 In the lower half of the window, set the Required property to *Yes*.

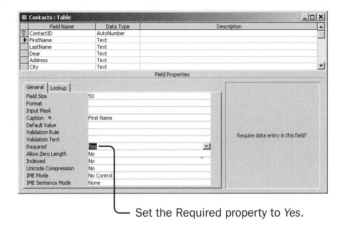

Set the Required property to *Yes*.

6 Click the LastName field, and set the Required property to *Yes*.

Now Access won't allow the user to save a contact without entering both a first and last name.

Require That Each Record Include a Phone Number

Because you often print a phone list, you'd like to make sure that users enter either a work phone number or a mobile phone number for every contact. If you wanted to require entry in both fields, you'd set the Required property as you did for the name fields. But because either one or both of the phone numbers is acceptable, you'll need to use a different strategy. To provide a validation rule that involves more than one field in a table, you set the table's ValidationRule property.

Properties

1 Click the Properties button on the toolbar.

2 In the property sheet, click the ValidationRule property, and then type **([WorkPhone] & [MobilePhone]) Is Not Null**.

This validation expression combines the two phone fields and then checks to make sure the resulting value is not Null (empty). You can think of this expression as saying, "Does the combination of the WorkPhone field and the MobilePhone field contain any text?"

If both phone fields are blank, then the entire expression is false, which tells Access that the record is invalid. Note that you must include the brackets around the field names you use in the validation expression, or else the property sheet will interpret them as string expressions instead of field names.

3   Click the ValidationText property, and then type **You must enter either a work phone or a mobile phone**.

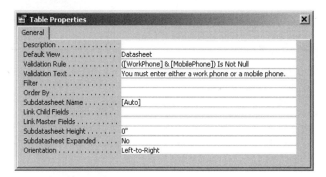

This is the message Access displays if the record is invalid.

4   Close the property sheet.

5   Close the *Contacts* table, choosing Yes when Access asks if you want to save changes, and choosing No when it asks if you want to check whether existing data follows the rules you set.

6   Minimize the Database window.

Test the Validation Rules

1   On the main *Switchboard* form, click Enter/View Contacts.

New Record

2   Click the New Record button on the toolbar.

3   In the First Name field, type **Carl**.

4   Press Shift+Enter to save changes to the record.

Access displays a message telling you that the Last Name field can't be null, and it doesn't let you save the record.

5   Click OK.

6   Click the Last Name field, and then type **Thorgerson**.

7   Press Shift+Enter.

This time, Access displays your phone number validation message—and it still won't let you save the record.

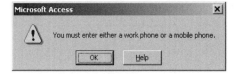

8 Click OK.

9 Click the Work Phone field, and then type **(212) 555-1314**.

10 Press Shift+Enter

This time, you can successfully save the record in the *Contacts* table.

Validating Data Using an Event Procedure

So far, the validation you've added hasn't required any code. But what if you want to provide validation that works differently in different situations? You may want to remind users that addresses should always have a postal (or ZIP) code. You could set the Required property for the PostalCode field in the *Contacts* table; then, every record would need this field filled in. But this would be too restrictive—some contact records won't have an address at all, so you don't want to always require a postal code.

To provide this type of custom validation, you write an event procedure that runs each time a record is saved. The procedure will check for a postal code and then display a message if necessary.

Create an Event Procedure That Checks for a Postal Code

When the user tries to save a record in the *Contacts* table, the *BeforeUpdate* event occurs. In a *BeforeUpdate* event procedure, your code can either allow the record to be saved, or cancel the event, requiring the user to fix the problem and try again.

Design View

1 Click the Design View button.

2 With the right mouse button, click the form selection box, and then click Properties on the shortcut menu.

3 Click the Event tab in the property sheet.

4 Click the BeforeUpdate property, and then click the Build button.

5 Select Code Builder, and then click OK.

Visual Basic displays the *Form_BeforeUpdate* event procedure.

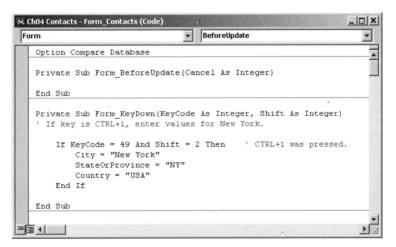

```
Option Compare Database

Private Sub Form_BeforeUpdate(Cancel As Integer)

End Sub

Private Sub Form_KeyDown(KeyCode As Integer, Shift As Integer)
' If key is CTRL+1, enter values for New York.

    If KeyCode = 49 And Shift = 2 Then    ' CTRL+1 was pressed.
        City = "New York"
        StateOrProvince = "NY"
        Country = "USA"
    End If

End Sub
```

You'll notice that the header for the *BeforeUpdate* procedure includes a *Cancel* argument. You'll use this argument in your event procedure to tell Access whether to allow the user to save the record.

6 Enter the following Visual Basic code for the procedure.

```
Private Sub Form_BeforeUpdate(Cancel As Integer)
' If the user entered an address, check for a postal code.

    If Not IsNull(Address) And IsNull(PostalCode) Then
        MsgBox "You must enter a postal code.", vbExclamation
        PostalCode.SetFocus    ' Go back to PostalCode field.
        Cancel = True          ' Cancel saving the record.
    End If

End Sub
```

Let's walk through the procedure line by line.

The first line uses a complex condition—*Not IsNull(Address) And IsNull(PostalCode)*—to determine whether or not the record that the user is saving is acceptable. This condition uses the *IsNull* function, which returns *False* if the field in parentheses contains a value, and *True* if it contains no value (also known as the *Null* value). You can read the statement like this: "If the Address field doesn't contain *Null* (if it has a value) and the PostalCode field does contain *Null* (it doesn't have a value), then execute the statements inside the block, otherwise skip over them."

If the user enters an address without a postal code, the next three lines run.

■ The first line uses the *MsgBox* statement to display a simple message to the user. You've used this statement before, but here it has a second argument which you can use to tell Access what type of box to display. The constant value *vbExclamation* tells Access to display a message box with an exclamation point icon.

■ The user must return to the PostalCode field to enter a postal code before saving the record. For convenience, the second line uses the *SetFocus* method to return the focus to this field automatically so that the user can just type in the postal code.

■ The final statement sets the value of the *Cancel* argument to *True* to cancel the *BeforeUpdate* event. Every *BeforeUpdate* event procedure—like many other event procedures—includes the *Cancel* argument. Setting this argument to *True* is equivalent to saying, "Pretend that the user action that caused this event didn't happen." In this case, the user is trying to save the record, and canceling this event causes the record not to be saved. Instead, the user must enter a postal code and try again.

Test the New Event Procedure

View Microsoft Access

1 Switch to Access.

2 Close the property sheet.

3 Click the Form View button on the toolbar.

Form View

New Record

4 Click the New Record button on the toolbar.

5 Fill in the fields as follows:

Field Name	Value
First Name	**Karl**
Last Name	**Sigel**
Address	**200 Bourbon St.**
City	**New Orleans**
State/Province	**LA**
Work Phone	**(404) 555-3933**

6 Press Shift+Enter to save changes to the record.

The *BeforeUpdate* event occurs, running the code in your event procedure. Because you filled in the Address field but not the Postal Code field, the code in the procedure displays the message—complete with the exclamation point icon—telling you why the record can't be saved.

7 Click OK.

The code in your procedure continues, canceling the *BeforeUpdate* event. This returns you to the form without saving the record—you must now either undo the record or enter a postal code.

8 In the Postal Code field, type **70130**.

9 Press Shift+Enter.

Asking the User a Question

Your procedure works just fine—if the user types an address but doesn't have the postal code, it is impossible to save the record. This design is still awfully restrictive. To be more flexible, it would be nice to simply warn the user that there's no postal code, and then allow the record to be saved.

To do this, you'll learn an important technique: using the *MsgBox* function to get a response from the user and performing different actions based on the response.

Let the User Leave the *PostalCode* Field Blank

1 Switch to Visual Basic.

2 Edit the code in the *BeforeUpdate* procedure to appear as follows:

```
Private Sub Form_BeforeUpdate(Cancel As Integer)
' If the user entered an address, check for a postal code.
```

```
    Dim strMessage As String
    Dim intOptions As Integer
    Dim bytChoice As Byte

    If Not IsNull(Address) And IsNull(PostalCode) Then
        strMessage = "You didn't enter a postal code. Save anyway?"
        intOptions = vbQuestion + vbOKCancel
        bytChoice = MsgBox(strMessage, intOptions)

        If bytChoice = vbCancel Then
            PostalCode.SetFocus    ' Go back to PostalCode field.
            Cancel = True          ' Cancel saving the record.
        End If
    End If
End Sub
```

The procedure now uses several new Visual Basic techniques.

The first three lines use *Dim* statements to tell Visual Basic about three variables you're going to use in this procedure. A variable is a temporary place to store information in the computer's memory—similar to the memory function on a calculator. Each *Dim* statement includes the name of a variable, along with the type of data it will store. As the procedure continues, your code can assign values to the variables, retrieving the values at any time later in the procedure.

You'll notice that the name of each variable has a prefix that indicates the type of data it stores: "*str*" for string data, "*int*" for integer data, "*byt*" for byte data. You'll use this convention to name variables throughout the book.

- The *If...Then* statement is the same as before, but the code block it runs if the user enters an address without a postal code is different. The first line in the block assigns a value to the *strMessage* variable. This variable stores the message you want to display, warning the user about the postal code and asking for a response. When you assign a value to a string variable, you surround the string data with quotation marks.

- The next line assigns a value to the *intOptions* variable. This variable stores a number representing options for the *MsgBox* function. You can add the values of several constants to specify more than one option—here, for example, you've specified that you want the Warning query icon to appear in the box (*vbQuestion*) and that you want the box to include OK and Cancel buttons (*vbOKCancel*).

- The next line uses the *MsgBox* function to display the question to the user. When you used the *MsgBox* statement previously, you placed the arguments to the statement—the message and options—after the statement, separated by a comma. Using the function, you do the same, but because it's a function, you surround the arguments with parentheses. In addition, the function returns a value that you want to store in the *bytChoice* variable. To assign the value of the function to the variable, you've put it after the variable name, separated by an equal sign (=). In effect, this line of code says, "Display the message text from the *strMessage* variable using the options from the *intOptions* variable, and put the result in the *bytChoice* variable." The result that the *MsgBox* function returns is a number representing which button the user chose in the message box, either OK or Cancel.

■ The next few lines use another *If...Then* structure to perform an action based on the user's response to the question. If the user responds by clicking the Cancel button, the value that gets stored in the *bytChoice* variable will equal the constant value *vbCancel*, and the block of code runs.

■ If the user responds by clicking Cancel, you want to move back to the Postal Code field and cancel the event so that the user still has to enter a postal code. If the user responds by clicking OK, the procedure skips this block of code, allowing the record to be saved without a postal code. Note that each *If...Then* structure ends with its own *End If* statement to indicate the end of that structure.

Tip

You may wonder how you can find out which constant values to use for specifying options for the *MsgBox* function and interpreting the response. You can read about all these constants in the Help topic for the *MsgBox* function, by clicking the *MsgBox* keyword in the Code window and pressing F1.

Test the Procedure Again

View Microsoft Access

1 Switch to Access.

2 Click the Postal Code field's label, and press the Delete key to delete the postal code.

3 Press Shift+Enter to save changes to the record.

The *BeforeUpdate* event occurs, running your new code. This time, the code in the procedure displays the question—and includes OK and Cancel buttons so that you can indicate a response.

4 Click Cancel.

The code in your procedure continues, canceling the *BeforeUpdate* event. But suppose you realize that you don't have the postal code and want to save the record anyway.

5 Press Shift+Enter.

6 Click OK.

This time, your response causes the code that cancels the *BeforeUpdate* event to be skipped, allowing the record to be saved as if the procedure weren't there at all.

As you can see, validation can be as simple or complex as necessary in your application. Even this procedure could be expanded to cover several different scenarios: if you had other rules for entering contacts in records, you would simply add additional blocks of code to the same *BeforeUpdate* event procedure to check all your rules before allowing the record to be saved.

Chapter Wrap-Up

1   Close the *Contacts* form, clicking Yes when Access asks if you want to save changes.

2   Close Access.

Create a standard module, page 91

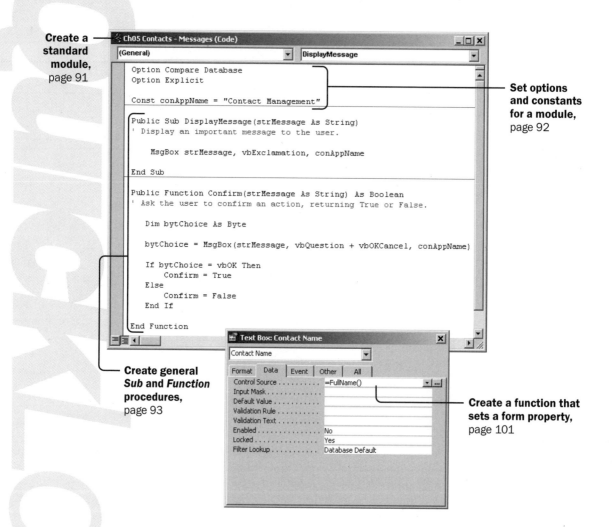

Set options and constants for a module, page 92

```
Ch05 Contacts - Messages (Code)                                    _ □ X
(General)                        ▼        DisplayMessage              ▼

    Option Compare Database
    Option Explicit

    Const conAppName = "Contact Management"

Public Sub DisplayMessage(strMessage As String)
' Display an important message to the user.

    MsgBox strMessage, vbExclamation, conAppName

End Sub

Public Function Confirm(strMessage As String) As Boolean
' Ask the user to confirm an action, returning True or False.

    Dim bytChoice As Byte

    bytChoice = MsgBox(strMessage, vbQuestion + vbOKCancel, conAppName)

    If bytChoice = vbOK Then
        Confirm = True
    Else
        Confirm = False
    End If

End Function
```

Create general *Sub* and *Function* procedures, page 93

```
Text Box: Contact Name                             X
Contact Name                              ▼
 Format   Data   Event   Other   All
Control Source . . . . . . . . . .   =FullName()          ▼ ...
Input Mask . . . . . . . . . . . . .
Default Value . . . . . . . . . . .
Validation Rule . . . . . . . . . .
Validation Text . . . . . . . . . .
Enabled . . . . . . . . . . . . . . .   No
Locked . . . . . . . . . . . . . .   Yes
Filter Lookup . . . . . . . . . .   Database Default
```

Create a function that sets a form property, page 101

Chapter 5
Write Your Own Functions

After completing this chapter, you will be able to:

✔ **Create a standard module.**

✔ **Write general *Sub* and *Function* procedures.**

✔ **Provide information to a procedure by adding arguments.**

✔ **Use general procedures in code and expressions on a form.**

Watching small children learn to speak is fascinating. Long before they're aware of grammar or sentence structure, they manage to build sentences. Without any understanding of the rules of language, they nevertheless communicate. Of course, before you can read or write, you need to learn *something* about the language—still, you can get by pretty well with a rudimentary understanding of grammar and a limited vocabulary.

Although a far cry from anyone's native tongue, computer programming languages share many characteristics with human language. Both have an extensive vocabulary and complex rules of grammar to follow. But you can learn to get things done using Microsoft Visual Basic and even create and customize applications, without bothering to learn much about the programming language. You can get a good start with a language before studying any grammar, but you won't be likely to write *War and Peace*. In order to use a language with confidence, you need to understand how it works—the basic rules and components, and how to combine them effectively. In this chapter, you'll learn about the fundamental building blocks of Visual Basic—modules and procedures—and how you fit them together to build flexible, well-organized applications. You'll pick up new vocabulary along the way, and you'll try using it in several different contexts.

Ch05
Contacts.mdb

This chapter uses the practice file Ch05 Contacts.mdb that you installed from the book's CD-ROM. For details about installing the practice files, see "Using the Book's CD-ROM" at the beginning of this book."

Getting Started

● Start Access, and open the Ch05 Contacts database in the practice files folder.

Understanding Modules and Procedures

So far, you may have been working exclusively with event procedures on existing forms. Because forms are so central to Access applications, this type of procedure is probably where you'll add most of the code you write. However, there is another important type of procedure you'll create in this chapter, called a *general* procedure. General procedures don't run automatically in response to events—instead, you have to run them yourself, either by referring to them in an expression on a form or report or by using them in Visual Basic code. General procedures come in two types: *Sub* procedures and *Function* procedures. Event procedures, by contrast, are all *Sub* procedures.

Why Create General Procedures?

You can think of general procedures as having a supporting role in your applications. While event procedures are the central force in Access programming, general procedures are helpers along the way. You could accomplish most anything in Access with event procedures alone, but using general procedures provides much better solutions as the complexity of your application increases. You can use general procedures in several ways.

Perform complex operations that don't fit in an expression. If you've used expressions as property settings on forms and reports, you know that they can quickly become unwieldy. You can hide this complexity by creating your own function to perform the operation you need and then referring to it in your expressions. Additionally, Visual Basic code can perform complex operations that aren't possible using expressions.

Reuse program code to repeat a task. Your event procedures often perform the same or similar actions at various times. For example, you might often display a message to the user. Although you could copy the same code into every event procedure that uses it, this would be extremely inefficient. Instead, you can create a general procedure that performs a common task and reuse it in every procedure that performs that task.

Break up programming tasks into manageable units. If you were to put all your code into event procedures, they could become very long, complicated, and difficult to understand. By creating separate procedures to perform each part of a large task, you can simplify your work and make each individual procedure easier to read and understand.

Standard Modules and Form Modules

You can put general procedures in one of two places: in a form or report module, where they share space with any event procedures you write; or in a *standard* module. Standard modules are separate database objects containing one or many procedures. They most often contain "utility" functions, so named because they are useful in many different circumstances. For example, one standard module might contain several general functions for working with dates in Visual Basic—you can copy such a module to any application in which you use dates.

If you add a general procedure to a form or report module, it belongs to that form or report. Most often, you'll use this type of procedure only in the form or report itself, either in expressions on the form or in other procedures in the same module. Create this type of procedure to perform a task that applies directly to the form—for example, to work with information in the fields on that form.

General procedures that you add to standard modules usually belong to the application as a whole. Create this type of procedure to perform a task that applies to more than one form or report—often, a task that could apply to any form or report.

Creating General Procedures in a Standard Module

A database can contain one or more standard modules, each of which can hold many procedures. You'll usually group all the procedures for a specific purpose into one module. In this section, you'll create a module to store two procedures that are used to display messages to the user.

Create a New Standard Module

1 In the Database window, click the Modules shortcut.

Standard modules are regular objects in the Database window, just like tables and forms.

2 Click the New button.

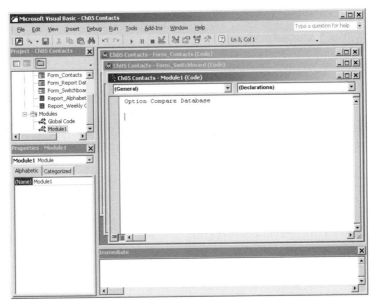

Access creates a new standard module and displays it in Visual Basic. From here, you can enter Visual Basic code and create general procedures.

Using the Declarations Section

A new module doesn't contain any procedures. However, like all modules, it has a special section called the *Declarations* section. In this section, you declare variables and constants and enter other preliminary code that applies to the entire module. In a standard module, code in the Declarations section can even apply to all modules in the application.

As you can see, Visual Basic automatically added the *Option Compare Database* statement to the Declarations section of your module. This statement uses the *Option* keyword to set an option for the whole module. It is one of several available statements that begin with the *Option* keyword.

The *Compare* option determines the method that Visual Basic uses for comparing strings in your module and can be set to *Database*, *Text*, or *Binary*. Using the *Database* option tells Visual Basic to compare strings using the sort order set in your database, as opposed to the traditional Visual Basic sort order, which distinguishes between uppercase and lowercase letters. Because *Option Compare Database* makes sense for most applications in Access, you should just leave this statement in your modules.

Set a Visual Basic Option for Your Module

There is another option that you'll want to set using the *Option* keyword: the *Explicit* option. This option tells Visual Basic to check all the variable names you use in the module, to make sure you've declared them. If you don't include this option in the *Declarations* section of a module, Visual Basic lets you enter just about anything in code—but doing this makes your code much more prone to errors, because a misspelling won't be caught before you run your code. Having the *Option Explicit* statement in your modules will help you avoid many headaches down the road. In fact, since it's such a good idea, you'll also set a special option for all of Visual Basic so that every module you create will have this option setting.

1   Press the Backspace key to move to the previous line in the module.

2   Type **Option Explicit**, and then press the Enter key twice.

    You've set the option for this one module. Next, you'll set it for all modules you create in the future.

3   On the Tools menu, click Options.

4   On the Editor tab, click the Require Variable Declaration box to select it.

5   Click OK.

    Now every module you create will include the Option Explicit line, so you'll always be informed of undeclared or misspelled names in your code.

Declaring Constant Values

One of the statements you can place in the *Declarations* section is the *Const* statement, which declares a *constant* for use in your code. A constant is like a variable, except that you can't change its value after you declare it. You've probably already used predefined constants such as *vbCancel*. Your own constants work the same way, except that you decide what name and value to give them. You can think of a constant as being a placeholder for a value, making it easier to refer to in your code.

Declare a Constant for the Name of Your Application

You might want to declare a constant to store the name of your application, which you plan to use in procedures in the module.

●   Type **Const conAppName = "Contact Management"**, and press Enter.

This tells Visual Basic that each time *conAppName* appears in code, it should be replaced with this string value. If you want to change the application name later, you'll only need to change it in one place, not throughout the module.

Here's what the completed Declarations section looks like.

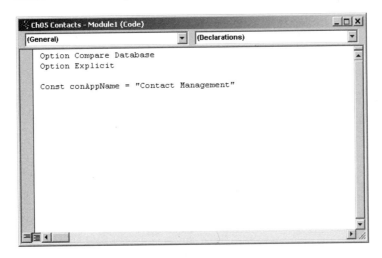

Tip

Declaring a constant in the *Declarations* section makes the constant available throughout the module. If you plan to use a constant value in only one procedure, it makes more sense to declare it in the procedure itself.

On the other hand, if you plan to use a constant value in more than one module, you can make it available to the entire database by using the *PublicConst* statement instead of *Const*. Place this statement only in the *Declarations* section of a standard module.

Creating a *Sub* Procedure

You've already seen how to create event procedures and write code for them in Visual Basic. Creating general procedures is much the same, except that you have more flexibility. While the attributes of an event procedure—its name, type, and arguments—are predefined by Visual Basic, you choose all these attributes for the general procedures you create.

Create the *DisplayMessage* Procedure

You'll create a general procedure that you can use to display a message to the user—a common task that the procedure will help make easier.

Insert Module

1 Click the arrow next to the Insert Module button on the toolbar (which displays the button face for the last button you selected here), and then click Procedure.

Visual Basic displays the Add Procedure dialog box, where you specify the name and type of the procedure you want to create.

2   In the Name box, type **DisplayMessage**.

3   Click OK.

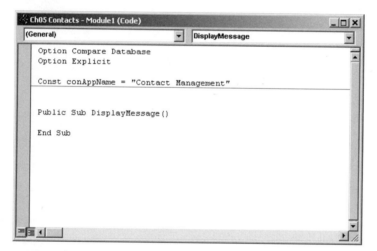

Because the default type of procedure is *Sub*, Visual Basic creates a new *Sub* procedure and displays its *Sub* and *End Sub* lines in the Code window, just underneath the Declarations section for the module.

Add Code to the Procedure

1   Enter the following code for the procedure:

```
' Display an important message to the user.

    MsgBox "This is important.", vbExclamation, conAppName
```

This code uses the *MsgBox* statement to display your message. It specifies a *MsgBox* option by including the *vbExclamation* constant as the second argument so that the message box will include the Warning Message icon. Additionally, it specifies a title for the message box by including the third argument—the constant value that provides the name of the application.

Save

2   Click the Save button on the toolbar.

3   In the Module Name box, type **Messages**, and then click OK.

Visual Basic saves the module in the Contacts database.

Test Your Procedure Using the Immediate Window

You can test general procedures such as the *DisplayMessage* procedure by using the Immediate window.

1   On the View menu, click Immediate Window.

The Immediate window can be docked at the bottom or sides of the Visual Basic window, or it can be an independent floating window. To give yourself more space in the module window, you'll make the Immediate window float on top of Visual Basic.

2   Drag the title bar of the Immediate window up to the center of the Visual Basic window, and then position and resize the window so that you can see as much of your code as possible.

The Immediate window stays on top of your code as long as it is open.

3   In the Immediate window, type **DisplayMessage**.

4   Press Enter.

Your procedure runs in Access, displaying a message in the center of the screen.

5   Click OK.

Now that your procedure has ended, Visual Basic returns to the front.

Adding Arguments to a Procedure

Your procedure works well so far, but it leaves something to be desired. The message it displays is always the same—and the user will get pretty tired of seeing it if it stays this way. What you want is a flexible procedure that allows you to specify which of several messages you want to display. You can achieve this by adding an argument to the procedure.

Add an Argument to the *DisplayMessage* Procedure

1   In the Ch05 Contacts – Messages (Code) window, click between the parentheses in the *Sub* statement, and then type **strMessage As String**.

```
Public Sub DisplayMessage(strMessage As String)
```

This tells Visual Basic that you want to be able to give some information to the *DisplayMessage* procedure, namely, the message you want to display. You're also saying that the piece of information you'll provide to the procedure will be a string, and that it will be called *strMessage*.

2 Edit the *MsgBox* line, replacing the message string with an argument—the *strMessage* variable you declared in the procedure's header:

```
MsgBox strMessage, vbExclamation, conAppName
```

Now, when Visual Basic runs the *MsgBox* statement, it will use the value of *strMessage* instead of a string that's always the same.

Run Your Procedure Using an Argument

When you run a procedure and provide an argument value, it's referred to as *passing* the argument to the procedure.

1 Switch to the Immediate window. (Click its title bar.)

2 Type **DisplayMessage "I can say anything I like!"** and press Enter.

Your procedure runs, using the string value you passed for the *strMessage* argument.

3 Click OK.

Creating a Function

The procedure you created performs an action, but it doesn't provide any information back to the program—this is the nature of a *Sub* procedure. A much more common type of general procedure is a *function*. Using a *Function* procedure allows you to *return* a value to the procedure that runs the function. You've probably already used lots of built-in functions in Access, such as the *IsNull* function, to get information back about something. Now you'll create your own function to use in Access or in Visual Basic code.

Create a Procedure That Asks a Question

In Chapter 4, you used the *MsgBox* function to ask for confirmation before saving a record. Now you'll create a general function, called *Confirm*, that performs this same task for any action that needs confirmation. The function returns a different value depending on the choice the user makes in the message box.

1 Switch to the Ch05 Contacts-Messages (Code) window.

Insert
Procedure

2 Click the Insert Procedure button on the toolbar.

3 In the Name box, type **Confirm**.

4 In the Type box, click Function, and then click OK.

Visual Basic creates a new function and displays its *Function* and *End Function* statements.

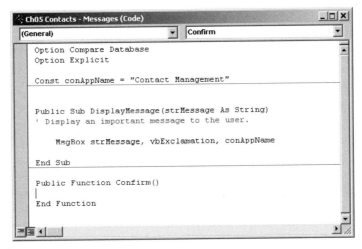

```
Ch05 Contacts - Messages (Code)                    _ □ ×

(General)                    ▼   Confirm                        ▼

    Option Compare Database
    Option Explicit

    Const conAppName = "Contact Management"


    Public Sub DisplayMessage(strMessage As String)
    ' Display an important message to the user.

        MsgBox strMessage, vbExclamation, conAppName

    End Sub

    Public Function Confirm()
    |
    End Function
```

5 Type **strMessage As String** within the parentheses of the *Function* statement, and type **As Boolean** at the end:

```
Public Function Confirm(strMessage As String) As Boolean
```

Let's take a close look at this function declaration:

- The *Public* keyword before the *Function* statement says that this function can be used from anywhere in the application. If you had used the Private keyword instead, you could only run the *Confirm* function from within the Messages module.

- The argument declaration in parentheses tells Visual Basic that you'll pass the message you want to display to the procedure, as you did for the *DisplayMessage* procedure.

- The *As* clause at the end of the *Function* statement tells Visual Basic that you want the function to return a certain type of value. Because you want the *Confirm* function to return either *True* or *False* depending on the user's choice, you'll use the Boolean data type for the function—variables of the Boolean type can have one of only two values, *True* or *False*.

6 Type the following code into the procedure between the *Function* and *End Function* statements:

```
' Ask the user to confirm an action, returning True or False.

    Dim bytChoice As Byte

    bytChoice = MsgBox(strMessage, vbQuestion + vbOKCancel, conAppName)

    If bytChoice = vbOK Then
        Confirm = True
    Else
        Confirm = False
    End If
```

Here's what the code does:

■ First it uses the *Dim* statement to declare the variable *bytChoice*, which will store the number returned by the *MsgBox* function.

■ Next it calls the *MsgBox* function, passing it the *strMessage* argument and specifying options using the predefined constants *vbQuestion* and *vbOKCancel*, which tell Visual Basic to display the message with a Help (question mark) icon and to include OK and Cancel buttons.

■ Finally the function uses an *If...Then* statement to check whether the user chose OK—the condition in the statement compares the *bytChoice* variable to the predefined constant *vbOK*. If the condition is true, the return value of the *Confirm* function gets set to *True*; otherwise, it gets set to *False*. To specify the value you want a function to return, all you have to do is type the function name followed by an equal sign and the value you want it to return. Of course, the value it returns must be consistent with the data type of the function—in this case, Boolean.

Test the *Confirm* Function

Now you can try out the *Confirm* function. To display the value of a function in the Immediate window, you type a question mark (?) before the function name. Also, remember to enclose the arguments to a function in parentheses.

1 Switch to the Immediate window.

2 Type **?Confirm("Is it OK?")**, and press Enter.

Your procedure runs, using the string value you passed for the *strMessage* argument and displaying the message box according to the options you specified in your function.

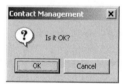

3 Click OK.

The Immediate window displays the return value of the *Confirm* function.

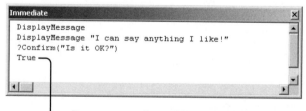

Because you chose OK, the Confirm function returned *True*.

4 Press the Backspace key six times to move back to the end of the line that calls the *Confirm* function, and then press Enter.

5 Click Cancel.

This time, the function returns *False*, indicating that you didn't confirm the action.

6 Close the Immediate window.

Save

7 Click the Save button on the toolbar.

You've created two useful general procedures, *DisplayMessage* and *Confirm*, that you can use in code throughout your database. Moreover, you could copy the Messages module to other databases you create so that you wouldn't have to redo this work in future applications. This is the advantage of standard modules—they're like a box of tools you can use when you need them, and you can carry them around wherever you go, increasing your programming productivity.

Using General Procedures on a Form

The next step is to put your new procedures to work. And because they're general procedures, declared as public, you can use them anywhere in your application. In this section, you'll simplify the code in the *Contacts* form's module by using general procedures where appropriate.

Open the *Contacts* Form's Module

You could open the *Contacts* form's module by setting event properties in the property sheet. However, an easy way to view the Visual Basic code for a form is to click the Code button.

View Microsoft
Access

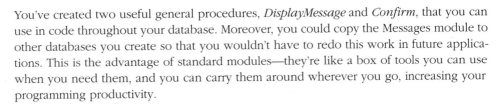

1 Switch to Access. (Click the View Microsoft Access button.)

Access returns to the front.

2 In the Database window, click the Forms shortcut, and then click the *Contacts* form.

Code

3 Click the Code button on the toolbar.

Access opens the *Contacts* form in Design view, and then opens its module in Visual Basic and displays the existing procedures in the module. From here, you can browse through procedures or add new Visual Basic code.

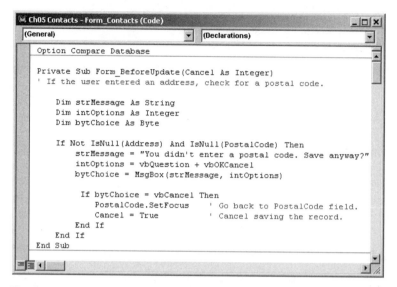

The first event procedure shown in the module is the *Form_BeforeUpdate* procedure. It displays a message if a user fails to enter a postal code for an address. If the user clicks Cancel in the message box, it cancels the update so that the record isn't saved.

Edit the Code to Use the *Confirm* Function

This procedure performs a simple action, but it uses several variables and lines of code that aren't really related to the task at hand—they're related to the problem of displaying a message box that asks the user a question. Now that you have a general function that does this for you, you can simplify this event procedure.

1 Replace the three *Dim* lines with a single *Dim* statement.

```
Dim blnOK As Boolean
```

This line of code declares a variable called *blnOK*, which stores the response you get from the *Confirm* function. Because the *Confirm* function returns a Boolean value (either *True* or *False*), you declare the variable with the Boolean data type.

2 Replace the three lines that set up and display the message (after the first *If...Then* statement) with the following line:

```
blnOK = Confirm("You didn't enter a postal code. Save anyway?")
```

This line calls the *Confirm* function, passing it the message you want to display and storing its return value—*True* if the user chose OK, *False* if the user chose Cancel—in the *blnOK* variable.

3 Replace the second *If...Then* statement, which tests what button the user chose, with the following line:

```
If Not blnOK Then' User chose Cancel.
```

This line checks to see whether the user chose the OK or the Cancel button. Because the value of *blnOK* is *True* if the user chose OK, the condition *Not blnOK* is *True* if the user chose Cancel. If the user chose Cancel, the code in the *If...Then* block runs, moving the focus to *PostalCode* and canceling the update.

The following illustration shows the much-simplified *BeforeUpdate* event procedure.

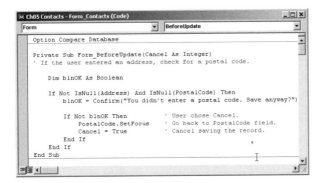

Try the Procedure

1 Switch to Access.

2 Click the Form View button on the toolbar.

3 Click the Postal Code field's label to select the text in the field, and then press the Delete to delete the postal code.

4 Press the Shift+Enter key combination to save the current record.

The *BeforeUpdate* event occurs, running your new version of the event procedure. The event procedure works just as it did before, displaying the message that asks if you want to save. This time, however, your general *Confirm* procedure displays the question.

5 Click OK.

Creating General Functions in a Form Module

You've created general functions, and you're using one of them on the *Contacts* form. Now, suppose you have some ideas for functions that would be useful on the *Contacts* form, but that would apply only to the form itself. For example, you might want to write functions that manipulate text values on the form.

There's no reason to put this type of procedure in a standard module, because no other form could use it. Additionally, from a standard module, it would be harder to work with values on the form: every time you referred to it, you'd have to specify the form name so that Visual Basic would know which controls you were referring to. Instead, you should put this type of procedure in the form module.

In this section, you'll create two general functions designed specifically for the *Contacts* form.

Create the *FullName* Function

The *Contacts* table has separate fields for last name and first name—and for good reason: in a database that has a single field for names, it's very difficult to search and sort by last name. But suppose you're finding that you often need a way to refer to the full name of the current contact, either in expressions or in code. You can write a very simple general function for the form that returns the full name so that you'll have a simple way to refer to it.

1 Switch to Visual Basic. (Click Microsoft Visual Basic in the Windows taskbar.)

Up to now, you've created a procedure by clicking a toolbar button. But you don't have to use a command to create a new procedure—you can also create a procedure by typing its header in the Code window.

2 Press the Ctrl+End key combination to move to the end of the module.

3 Type the following function header.

```
Private Function FullName() As String
```

When you press Enter, the new procedure gets created, and Visual Basic automatically adds an *End Function* statement for it. (You might need to scroll down in the window to see this line.) As its procedure header declares, the *FullName* function returns a string value. The function is private to the *Contacts* form module, because you won't need to call the function from outside the form.

4 Type the following line of code for the function.

```
FullName = FirstName & " " & LastName
```

This line concatenates the value of the FirstName field with a space, followed by the value of the LastName field, and specifies that this is the value for the function to return.

Use the *FullName* Function in an Expression

The *Contacts* form has a calculated field that displays the full name of the contact—it's at the top of page 2 of the form. The ControlSource property of this field is set to an expression that combines the two name fields. But now that you have a function to perform this task, you can refer to the function as the source of the control. This is one of the common situations for including a private function in a form module—when you need to refer to a calculation in expressions on the form.

View Microsoft Access

1 Switch to Access.

2 In the *Contacts* form footer, click the Page 2 button.

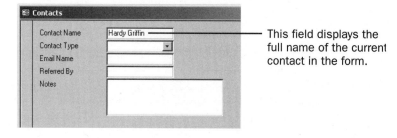

This field displays the full name of the current contact in the form.

Now you'll change the control to use your new function.

Design View

3   Click the Design View button on the toolbar.

4   Scroll down a bit in the form, and then click the Contact Name text box.

Properties

5   If the property sheet isn't open, click the Properties button on the toolbar.

6   In the property sheet, click the Data tab.

The ControlSource property has a long setting, which you can simplify by using your new function.

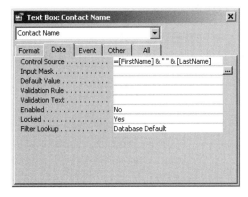

7   Change the ControlSource property setting to **=FullName()**.

This setting tells Access to run your function each time it refreshes this control and to display the return value of the function in the control.

8   Close the property sheet.

Form View

9   Click the Form View button on the toolbar.

10 Click the Page 2 button in the form footer.

The Contact Name control still shows the full name, but now it uses your function to fill in the name.

In this case, you could have done without the function—after all, the wizard wrote the control's expression for you. But now that you have a function, you can use it in expressions or code throughout the form.

Create the *FullAddress* Function

You might want to combine the address fields for a contact into a single value, such as the full address you'd type on an envelope. But unlike the *FullName* function, which you'll only use on the *Contacts* form itself, you may want to call this function from outside the form—to put the address on another form or report, for example. To make a function available outside the form, you declare it using the *Public* keyword.

1   Switch to Visual Basic.

2   Click below the *End Function* line in the *FullName* function, and then type the following function (except the *End Function* line, which Visual Basic enters after you type the function header).

```
Public Function FullAddress() As String
' Return a string containing the full name and address.

    ' If no name or address, return an empty string.
    If IsNull(LastName) Or IsNull(Address) Then
        FullAddress = ""
    Else
        ' Build the address string.
        FullAddress = FullName & vbNewLine & _
            Address & vbNewLine & _
            City & ", " & _
            StateOrProvince & " " & PostalCode
    End If
End Function
```

Here are some things to notice in the function.

- First, the function uses the *If...Then* statement to determine whether there are *Last-Name* and *Address* values on the form. If there aren't, it returns an empty string (""). If there are, it builds the address string by concatenating the contact's name, address, city, state, and postal code. (Note that this function applies to U.S. addresses only.)

- Take a closer look at the *Else* statement, which builds the address string. Because the code is much too long to fit on a single line, it's broken up into four lines using the Visual Basic line-continuation character, the underscore (_). Any time you want to continue a line of code on a second line, you can type a space followed by this character and then continue on a new line—Visual Basic interprets the code as if it were all on one line.

- The *Else* statement uses the *FullName* function you already created to represent the first and last names. You'll recall that in the expression for the ContactName control, you had to include an equal sign before the function and then follow the function name with a pair of parentheses; in code, by contrast, you can run a function that has no arguments by simply entering its name.

- The code then goes on to concatenate the fields in the address, separating them with correct formatting. In order to format the address on three separate lines, it uses the Visual Basic constant *vbNewLine*, which is a short way of specifying a carriage return character followed by a line feed character. It places the *vbNewLine* value after the name and address, places a comma and a space after the state, and includes a space before the postal code. This whole string value gets assigned to the return value of the *FullAddress* function.

Try the *FullAddress* Function from the Immediate Window

Now that the function is complete, you can use it in expressions or code throughout the form. For example, you could create a control on the form that displays the full address. But because you declared the *FullAddress* function using the Public keyword, you should also be able to use it from outside the *Contacts* form—for example, from the Immediate window.

1 On the View menu, click Immediate Window.

The Immediate window still displays the text you assigned earlier.

2 Type **?Forms!Contacts.FullAddress.**

The expression *Forms!Contacts* refers to the *Contacts* form. To use a public function of a form, you type the form reference, followed by a period (.), followed by the function name (and its arguments, if any, in parentheses).

3 Press Enter.

The *FullAddress* function runs, combines the address fields for the current record on the *Contacts* form, and displays the function's return value in the Immediate window.

Important

Since the *FullAddress* function refers to the values of several fields on the *Contacts* form, the form must be open in Form view whenever you use the function. If the *Contacts* form is in Design view instead of Form view, the previous procedure causes an error. If you encountered an error running the *FullAddress* function, switch the *Contacts* form into Form view and then go back to the Immediate window and try again.

Try the *FullName* Function from the Immediate Window

As you've seen, you can run a public function from outside the form. But what about the *FullName* function, which you declared using the Private keyword?

1 Type **?Forms!Contacts.FullName**, and press Enter.

An error message appears, telling you that there was an object-defined error. In plain English, this means that you asked the form to do something it isn't allowed to do—and it responds, "Sorry, that's private!"

2 Click OK.

3 Close the Immediate window.

As you can see, you can't refer to a private function from outside its module. Note, however, that if a public function in the module uses the private function, you can end up running the private function from elsewhere. This is the case with the *FullAddress* function, which uses the *FullName* function in its code—so although *FullName* isn't directly available from the Immediate window, we actually ran it courtesy of the *FullAddress* function, because *FullName* is available to any other function in the *Contacts* form's module.

The Many Ways to Declare Variables

Like procedures, the variables you use can be public or private and can live in various places in your database. How variables work depends entirely on where and how you declare them. It may be that all the variables you've used so far have been private variables, declared using the *Dim* keyword inside a procedure and used only in that procedure. When the procedure finishes running, a variable declared in this way disappears, along with its contents.

There are several other ways to declare variables that you'll want to keep in mind.

Dim To declare a variable that you'll use throughout a module, use the *Dim* statement in the *Declarations* section of the module—outside any one procedure. The variable will keep its value between procedure calls. Use this type of variable when several procedures in the module all work with the same data.

Public To declare a variable that you'll use throughout your application, use the *Public* statement instead of the *Dim* statement, placing it in the *Declarations* section of any module. The variable will keep its value during the entire time your application is running. You can declare a public variable in a form or report module, but you'll have to include the object's name in every reference to the variable that occurs outside that object. Public variables are useful for application-wide information, such as the names of the application users.

Static Variables you declare within a procedure normally lose their values when the procedure ends. However, if you want Access to preserve the value of a variable between calls to the procedure, replace the *Dim* keyword with the *Static* keyword. This is useful for a procedure that accumulates a value each time it is called.

In later chapters, you'll use some of these techniques. However, except in special cases, you should stay in the habit of using only private, procedure-level variables—they take up space in memory only while their procedure is running, and they don't conflict with variables of the same name in other procedures.

So Many Options, So Few Rules

Visual Basic gives you nearly unlimited freedom as a programmer to put code all over the place—in standard modules, form and report modules, and event procedures—and to specify various options, such as public and private procedures. How do you decide where to put your code and how to declare it? Here are some guidelines.

Break procedures into separate tasks. Try to follow the rule of one task per procedure—your applications will be much easier to maintain. If you're writing code for an event procedure and it's getting complex, consider writing a general function for each subtask.

Generalize procedures whenever possible. If you can write a procedure so that it could apply to any form or report, do so—and put it in a standard module. One way to achieve this is to add arguments to the procedure so that you can provide the specifics when you call the procedure.

Put object-specific procedures in the object's module. For tasks or procedures that you know will only be used by a single form or report, be sure to put them in the form or report modules where they belong. You'll avoid having stray procedures, and it will be easier to refer to objects, properties, and controls on the form.

Choose *Private* over *Public* to avoid conflicts. In a form or report module, declare procedures using the *Private* keyword unless you have a reason to call them from outside the form. In a standard module, most procedures will need to be declared using *Public*, because you'll want to use them throughout your database; however, if they're only used to perform subtasks for other procedures in the module, be sure to declare them using *Private*. Making procedures private whenever possible uses less memory and can help avoid conflicts.

Chapter Wrap-Up

1 Close Visual Basic.

2 Close the *Contacts* form, clicking Yes when Access asks if you want to save changes.

3 Close Access.

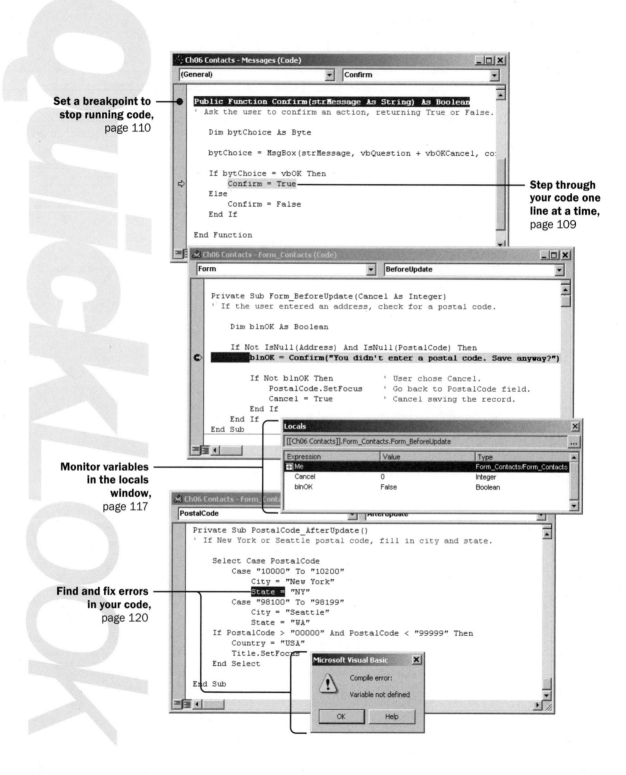

Set a breakpoint to stop running code, page 110

Step through your code one line at a time, page 109

Monitor variables in the locals window, page 117

Find and fix errors in your code, page 120

Chapter 6
Monitor and Debug Your Code

After completing this chapter, you will be able to:

✔ Watch Visual Basic code run line by line.

✔ View the values of variables in your code.

✔ Compile procedures to ensure that they follow the rules.

✔ Find and fix programming errors using Visual Basic debugging tools.

In trying to stay on course to reach a destination, a navigator uses various tools to keep track of a vessel's location and heading—and keeps a constant eye on the charts. Because of obstacles, wind conditions, or currents, changes in course are common, and the navigator has to anticipate problems and adjust accordingly. A change in course doesn't necessarily indicate a mistake; it's just part of the job.

When you program in Microsoft Visual Basic, you have to anticipate that errors will pop up here and there, both while you're programming and when you run your application. Microsoft Access comes equipped with many tools that, like a ship's compass, help you keep track of where your application is and where it's heading. In this chapter, you'll learn to monitor your Visual Basic code as it runs and to understand what's really happening inside the computer when your application is running. You'll use Visual Basic tools to find bugs and then fix them and test to make sure they're taken care of.

Ch06 Contacts.mdb

This chapter uses the practice file Ch06 Contacts.mdb that you installed from the book's CD-ROM. For details about installing the practice files, see "Using the Book's CD-ROM" at the beginning of this book.

Getting Started

● Start Access, and open the Ch06 Contacts database in the practice files folder.

Stepping Through Code Line by Line

In previous chapters, you've written quite a bit of Visual Basic code and seen the results of running your procedures. But so far, you haven't actually *seen* the code run—you've taken it on faith that your code was running behind the scenes. In this section, you'll see your code run for the first time.

Visual Basic provides tools that let you stop your code while it's running and step through Visual Basic statements one by one. This way, you can see what's really going on in your code.

Open the Messages Module

In order to watch code run, you first need to open it up and tell Visual Basic where you want to start watching it. First you'll open the Messages module and move to the *Confirm* function, which you created in Chapter 5. You'll also tell Visual Basic to display the Debug toolbar, which contains tools to help you step through your code.

1 In the Database window, click the Modules shortcut.

2 Double-click the Messages module.

Access opens Visual Basic and displays your code.

3 Scroll down in the Code window to view the *Confirm* function.

4 On the View menu, point to Toolbars, and then click Debug.

Visual Basic displays the Debug toolbar, which has buttons that help you step through your code.

5 Drag the Debug toolbar to the top of the Visual Basic window, out of the way of the Code window.

Setting a Breakpoint to Stop Running Code

When you want Visual Basic to stop running your code midstream so that you can take a look at it, you set a *breakpoint* at the line of code you want to check. A breakpoint tells Visual Basic, "When you get to this line—but before you run it—stop everything and display the code." It's like calling time out in a basketball game: the action stops so that you can regroup, consider what you're doing right or wrong, and make adjustments. Then when the time-out is over, you allow your code to continue, letting the game go on as before.

Set a Breakpoint at the Beginning of a Procedure

You'll set a breakpoint at the very beginning of the *Confirm* function, on the *Function* statement itself. This way, you can take a look at the function each time it runs. To set and clear breakpoints, you use the gray margin that runs down the left side of the Code window.

● Click the gray margin to the left of the *Confirm* function header line (the line that begins with Public Function Confirm).

Click the margin to set a breakpoint for this line.

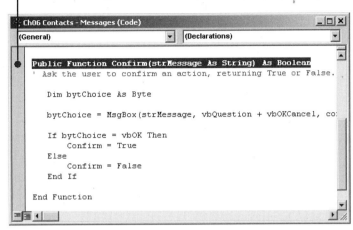

```
Ch06 Contacts - Messages (Code)                          _ □ ×
(General)                          ▼   (Declarations)              ▼

Public Function Confirm(strMessage As String) As Boolean
' Ask the user to confirm an action, returning True or False.

    Dim bytChoice As Byte

    bytChoice = MsgBox(strMessage, vbQuestion + vbOKCancel, co

    If bytChoice = vbOK Then
        Confirm = True
    Else
        Confirm = False
    End If

End Function
```

A red dot appears in the margin, and the line of code changes to white text on red. This indicates that Visual Basic will stop when it encounters this code—in other words, as soon as it tries to run the *Confirm* function.

Tip

If you set a breakpoint on the wrong line of code, click the red dot to clear the breakpoint, and then click next to the correct line.

Run the Procedure

1 Now try running the *Confirm* function from the Immediate window.

Immediate
Window

2 Click the Immediate Window button.

3 Type **?Confirm("Isn't it wonderful?")**, and press the Enter key.

The *Confirm* function runs, but as soon as it starts, Visual Basic encounters the breakpoint you set. It then switches back to the *Confirm* function in the Code window. When you view running code, you'll notice that Visual Basic displays a *current statement indicator*: a yellow arrow in the margin and a yellow background highlighting the current statement.

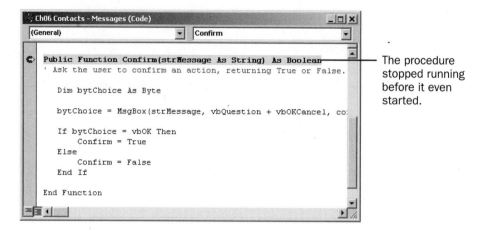

The procedure stopped running before it even started.

Step Through the Code One Line at a Time

Nothing is happening right now because of the breakpoint—but in a sense, your code is still running. Information about the procedure, such as the values of local variables and arguments, is stored in your computer's memory. Visual Basic is ready to continue running the function as soon as you say so. You'll use the Step Into command, which tells Visual Basic to run one line of code and then display the Code window again and return control to you.

Step Into

1   Click the Step Into button.

When you click the button, Visual Basic moves the current statement indicator to the statement that uses the *MsgBox* function. Note that Visual Basic skips over two lines of code: the comment statement and the *Dim* statement. Because these lines of code don't actually perform an action, they never become the current statement.

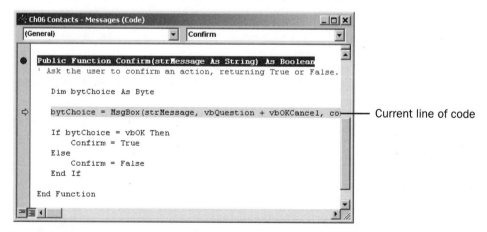

Current line of code

This line of code uses the *MsgBox* function to display a message to the user and assigns the return value of the function to the *bytChoice* variable. When you start the code running again, you can expect to see the message on the screen.

2 Click the Step Into button again.

Access returns to the front, and the current statement runs, which displays your message on the screen.

3 Click OK.

When you answer the question in the message box, Visual Basic finishes running the statement by assigning your choice to the *bytChoice* variable. It then returns to the Code window and moves the current statement indicator to the next line of code: the *If...Then* statement that determines whether you clicked the OK button.

4 Click the Step Into button again.

Because the condition in the *If...Then* statement is true—the *bytChoice* variable is equal to the *vbOK* constant—Visual Basic moves to the line of code directly underneath the *If...Then* statement.

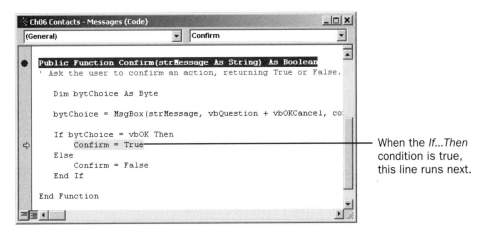

When the *If...Then* condition is true, this line runs next.

5 Click the Step Into button again.

Visual Basic sets the return value of the *Confirm* function to *True*, and then skips over the *Else* block, moving the current statement indicator to the *End If* statement.

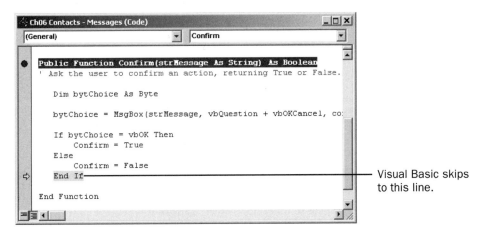

Visual Basic skips to this line.

Here's where you can really see the value of stepping through your code. If the condition in the *If...Then* statement were false—if you'd chosen Cancel instead of OK—Visual Basic would have taken a different path through the code. By stepping through your code, you can see exactly which lines of code actually run, rather than trying to guess what's happening in your procedures.

6 Click the Step Into button two more times.

The last two statements in the function run. When you step past the *End Function* statement, the Immediate window becomes active again. This is where you started running the code—before it was stopped by the breakpoint—so this is the place Visual Basic returns you to when the code finishes running.

The Immediate window displays the return value of the function, which is *True*.

7 Close the Immediate window.

8 In the margin, click the red dot next to the line with the breakpoint (the *Confirm* function's header line).

This clears the breakpoint you set so that Visual Basic will allow the *Confirm* function to run without interruption in the future.

Stepping from One Procedure to Another

So far, you've stepped through code in just one procedure. Of course, your application might contain separate procedures for each of the tasks you want to complete. When you step through code in your application, Visual Basic can automatically step into each procedure you call so that you can follow the progression of your code.

To see this, you'll step through the *BeforeUpdate* event procedure on the *Contacts* form. This event procedure calls the *Confirm* function, so you'll get to see how Access runs both procedures.

Open the *Contacts* Form's Module and Set a Breakpoint

Before you can step through the code in an event procedure, you need to set a breakpoint in the function.

View Microsoft
Access

1 Switch to Access. (Click the View Microsoft Access button on the toolbar.)

2 In the Database window, click the Forms shortcut.

3 Click the *Contacts* form, and then click the Code button.

Visual Basic returns to the front and displays the *Contacts* form's module. The first procedure in the window is the *Form_BeforeUpdate* event procedure.

Code

4 If necessary, resize the Code window so that it displays most of the code in the procedure. (Drag the bottom right corner of the window to make it larger.)

5 In the gray margin, click next to the fifth line in the procedure—the one that calls the *Confirm* function.

This sets a breakpoint on the statement, so code will stop running there.

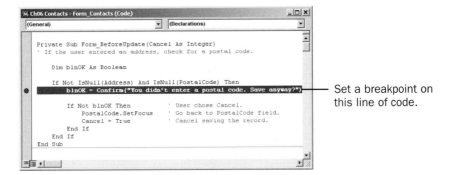

Set a breakpoint on this line of code.

Step Through the Event Procedure

To run an event procedure on a form, you don't use the Immediate window—instead, you make the event occur on the form in Access, and the event procedure runs automatically.

1 Switch to Access.

Form View

2 Click the Form View button.

3 Click the Postal Code field, and delete the value in the field.

4 Press the Shift+Enter key combination to save the current record.

The *BeforeUpdate* procedure runs, and when Visual Basic encounters the breakpoint you set, it displays the event procedure in the Code window.

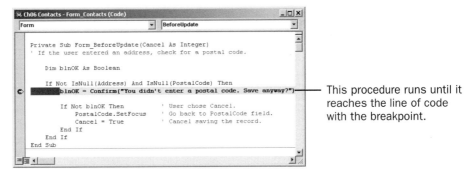

This procedure runs until it reaches the line of code with the breakpoint.

This line of code, which is the next statement that will run, calls the *Confirm* function in the Messages module. When you step through this statement, Visual Basic will pass control to the *Confirm* function.

Step Into

5 Click the Step Into button.

Visual Basic switches to the Messages module and displays the *Confirm* function.

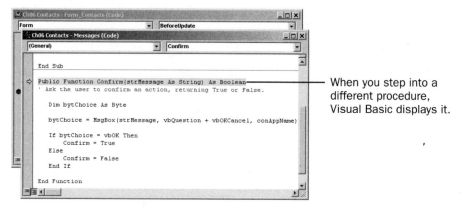

When you step into a
different procedure,
Visual Basic displays it.

Now that you're in the *Confirm* function, you could step through the code line by line. Instead, you'll use another new technique to run several lines of code at once, stepping through the entire *Confirm* function.

Step Out

6 Click the Step Out button.

The Step Out command tells Visual Basic to run code until it finishes the current procedure, then pause again when it returns to the procedure that called it. When you click the button, the code in the *Confirm* function displays your message in Access, asking whether you want to save the record without a postal code.

7 Click Cancel.

When the *Confirm* function ends, Access returns control to the *Form_BeforeUpdate* event procedure—remember, this is the procedure that called the *Confirm* function. Starting up where it left off, it moves the current statement indicator to the *If...Then* statement after the line that called the function.

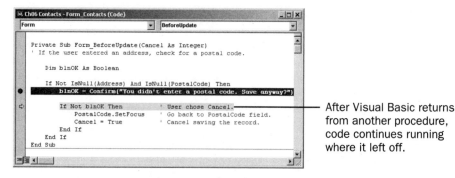

After Visual Basic returns
from another procedure,
code continues running
where it left off.

You can now continue stepping through the event procedure, or you can just tell Visual Basic to continue.

Continue

8 Click the Continue button.

The *BeforeUpdate* event procedure finishes running.

9 Switch to Access.

Because you chose the Cancel button in the message box, your code didn't allow the record to be saved—the Pencil icon is still displayed in the record selector. In the next section, you'll try to save the record again.

Tip

When you're stepping through code in an event procedure, you can't switch back to the form until the event procedure finishes running. If you want to stop code from running, use the Reset command (on the Run menu) to end the procedure and reset all variables. The Reset command is also useful if an error occurs while you're stepping through code, when you may seem to be "stuck" in the procedure. If you can't fix the error and move on, use the Reset command to stop all code from running.

Monitoring Variables and Other Values

Stepping through your code can help you figure out where it's going. But as your application progresses, the values of variables and fields stored in the computer's memory change, affecting how your application works. To really understand what's happening as your code runs, you'll want to find out the values of variables and fields along the way. You need a window into the computer's brain.

Using the debugging tools built into Visual Basic, you can find out the value of a variable, control, or other expression. In fact, you've already done this: in Chapter 3, you used the Immediate window to find out the value of a property. However, there are more efficient ways to monitor values while your code is running, such as using the Locals window. In the Locals window, Visual Basic displays the values of all variables and objects that apply to the currently running procedure—the *local* variables and objects, as they're called. As code runs, the Locals window automatically reflects the changing values of the variables it shows.

Step Through the Event Procedure Again

To see how the Locals window works, you'll run the form's *BeforeUpdate* procedure one more time by trying to save the record again with the Postal Code field blank. Then, you'll monitor the value of a variable while the procedure runs.

1 Press Shift+Enter to save the current record.

When Visual Basic encounters the breakpoint you set in the *BeforeUpdate* event procedure, it displays the Code window. Now that the procedure is running, you can check the Locals window to see the value of the *blnOK* variable, which the procedure uses to determine which choice you make in the message box.

Locals
Windows

2 Click the Locals Window button.

Like the Immediate window, the Locals window can be docked at the side or bottom of the Visual Basic window, or it can be a floating window.

3 Drag the title bar of the Locals window up to the center of the Visual Basic window, and then position and resize the window so that you can see as much of your code as possible.

The Locals window lists three objects, the third of which is the *blnOK* variable. As you can see, the *blnOK* variable is currently set to *False*.

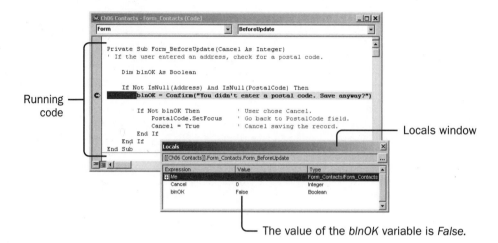

Running code

Locals window

The value of the *blnOK* variable is *False.*

Tip

In the Locals window, you may notice the entry for "Me" listed above the two variables. This entry, which you'll find at the top of the Locals window whenever an event procedure is running, represents the current Form or Report object—in this case, the *Contacts* form—with all its controls and properties. Using this entry, you can view properties of the form and its controls as you monitor your application. To display properties of the form, click the small box with a plus sign to the left of the Me entry. This expands a long list of properties and objects belonging to the form. To view the properties of controls on the form, locate them in the expanded list and click their plus signs.

You're ready to step through the event procedure and watch its variables. In the previous run through this code, you stepped into the code of the *Confirm* function. This time, you'll learn how to save time by skipping *over* procedures that you aren't interested in. To run a line of code without stepping into the procedure it calls, use the Step Over command—it works just like the Step Into command, except that it runs procedures without pause.

Step Over

4 Click the Step Over button on the toolbar.

The *Confirm* function runs, displaying its message box.

5 Click OK.

Visual Basic displays the *BeforeUpdate* event procedure again—although you stepped over the *Confirm* function, you are still stepping through code line by line. The *Confirm* function in the line you just stepped over should have set the *blnOK* value based on your choice in the message box.

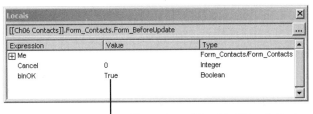

                          — The value of the *blnOK* variable is now *True.*

Sure enough, the Locals window shows that the *blnOK* variable is now set to *True*—indicating that you chose OK in the message box. You can now continue stepping through the event procedure.

6   Click the Step Over button again.

Because the value of the variable is *True*, which means that the value of *Not blnOK* is *False*, the *If...Then* block doesn't run.

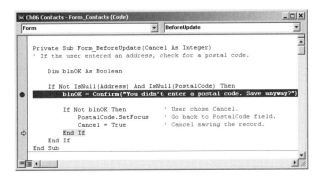

7   Click the Step Over button three more times.

The *BeforeUpdate* event procedure finishes running, allowing the record to be saved in the *Contacts* form.

8   Close the Locals window. (Click the "X" in its upper-right corner.)

Other Techniques for Monitoring Code

The Locals window is useful when you want to monitor the value of a variable or other object continuously while your code runs. But there are several other techniques you can use for monitoring the progress of your code.

Set watch expressions in the Watch window. The Locals window shows only the variables and objects in the current procedure. Sometimes, you may want to view the values of variables or objects outside the current procedure—variables shared by your entire application, for example. To specify exactly what data you want to monitor, use the Add Watch or Quick Watch command (on the Debug menu). When you run your code, the values of each expression you've specified are displayed in the Watch window.

Send values or messages to the Immediate window. If there is a certain point in your code where you want to check the status of your procedure or the value of a variable, you can send a message to the Immediate window by using the *Print* method of the *Debug* object. Anywhere you want to send output to the Immediate window, insert a line and type **Debug.Print** followed by the expression you want to display. For example, you might add the following line of code in the *BeforeUpdate* procedure instead of using a watch expression.

```
Debug.Print "The Confirm function returned: "; blnOK
```

This way, each time the procedure runs, it reports the value of *blnOK* in the Immediate window. You don't need to set a breakpoint or step through code at all—you can just check the Immediate window after the procedure finishes running.

Display message boxes. If you want to report on the progress of a procedure while it runs, but you don't want to check the Immediate window each time, you can instead display messages to yourself using the *MsgBox* function. For example, you could place the following line of code in the *BeforeUpdate* procedure.

```
MsgBox "The Confirm function returned: " & blnOK
```

Change code as it runs. In most programming systems, you can't change code while it's running. But in Visual Basic, you have the flexibility to change the values of variables or code itself while you step through line by line. Suppose you're monitoring a variable and you notice it doesn't have the value you expect. If necessary, you can add a line of code to your procedure and continue running it.

Set the current statement. Normally, when stepping through code, you don't control the order in which Visual Basic statements occur. However, if you're stepping through code and would like to change which statement runs next, you can use the Set Next Statement command (on the Debug menu). This is especially useful if you change a line of code that didn't work as expected and you want to run it again without restarting the procedure.

The strategy you select to monitor and debug your code depends on what problems you're trying to diagnose and how often you need to check what's happening. As you program in Visual Basic, you'll learn which techniques are most appropriate for each debugging task.

Finding and Fixing Bugs in Your Code

The procedures you've stepped through so far aren't broken—although you've learned more about how they work by monitoring them more closely, they seem to be working just fine. But what if code isn't working as you'd planned? This is when Visual Basic tools come in especially handy. In this section, you'll learn to check your Visual Basic code as you enter it, and then fix any errors you find.

Suppose that most of your contacts are in either New York City or Seattle, and you'd like to make it easier for users to enter addresses from these cities. One approach is to write an event procedure that runs after you enter a postal code, filling in the correct *City* and *State* values. This way, users who know about the shortcut can skip over the City and State fields when they're entering New York City or Seattle addresses. While you're at it, you'll also have the event procedure fill in the Country field if the user enters a U.S. postal code.

Write an Event Procedure That Fills in Values for You

You want to set the City, State, and Country fields each time the user enters a value in the Postal Code field. To do this, you need to create an event procedure for the control's *AfterUpdate* event.

1 In the Object box at the top of the Code window (on the left), click PostalCode.

2 In the Procedure box (on the right), click AfterUpdate.

The Code window shows the *PostalCode_AfterUpdate* event procedure.

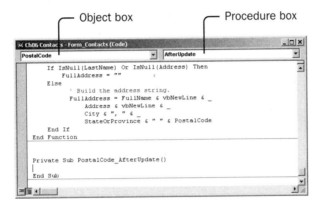

Object box — Procedure box

3 Type the following code for the event procedure:

```
' If New York or Seattle postal code, fill in city and state.

Select Case PostalCode
    Case "10000" To "10200"
        City = "New York"
        State = "NY"
    Case "98100" To "98199"
        City = "Seattle"
        State = "WA"

End Select
```

So far so good! This code introduces a new Visual Basic statement for controlling the flow of code: the *Select Case* statement. You use this statement when you want to perform one of several different actions based on the value of a single variable or expression. Each *Case* statement underneath it introduces a different block of code—which block of code runs depends on which value the *Select Case* expression has. As you've seen before, indenting each block of code helps to show how the statement works.

In this example, you're telling Visual Basic, "OK, look at the value of the *PostalCode* field—if it's between 10000 and 10200 (most New York City addresses), run this first block of code; if it's between 98100 and 98199 (most Seattle addresses), run this second block of code." You can set up as many "cases" as necessary; if you want, you can finish with the *Case Else* statement followed by a block of code, which runs if none of the cases match the value of the *Select Case* expression.

Next, you'll add code that checks whether the postal code is a U.S. ZIP Code and fills in the Country field if it is a U.S. ZIP code.

4 Just above the line with the *End Select* statement, enter the following line of code:

```
If PostalCode > "00000" And < "99999" Then
```

When you press Enter, the text of this line turns red and a message appears. You made an error! (Of course, you were only following instructions.) The error message, "Expected: expression," tells you that Visual Basic requires an expression—such as a variable—that's missing somewhere in this line.

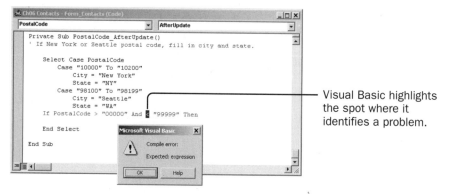

Visual Basic highlights the spot where it identifies a problem.

You'll notice that the "<" symbol is highlighted—this is the point in the line that Visual Basic doesn't like—and the line is still shown in red text.

5 Click OK.

You may not have known it, especially if you're a good typist, but every time you've entered a line of code in a code window, Visual Basic has checked to make sure it follows the rules. In this case, you've entered something that isn't allowed, even though it looks like it should work. The line seems to say, "If the PostalCode field is greater than five zeros and less than five nines, then..." Why doesn't it work? Unlike the English language, where you can skip the subject if it's repeated after a conjunction such as "and"—as in "Buzz went to the moon and returned"—the Visual Basic language requires you to repeat the subject. In other words, you have to say, "If the *PostalCode* field is *this* and the *Postal-Code* field is *that*..."

Fix the Error and Finish the Procedure

Before going any further, you should fix the error. Incidentally, if you don't fix a line of code that contains a syntax error, Visual Basic continues to display the line in red text to indicate that it isn't valid.

1 Press the Left Arrow key, type **PostalCode**, and then click the next line.

No error this time!

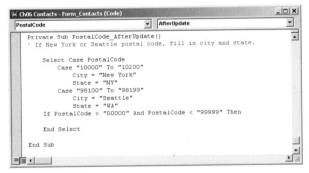

```
Ch06 Contacts - Form_Contacts (Code)                          _ □ ×
PostalCode                            ▼    AfterUpdate                 ▼
    Private Sub PostalCode_AfterUpdate()
    ' If New York or Seattle postal code, fill in city and state.

        Select Case PostalCode
            Case "10000" To "10200"
                City = "New York"
                State = "NY"
            Case "98100" To "98199"
                City = "Seattle"
                State = "WA"
            If PostalCode > "00000" And PostalCode < "99999" Then

        End Select

    End Sub
```

2 Enter the following two lines of code underneath the *If...Then* statement.

```
Country = "USA"
Title.SetFocus
```

These two lines set the value of the Country field and then move the focus to the Title field, because the user no longer needs to enter a value in the Country field.

Types of Errors

Errors are bound to occur when you write or run code—which is why Visual Basic offers so many tools to help you deal with them. Still, it isn't always easy to figure out what's wrong. To know where to look, it helps to know the types of errors that can occur. Most errors fall into the following categories.

Syntax errors When you type a keyword incorrectly or leave off punctuation in code, Visual Basic displays a message as soon as you try to leave the line. Usually, the message tells you exactly what is wrong with the line of code. Until you fix a line of code with a syntax error, Visual Basic displays the line in red.

Invalid references If you misspell the name of a variable, field, or procedure, or if you forget to declare a variable you use, Visual Basic displays an error when you try to run the code.

Incomplete code If your code isn't complete—for example, if you have an *If...Then* statement block without an *End If* statement—Visual Basic displays an error when you try to run the code.

Logic errors If your code runs without errors but doesn't do what you had planned, you've probably made an error in the logic of your program. Remember, the computer only does what you tell it—you can't make any assumptions about how things will work! The toughest kind of error to figure out, a logic error '1q2 requires that you step through code to watch what's happening and then correct any mistakes you find.

Run-time errors There are many errors that Visual Basic can't detect until your application is running. For example, if your code passes an invalid value as the argument to a Visual Basic function, an error occurs and code stops running. A run-time error sometimes indicates that your code needs rethinking—especially if you made incorrect assumptions about how the user interacts with your application. In many cases, however, run-time errors are to be expected. In Chapter 7, you'll see how your code can anticipate errors and respond to them before an error message disrupts your application.

You'll see examples of all these types of errors in this chapter—and you're guaranteed to keep seeing them, just about every time you program. However, as you gain experience with Visual Basic programming, you'll become better at avoiding errors or handling them as they come up.

Telling Visual Basic to Check Your Code

You've already seen how Visual Basic checks each line of code you enter to make sure that it doesn't contain any errors. But many errors aren't obvious in a single line. To see them, you have to look at the line of code in the context of the rest of the procedure or application. Although it doesn't do so automatically while you enter code, Visual Basic does check your procedures thoroughly before it runs them. It checks for various types of consistency—for example, whether the variables you've used in your code are all declared and whether the procedures you call exist in your application. This process is called *compiling*, because it involves putting together information from various sources in your application, preparing to run the code.

One way to compile a procedure is to try running it. But you won't always want to wait until you run your code to make sure it's all right—that would be like checking to see if you have air in your tires only *after* leaving on a long trip. Fortunately, you can ask Visual Basic to compile your procedures at any time.

Compile Your Event Procedure and Resolve Errors

Believe it or not, there are a couple of errors in the *PostalCode_AfterUpdate* procedure. If you try to run the procedure as it is, it won't work. To find out what they are, you'll ask Visual Basic to compile your code.

1 On the Debug menu, click Compile Ch06 Contacts.

Visual Basic displays the error message "Variable not defined." This message means, more or less, that Visual Basic isn't familiar with an expression in your code and can't find anything in your Access application that the expression refers to.

2 In the message box, click OK.

The expression it can't figure out is highlighted in the Code window. In this case, the "variable" that Visual Basic doesn't recognize is *State*.

The code that caused the error is selected.

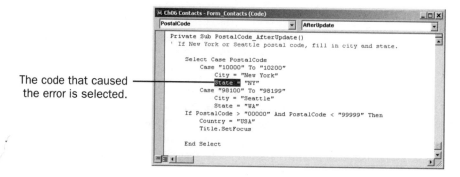

In this line of code, you're not actually referring to a variable at all. You're trying to refer to the *State* field on the *Contacts* form. The reason for this error? The field is actually called *StateOrProvince*—a simple mistake, but one we'll need to correct before going on. In cases like this one where you've misspelled something, you'll notice that Visual Basic isn't always as helpful as it could be. At least it isn't judgmental, just matter-of-fact.

3 Click the end of the word *State*, and type **OrProvince**.

4 Two lines down, at the other reference to *State*, click the end of the word, and type **OrProvince**.

Now that you've fixed the error, you should compile again to make sure that everything's just right.

5 On the Debug menu, click Compile Ch06 Contacts.

It's still not right. This time, Visual Basic displays the message "End Select without Select Case." This message indicates that at least one block of code in the procedure isn't set up correctly and that Visual Basic encountered a *Case* or *End Select* statement when it expected something else. Here is the problem: You used the *If...Then* statement, included a block of code after it, but didn't include the *End If* statement to indicate the end of the block. To successfully compile and run this procedure, you'll have to make sure each block of code has a beginning and an end (just as a parenthetical remark has an opening and a closing parenthesis).

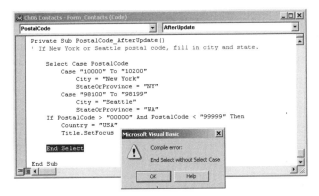

6 Click OK.

The statement that's selected is the one immediately *after* the point where Visual Basic expects to see the *End If* statement.

7 Click the blank line above the *End Select* statement, and type **End If**.

8 On the Debug menu, click Compile Ch06 Contacts.

No surprises this time; your house is in order.

Tip

In any Visual Basic error message, you can click the Help button to see a Help topic giving you more information about the error and how to fix it.

Run the Event Procedure from the *Contacts* Form

Now that the code compiles fine, you can test the procedure to see if it works correctly. You'll want to step through the code, so you should set a breakpoint in the event procedure.

1 In the Code window, click the gray margin next to the *Select Case* line.

The now-familiar breakpoint indicator appears in the margin.

2 Switch to Access.

New Record

3 Click the New Record button on the toolbar.

▶∗

4 Fill in the fields in the record as follows:

Field Name	Value
First Name	**Fiona**
Last Name	**McNair**
Address	**102 W. 86th St.**
Postal Code	**10024**

5 Press the Tab key to leave the Postal Code field.

When you leave the field, your event procedure runs. When Visual Basic reaches the breakpoint, it suspends the running code and displays the current statement with a yellow background.

Before you step through the code, you'll check to see what the *PostalCode* value is. Earlier in the chapter, you checked values using the Locals window. Here, you'll use an even easier method. When code is suspended as it is now, you can point to any variable or field in your code to bring up a *Data Tip*—a small box that tells you the current value of the variable or field.

6 Point to the *PostalCode* field anywhere in the event procedure.

A Data Tip appears just underneath the variable, showing the value you entered for the *PostalCode* field: *10024*.

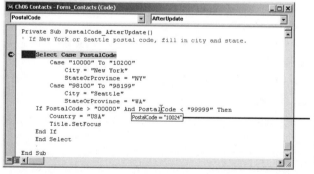

When code is running, Data Tips display the current value of variables or fields you point at.

Now that you've verified that the value of the *Select Case* expression is *10024*, step through the code and watch what happens.

Step Into

7 Click the Step Into button on the toolbar.

The current statement indicator moves to the *Case* statement for the first block of code, where it will check whether the value *10024* falls in the range of *10000* to *10200*.

8 Click the Step Into button again.

As expected, the current statement indicator moves into the first block of code, because the value *10024* does fall in the range of *10000* to *10200*. When you allow it to continue, Visual Basic will run the two lines underneath the *Case* statement, which set the *City* and *StateOrProvince* values for New York City.

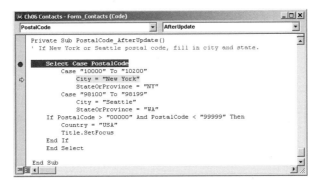

Continue

9 Click the Continue button on the toolbar.

10 Switch to Access.

The City and State/Province fields are filled in as you'd planned. However, look at the Country field. Your code was supposed to set it for you, but it doesn't have a value. Something in the event procedure isn't working correctly.

Fix a Bug in Your Code

To figure out the problem, you need to run the event procedure again. This time, you'll try a different postal code and see what happens in the code.

1 Click the Postal Code field, and type **02134**.

2 Press Tab.

The *PostalCode_AfterUpdate* event procedure runs and stops at the breakpoint.

Step Into

3 Click the Step Into button twice.

Visual Basic steps over the *Case* statements, because the postal code you entered doesn't fall in the range.

4 Click the Step Into button a third time.

As you expected, the two lines underneath the second *Case* statement didn't run. But look where the current statement indicator jumped to: it skipped over not only the two lines under the *Case* statement, but also the entire block of code that sets the Country field, and ended up on the *End Select* statement at the very end of the procedure.

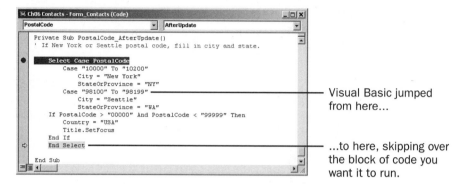

Visual Basic jumped from here...

...to here, skipping over the block of code you want it to run.

You've found the mistake in the code. Because the block of code is between the second *Case* statement and the *End Select* statement, Visual Basic assumes it is part of that "case," and runs it only when the postal code is in that range. To make the *If...Then* block run independently, you need to move it completely outside the *Select Case...End Select* structure.

5 If the *End Sub* statement isn't showing in the Code window, scroll down to bring it into view.

6 Click to the left of the *If...Then* statement (but *not* in the gray margin) and drag down to the *End If* statement to select the entire block of code.

The four lines appear highlighted.

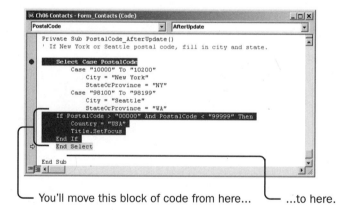

You'll move this block of code from here...   ...to here.

To move code, you just drag it to the new location.

7 Click the highlighted block of code, and then drag it down below the *End Select* line and release the mouse button.

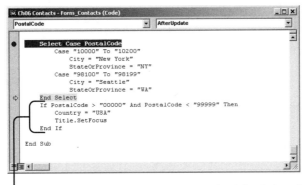

Now this block will run independently of the *Select Case* block.

Retest the Procedure

Debugging your code is all about testing and retesting your procedures—and it's time to test it once more. First, however, you'll need to stop the code that's currently running and clear the breakpoint so that the procedure can run without interruption.

Reset

1   Click the Reset button on the toolbar.

Visual Basic ends the procedure and resets all variables.

2   On the Debug menu, click Clear All Breakpoints.

3   Switch to Access.

4   Click the Postal Code field, and then type **10024**.

5   Press Tab.

This time, the Country field gets filled in with the value *USA*, and the focus moves to the Title field. The bug is fixed!

As you continue to program in Visual Basic, you're guaranteed to get all sorts of unexpected results from your code: some because of typos, some because of mistakes in program logic, and still others because of misunderstandings about how Access and Visual Basic work. But using the debugging tools available in Visual Basic—along with a healthy dose of patience and diligence in testing and retesting your procedures—you'll be able to solve these problems and get your application working just right.

Chapter Wrap-Up

1   Close the *Contacts* form, clicking Yes when Access asks if you want to save changes to the form.

2   On the File menu, click Exit.

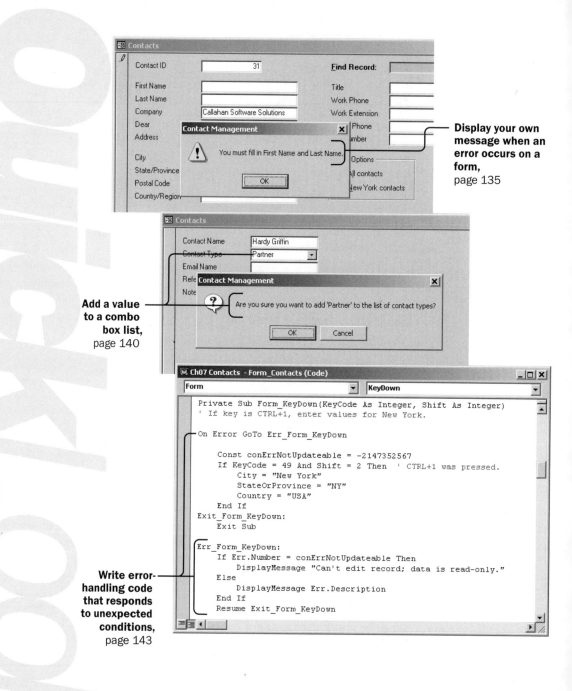

Display your own message when an error occurs on a form, page 135

Add a value to a combo box list, page 140

Write error-handling code that responds to unexpected conditions, page 143

Chapter 7
Respond to Errors and Unexpected Conditions

After completing this chapter, you will be able to:

✔ Replace standard Microsoft Access error messages with your own.

✔ Write code that responds to errors and unexpected conditions.

✔ Add a value to a combo box list.

If you've ever been on a trip into the wilderness, you know that there's quite a bit of work involved in preparation. You need to be ready for anything. Confusing trails make it easy to get lost, unexpected weather can catch you off guard, and even a minor injury can be a big deal away from civilization. You don't mind the risks, of course; it wouldn't be any fun if it were as safe as sitting in your living room! But for safety, you bring maps, a compass, first aid supplies, and extra food and clothing in case of a prolonged stay. Most of the time, you won't take advantage of your precautions—but who wants to be stuck in the middle of nowhere without these bases covered? Planning for the unexpected has its place in Microsoft Visual Basic programming as well. The nature of an event-driven system such as Microsoft Access is that your application waits around for things to happen. Most of them are what you expect: the user adds data here, clicks a button there. But computer users have a way of trying everything, and sooner or later, someone will try something you didn't anticipate. Although the errors that can occur in your application are less exciting than being stuck in the wilderness, it nevertheless pays to prepare your application for anything before sending it out into the wild world of daily use.

The Visual Basic language provides sophisticated ways to control what happens when errors occur. Normally, errors can interrupt your application, causing it to appear unpolished or even making it unusable. In this chapter, you'll learn to respond to special events that occur when users perform unexpected actions on your forms. Additionally, you'll learn to use Visual Basic statements to intercept errors that occur while your procedures are running. Overall, you'll discover strategies for making your application foolproof—so that whatever comes its way, it can respond gracefully and effectively.

Ch07
Contacts.mdb

This chapter uses the practice file Ch07 Contacts.mdb that you installed from the book's CD-ROM. For details about installing the practice files, see "Using the Book's CD-ROM" at the beginning of this book.

Getting Started

● Start Access, and open the Ch07 Contacts database in the practice files folder.

Replacing Standard Error Messages

There are many errors that can occur when users interact with the forms in your application. Some of these errors will come as a complete surprise, and there may be nothing you can do about them. On the other hand, you occasionally *intend* to have a specific error occur. For example, suppose you set the Required property to Yes for a field in a table, and then the user tries to leave the field blank when entering data. As you would expect, Access displays an error message saying that the field can't be blank. In Chapter 4, you did this very thing for the *LastName* and *FirstName* fields in the *Contacts* table.

If you expect that users will commonly encounter a specific error in a form, such as the error for leaving a required field blank, you'll want to ensure that the message they receive makes sense to them so that they can fix the problem and continue with their work. But the standard error messages that Access displays won't always make sense to your users. In this section, you'll learn to replace the standard error messages that occur on your forms with your own messages. Specifically, you'll respond to the error that occurs when a user leaves a required field blank, creating an event procedure that displays your own message for this situation.

Responding to the Error Event

Each time an error occurs in a form, the form's *Error* event occurs. You can place code in an *Error* event procedure to display a message, or even to fix the problem that's causing the error. But to respond, you'll need to know what error has occurred. For this purpose, the *Error* event procedure includes an argument called *DataErr*, which contains the code number of the error that occurred. You'll use this number to determine whether it's the error you're expecting so that you can respond appropriately.

But first you must do a little detective work. You need to find out what the code number is for the error you want to respond to. To do this, you'll add code to the *Error* event procedure telling Visual Basic to display the error number in the Immediate window. Then you'll cause the error to occur so that you can discover the number. After you know the code number of the error that occurs when the user leaves a required field blank, you'll change the code to respond to this specific error.

Find Out the Code Number for an Error in a Form

You'll first open the *Contacts* form and then add a line of code to the *Error* event procedure.

1   In the Database window, click the Forms shortcut.

2   Click the *Contacts* form, and then click the Design button.

Properties

3   If the property sheet isn't open, click the Properties button on the toolbar.

4   Click the Event tab in the property sheet.

5   Click the OnError property, and then click the Build button.

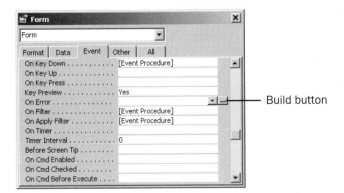

Build button

6 Click Code Builder, and then click OK.

Access displays the *Form_Error* event procedure in Visual Basic.

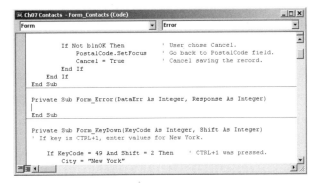

Note the two arguments in the *Sub* header for the *Form_Error* procedure, *DataErr* and *Response*.

7 Press the Tab key, and type the following line of code:

```
Debug.Print "DataErr = "; DataErr
```

8 If the Debug toolbar isn't displayed, point to Toolbars on the View menu and click Debug.

Immediate Window

9 Click the Immediate Window button.

This opens the Immediate window so that your code will have somewhere to send its message.

Cause the Error to Occur

Now you'll jump back to the *Contacts* form and cause the error to occur by trying to save a record without a name.

View Microsoft Access

1 Switch to Access. (Click the View Microsoft Access button on the toolbar.)

133

Form View

2   Click the Form View button on the toolbar.

3   Press the Delete key to delete the data in the First Name field.

┌─ Delete the data in this field.

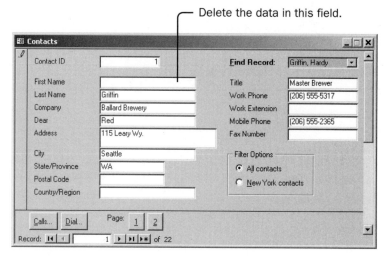

4   Press Tab.

Because the First Name field is required, Access displays an error message.

As you can see, the error message isn't all that friendly—but you'll replace it with your own message.

5   Click OK.

6   Press the Esc key to undo your change.

When you caused the Error event to run the event procedure, your code sent a message to the Visual Basic Immediate window. Let's take a look.

7   Switch back to Visual Basic. (Click Microsoft Visual Basic – Ch07 Contacts on the Windows taskbar.)

The error number for this error—leaving a required field blank—is 3314.

Displaying Your Own Message for a Specific Error

Now that you know the error number, you can write code to respond to the error. In the *Error* event procedure, you'll check to see if the error is caused by the user leaving a required field blank. If it is, you'll display an appropriate message; if not, you'll allow Access to display the standard error message.

In addition to the *DataErr* argument that provides you with the number of the error that occurred, the *Error* event procedure has another argument: the *Response* argument. You use this argument to tell Access how to proceed after your code runs. You have two options: you can tell Access to display the standard message for the error, or you can tell it to ignore the error (because you've either solved the problem or displayed your own custom error message).

Write Code That Displays a Custom Error Message

You'll replace the *Debug.Print* code you wrote before with code that displays your own message.

1   Close the Immediate window.

The Code window still shows the *Form_Error* event procedure.

2   Enter the Visual Basic code for the *Form_Error* event procedure, replacing the line containing *Debug.Print* with the following:

```
Private Sub Form_Error(DataErr As Integer, Response As Integer)
' If error is because of name, display a custom error message.

    Const conErrFieldRequired = 3314

    If DataErr = conErrFieldRequired Then
        DisplayMessage "You must fill in First Name and Last Name."
        Response = acDataErrContinue
    Else
        Response = acDataErrDisplay      ' Display standard message.
    End If
End Sub
```

Let's walk through the procedure line by line.

■   The *Const* statement declares a constant value for the error code you discovered. This helps to make your code more readable because it clarifies what the number 3314 means. You can use the constant *conErrFieldRequired* in place of the number later in the procedure.

■   The condition in the *If...Then* statement checks whether the *DataErr* value passed to the event procedure is equal to the error value *conErrFieldRequired*. If it is, the procedure runs the first block of code, displaying your custom message.

■   The *DisplayMessage* line of code uses the general procedure you created in Chapter 5 to display a message box. The message tells users what to do to solve the problem— fill in both the first and the last name before saving the record.

135

■ The next line sets the *Response* argument of the *Error* event procedure, using the pre-defined constant *acDataErrContinue*. Setting the *Response* argument to this value tells Access to skip displaying the standard error message—which is what you want in this case because you displayed your own message.

■ The *Else* block of code, which runs if the error is something other than the one you want to respond to, sets the *Response* argument to *acDataErrDisplay*. This tells Access to display the standard error message for the error because you don't know what the error is.

Try the New Message

If you cause the error again, it should display your new message.

View Microsoft Access

1   Switch to Access.

2   Click the label of the First Name field to select the data in the field.

3   Press Delete to delete the data in the field.

4   Press Tab.

Access displays the new error message.

5   Click OK.

6   Press Esc.

This simple use of the Error event shows how you can make life easier for users by anticipating problems they may encounter. Of course, this code responds only to a single error. By writing more complex code for the Error event, you can respond to errors in various ways. For example, you might want to use a *Select Case* statement to branch to several different blocks of code, providing your own error message for several errors. Or you might write code to help the user solve the problem—for example, your code could enter a required value automatically so that the record could be saved. The possibilities are endless; the main thing to remember is that when an error occurring in a form causes confusion, the *Error* event procedure is there as a resource to help you solve the problem.

Responding to a Combo Box Error

While the Error event helps you respond to many errors, there's one error that you respond to using a different event—an error that commonly occurs if you use combo boxes on your application's forms. Combo boxes and list boxes are one of the most powerful features of Access because they provide a way to look up values stored in different tables. In this section, you'll learn how to make combo boxes and list boxes work even better by responding to the *NotInList* event.

The *Contacts* form has a lookup field courtesy of the Database Wizard: the Contact Type field. This field displays values from the *Contact Types* table, so you can easily specify the type of each contact you enter by selecting from the list. For many fields, you'll want to ensure that only certain values are entered in the list. Combo boxes do this automatically if their LimitToList property is set to Yes—if you try to type a value in the Contact Type field that isn't in the list, you get an error.

Try Typing a New Value in the Contact Type Field

Suppose you want to enter the contact type for the first record in the *Contacts* form.

1 Click the Page 2 button in the *Contacts* form footer.

2 Click the Contact Type field, and then click the down arrow next to the combo box.

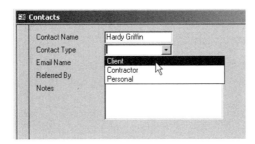

You don't see the contact type you want.

3 Click the drop-down arrow again to close the list, and then type **Vendor** and press the Enter key.

Access displays an error message, telling you that this value isn't in the list.

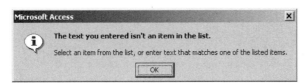

4 Click OK.

5 Press Escape twice to undo your changes.

This error message is a form of validation; Access makes sure you don't type an incorrect value. But what if you want users to be able to add their own contact types? They could do this by opening the *Contact Types* form, but this would interrupt their task of entering a contact. Ideally, you'd like them to do this easily from within the *Contacts* form. What you want to do is run an event procedure any time the user enters a value that isn't in the list. You can do this by responding to the *NotInList* event, which occurs when the user tries to enter the value—but before the error message tells the user the value must be in the list.

Let Users Add a Contact Type to the List Automatically

When a user enters a contact type value that isn't in the list, you want to ask if the user really wants this value to appear in the list permanently. To ask the question, you'll use the *Confirm* function you wrote in Chapter 5. If the user does want to add the new type, you'll use Visual Basic code to add the value to the *Contact Types* table behind the scenes.

Design View

1 Click the Design View button.

2 Scroll down in the form window so that you can see the *ContactTypeID* combo box.

3 Click the *ContactTypeID* control.

Access displays the event properties for the *ContactTypeID* control.

4 Click the OnNotInList property, and then click the Build button.

5 Click Code Builder, and then click OK.

Access opens the form module for the *Contacts* form and creates the *ContactTypeID_NotInList* event procedure.

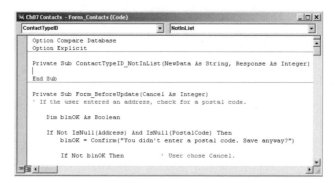

You'll notice that the header for the *NotInList* procedure includes two arguments: *NewData* and *Response*. The *NewData* argument contains the value the user entered in the field—the value that isn't yet in the list. The *Response* argument lets you tell Access what to do after your procedure ends, just like the *Response* argument you saw earlier in the *Error* event procedure.

6 Enter the following Visual Basic code for the procedure:

```
Private Sub ContactTypeID_NotInList(NewData As String, Response As Integer)
' Ask the user whether to add a value to the list.

    Dim strMessage As String
    Dim dbsContacts As Database
    Dim rstTypes As DAO.Recordset

    strMessage = "Are you sure you want to add '" & NewData & _
        "' to the list of contact types?"

    If Confirm(strMessage) Then

        ' Open the Contact Types table and add the NewData value.
```

```
            Set dbsContacts = CurrentDb
            Set rstTypes = dbsContacts.OpenRecordset("Contact Types")
            rstTypes.AddNew
            rstTypes!ContactType = NewData
            rstTypes.Update
            Response = acDataErrAdded      ' Requery the list.
        Else
            Response = acDataErrDisplay    ' Display the error.
        End If
    End Sub
```

This event procedure uses the same type of code you've seen before to ask the user a question. However, there are several important new elements.

■ The procedure has three Dim statements declaring variables you're going to use later in the procedure. The first declares a string variable you'll use to store your message to the user. The other two are *object variables*—so named because they store whole database objects, not just values—which you'll use when you add a record to the *Contact Types* table. The first of these is *dbsContacts*, a Database-type variable that will store information about the database; the second is *rstTypes*, a Recordset-type variable that will represent the *Contact Types* table when you add records.

■ The line that sets the value of the *strMessage* variable concatenates string values with the ampersand (&) operator. In this case, the line of code combines your message text with the value of the *NewData* variable, so the message can include the new value in the question it asks: "Are you sure you want to add '*this value*' to the list of contact types?" You'll notice that this line is broken in two for easier reading with a *line-continuation character*—an underscore (_) that tells Visual Basic to treat the next line of code as a continuation of the current line.

■ The condition in the *If...Then* statement is actually a call to your own *Confirm* function, which asks the user a question and returns *True* or *False*. If the *Confirm* function returns *True*, it means the user chose OK in the message box, and the first block of code runs.

■ The key to this procedure is the block of code that runs if the user chooses OK. These five lines are known as *data access object* (DAO) code because they utilize methods and statements belonging to the DAO code library, which you use when working directly with databases. For example, the first line uses the *Set* statement to assign an object to the *dbsContacts* variable—in this case it assigns the current database object, which is returned by the *CurrentDb* function. Before you can work with data in Visual Basic, you have to open a database in this way.

■ The next line uses the *OpenRecordset* method of the new database object to open the *Contact Types* table. To add or edit records using Visual Basic, you need to open a recordset object, either a table or a query. The *Set* statement assigns the recordset object to the *rstTypes* variable. As with other methods, you type the method after the object, separated by a period.

■ The next line uses the *AddNew* method of the *rstTypes* recordset to add a record to the end of the table.

- The next line assigns the value of the *NewData* argument, which is the value the user wants in the list, to the *ContactType* field in the table. To refer to the value of a field in a recordset, you follow the recordset name with the field name, separated by an exclamation point (!).

- The final line of DAO code uses the *Update* method to save the change to the recordset, adding the new record to the *Contact Types* table.

- After your procedure adds the record to the table, the last task is to tell Access how to proceed. Setting the *Response* argument to the constant *acDataErrAdded* tells Access that you've added the value and you want Access to requery the list box so that the value will show up in the list.

- The line after the *Else* keyword runs if the condition is *False*, in which case it sets the *Response* argument to *acDataErrDisplay*. This setting tells Access that you didn't add the value and that you want Access to display the standard error message and require the user to enter a value in the list.

The *NotInList* procedure gives a simple example of DAO code for manipulating a database—in later chapters, you'll learn advanced techniques for working with databases in Visual Basic. But this procedure does the trick for now—it adds a new record to the list. Perhaps most importantly, it allows your users to avoid a potentially annoying error message every time they try to type something in this box.

Tip

In order for the code to work, the Visual Basic project you're using needs a special setting—called a *reference*—telling it you are using DAO. The practice database already has this setting; however, if you want to use DAO code in your own databases, you'll need to tell Visual Basic by using the References command (on the Tools menu). For more information, see Chapter 12.

Try the *NotInList* Event Procedure

View Microsoft
Access

1   Switch to Access.

2   Click the Form View button on the toolbar.

3   Click the Page 2 button in the form footer.

4   Click the Contact Type field, type **Vendor,** and then and press Enter.

The *NotInList* event occurs, and your event procedure displays the message box, asking if you want to add your entry to the list.

Contact Management	✕
？ Are you sure you want to add 'Vendor' to the list of contact types?	
OK Cancel	

5 Click OK.

Your code opens the *Contact Types* table, adds the new record, and then tells Access to requery the list to include your new value.

6 Click the down arrow next to the Contact Type box.

The list now includes your new entry.

Adding a record to the list behind the scenes is just one possible strategy for responding to the *NotInList* event; you may need to choose another strategy based on your application's needs. For example, if the records shown in a combo box list are just part of a complete set of records that includes other values—a list of contacts' names, perhaps, taken from a complete table with addresses and phone numbers—you couldn't add records automatically. In a case like this, your *NotInList* event procedure might display another form where users could enter contact information.

Creating Error-Handling Routines

Up to this point, you've learned how to respond to errors that occur due to users' actions on a form, particularly when they enter data that isn't allowed. These errors are easy to respond to because form events occur whenever they happen. When you program in Visual Basic, there's an even more important class of errors—those that happen as a result of actions your code performs, rather than as a result of users' actions. Some errors occur because of mistakes in the code you've written; these you should fix. But others happen not because of an error in your code, but just because your code can't anticipate every possible condition that might be in place when it runs.

For example, suppose your code works with a database on a network and the network suddenly goes down. Obviously, this would cause an error. Or what if your code makes changes to a database, but the user opens the database using the read-only option so that changes can't be made? These unexpected conditions will cause run-time errors and would normally cause your application to stop abruptly, showing a message that would mean very little to a user who doesn't know much about programming.

Fortunately, Visual Basic provides a mechanism with which you can respond to any type of error that occurs while your code is running. It's called *error handling*. Error handling allows you to avoid abrupt interruptions of your application whenever unexpected things happen. By handling errors, you can either solve problems that come up and move on with your business, or give the user appropriate feedback about the problem and bow out gracefully. In this section, you'll learn how to use the *On Error GoTo* statement along with other Visual Basic statements to respond to run-time errors.

Handling Errors That Occur When Your Application Is Read-Only

When testing your application, it's a good idea to think of all the different conditions that might arise when users run it. One situation is that the user might open the application database in read-only mode. This isn't a common case, but it is certainly possible, and you want your application to be able to cope with it gracefully. Fortunately, when users open an application as read-only, Access automatically forbids them to change data in forms—you don't have to do anything special to make it work. You only have to worry if your code itself tries to make changes to data.

But guess what? In Chapter 4, you wrote code that sets the value of controls on the form. It's the *Form_KeyDown* procedure, which sets city, state, and country values on the form for New York City whenever a user presses the Ctrl+1 key combination. If the data can't be updated—for example, if the database is read-only—this code will cause a run-time error.

Set Up a Run-Time Error in Your Code

Before you write code to handle this error, let's see what happens if you don't handle it at all. Rather than closing the database and reopening it in read-only mode, you'll simulate this condition by making just the data in the *Contacts* form read-only. To do this, set the RecordsetType property for the form to Snapshot.

Design View

1 Click the Design View button on the toolbar.

2 Click the Data tab in the property sheet.

3 Click the RecordsetType property, and click Snapshot in the list of values.

Form View

4 Click the Form View button on the toolbar.

5 Press Ctrl+1.

An error occurs—and not one you'd like your users to see.

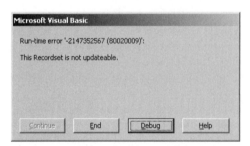

As with all run-time errors, you have two choices: Debug or End. (You can also get Help on the message, but eventually you still have to choose one of the other two options.) If you click Debug, Visual Basic displays the procedure that caused the error, highlighting the specific line of code that caused it. If you click End, the procedure that caused the error stops running.

Note the code number of the error at the top of the dialog box text: –2147352567. You'll use this number in your error-handling code.

6 Click Debug.

The Code window shows the existing *Form_KeyDown* event procedure, which you wrote in Chapter 4.

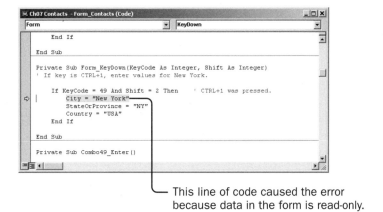

This line of code caused the error
because data in the form is read-only.

Tip

When you click the Debug button in a run-time error message, the procedure stops running temporarily, but it doesn't end. It's just as if you'd set a breakpoint on the statement that caused the error—except that you can't keep stepping through this code unless you first take care of the error. If you want to end the procedure that caused an error rather than stop and view it, click the End button in the run-time error message.

Add Error-Handling Code to the Event Procedure

Because you want to avoid having users see an error message like this—especially one that lets them dive right into your code—you'll add error-handling code to the procedure. But first you'll want to reset the code that you left running when the error occurred.

Reset

1   Click the Reset button on the toolbar.

2   Edit the existing *KeyDown* event procedure to appear as follows:

```
Private Sub Form_KeyDown(KeyCode As Integer, Shift As Integer)
' If key is CTRL+1, enter values for New York.

On Error GoTo Err_Form_KeyDown

    Const conErrNotUpdateable = -2147352567

    If KeyCode = 49 And Shift = 2 Then   ' CTRL+1 was pressed.
        City = "New York"
        StateOrProvince = "NY"
        Country = "USA"
    End If
Exit_Form_KeyDown:
    Exit Sub
```

(continued)

143

continued

```
Err_Form_KeyDown:
    If Err.Number = conErrNotUpdateable Then
      , DisplayMessage "Can't edit record; data is read-only."
    Else
        DisplayMessage Err.Description
    End If
    Resume Exit_Form_KeyDown
End Sub
```

Here's what the code does:

- The *On Error GoTo* statement says that if an error occurs while the procedure is running, Visual Basic should jump to the line labeled *Err_Form_KeyDown*, rather than halt the code and display an error message.

- The *Const* statement declares a constant value for the error code you saw earlier (–2147352567), which signifies the "This Recordset is not updateable" error.

- The *Exit_Form_KeyDown* line is a *label*, a name followed by a colon that you can use to identify a line of code you want Visual Basic to jump to. The *Exit Sub* statement below the label makes sure that if the procedure runs normally without error, it will exit after running the main code, rather than continuing with the error-handling code below. You should always add the *Exit Sub* or *Exit Function* statement before error-handling code so that the error-handling code won't run unless an error actually occurs.

- The *Err_Form_KeyDown* label introduces the error-handling code and provides a place for Visual Basic to jump to if an error does occur.

- The *If...Then* statement on the next line checks to see if the error is in fact the one you expected. It uses the Number property of the *Err* object, which always contains the number of the last error that occurred in your application.

- If the error is caused by read-only data, the following line displays your custom message using the *DisplayMessage Sub* procedure you created in Chapter 5. If the error is caused by something else you didn't expect, the line under the *Else* statement displays the standard Access error message, which you can find using the Description property of the *Err* object.

- Finally the *Resume* statement in the last line tells Visual Basic that your error-handling code is finished and that you want to continue running your procedure at the line labeled *Exit_Form_KeyDown*. Resuming at this line runs the *Exit Sub* line, causing the procedure to end.

Now, if this procedure can't set values in the form for any reason, the user will receive a message explaining the problem but your application will continue running instead of ending abruptly with an error message.

Step Through the Error-Handling Code

To try out the new error-handling code, you'll cause the error to happen again. However, before you start, you'll set a breakpoint in the procedure so that you can step through and see how it works.

1 Set a breakpoint on the sixth line of the procedure—the line that sets the City field to "New York"—by clicking the gray margin to the left of the line.

Now the procedure will stop at this line, regardless of whether an error occurs.

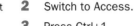
View Microsoft
Access

2 Switch to Access.

3 Press Ctrl+1.

The *KeyDown* event procedure runs, reaches your breakpoint, and appears again in the Code window. The next statement to run will try to set a value in the form. Because data in the form is still read-only, you can expect that this statement will cause an error.

4 Click the Step Over button.

Instead of moving to the next statement, the current statement indicator jumps all the way down to the line below the label *Err_Form_KeyDown*—the line you specified in the *On Error GoTo* statement at the beginning of the procedure.

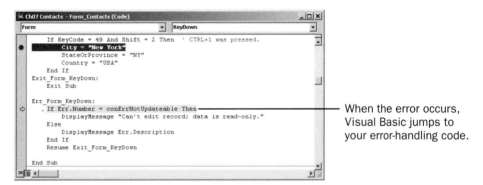

When the error occurs, Visual Basic jumps to your error-handling code.

In effect, the error-handling code you wrote is now interrupting the normal flow of code—you might say your procedure is in "error-handling mode."

5 Click the Step Over button twice.

Your code displays the error message.

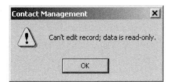

6 Click OK.

7 Click the Step Over button two more times.

When your error-handling code finishes running, the *Resume* statement sends the current statement indicator up to the line under the *Exit_Form_KeyDown* label: the *Exit Sub* line.

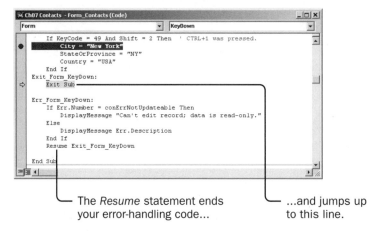

     The *Resume* statement ends   ...and jumps up
     your error-handling code...   to this line.

8   Click the Step Over button a final time.

9   Close Visual Basic.

Stepping through your error-handling code helped you to see how this technique works. For your users, this is all hidden—but the important difference is that now they won't see the run-time error message that appeared before your error-handling code was in place.

Anticipating Other Problems That Cause Errors

Having data turn out to be read-only is just one of many unexpected conditions that can occur in your application—the possibilities for errors are endless. And there are plenty of other procedures in the application that don't yet have error-handling code in them. To be thorough, you would want to provide error-handling code in every procedure you write so that users will never see your application halt abruptly with an error message. However, most procedures you write won't perform any actions that are likely to cause errors. To save time and effort, you can concentrate on providing error handling only where errors are likely to occur.

Although by no means complete, the following list shows a few actions for which you should be sure to provide error handling. You should anticipate that errors could occur any time your code attempts to do any of the following functions:

- Access any file on disk, directly or indirectly
- Run queries or change data in a database
- Set properties of objects
- Perform mathematical calculations

Additional Error-Handling Techniques

You've seen one simple way to handle errors using the On Error GoTo statement. But there are several other techniques you can use to handle errors. Here's a sampling.

Resume code at the statement that caused the error. If your code can diagnose and solve the problem that occurred, you'll want to allow your code to continue running with the statement that caused the error. By using the *Resume* statement on a line by itself at the end of your error-handling code, you can tell Visual Basic to return to the line that caused the error and try it over again.

For example, if your code tries to access a file on a floppy disk drive and an error occurs because the disk isn't in the drive, your code could display a message telling the user to insert the correct disk. At the end of the error-handling code, you'd use the *Resume* statement so that the statement that tried to access the disk could run again.

Skip over the statement that caused the error. If the statement that causes an error is not critical to your application, you can use the *Resume Next* statement to tell Visual Basic to continue running code at the statement *after* the one that caused the error. In this type of situation, you might even *expect* the error to occur on a regular basis, and you might want the statement to run only if it doesn't result in an error. For example, suppose you have a procedure that sets a value on a form that may or may not be open. If the form is open, the line of code that sets the value runs as expected. If it's not, the line causes an error—but because you don't want to set the value unless the form is open, you're content to simply skip the statement altogether using *Resume Next*.

Tell Visual Basic to ignore errors temporarily. If you know that an error is likely to occur on a particular statement and you don't want to suspend the running code at all, you can use the *On Error GoTo Next* statement to suspend error handling altogether. This causes Visual Basic to skip over a line that causes an error as if the error didn't occur. For example, if you want to set a property for a control only if the control has the property, you could use *On Error GoTo Next* before setting the property so that an error won't occur if the property doesn't exist.

If you use this strategy, you'll usually want to check the *Err.Number* value immediately following the statement to determine what error occurred, if any. Additionally, be sure to turn error handling back on by including another *On Error GoTo* statement, or additional errors could occur without your knowledge, causing problems in your application.

The technique you choose will depend on the types of errors you anticipate and what you want to do with them. If you don't know how you want to handle an error, the best fallback position is the strategy you used in this chapter—display the description of the error in a message box, and then exit the procedure.

Chapter Wrap-Up

1   Close the *Contacts* form, clicking Yes when Access asks if you want to save changes to the form.

2   On the File menu, click Exit.

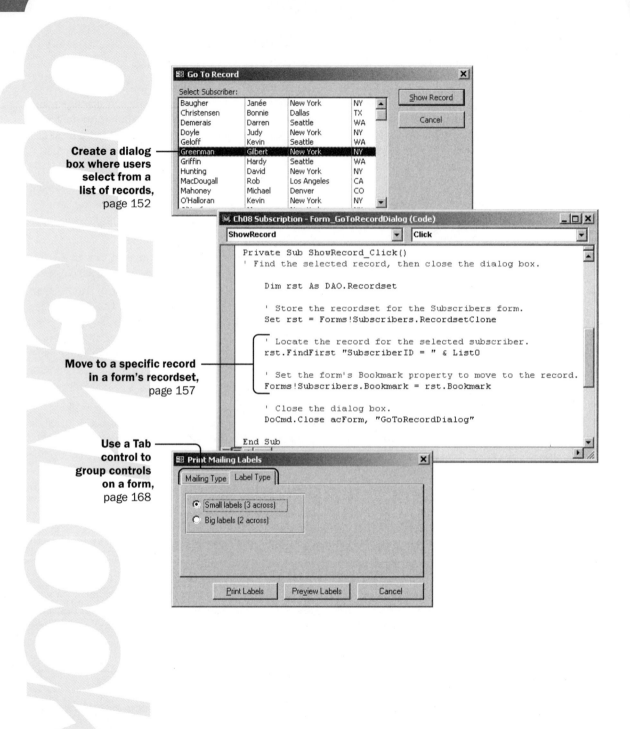

Create a dialog box where users select from a list of records, page 152

Move to a specific record in a form's recordset, page 157

Use a Tab control to group controls on a form, page 168

Go To Record

Select Subscriber:

Baugher	Janée	New York	NY
Christensen	Bonnie	Dallas	TX
Demerais	Darren	Seattle	WA
Doyle	Judy	New York	NY
Geloff	Kevin	Seattle	WA
Greenman	Gilbert	New York	NY
Griffin	Hardy	Seattle	WA
Hunting	David	New York	NY
MacDougall	Rob	Los Angeles	CA
Mahoney	Michael	Denver	CO
O'Halloran	Kevin	New York	NY

Show Record

Cancel

Ch08 Subscription - Form_GoToRecordDialog (Code)

ShowRecord / Click

```
Private Sub ShowRecord_Click()
' Find the selected record, then close the dialog box.

    Dim rst As DAO.Recordset

    ' Store the recordset for the Subscribers form.
    Set rst = Forms!Subscribers.RecordsetClone

    ' Locate the record for the selected subscriber.
    rst.FindFirst "SubscriberID = " & List0

    ' Set the form's Bookmark property to move to the record.
    Forms!Subscribers.Bookmark = rst.Bookmark

    ' Close the dialog box.
    DoCmd.Close acForm, "GoToRecordDialog"

End Sub
```

Print Mailing Labels

Mailing Type | Label Type

- ● Small labels (3 across)
- ○ Big labels (2 across)

Print Labels | Preview Labels | Cancel

Chapter 8
Gather Information in a Dialog Box

After completing this chapter, you will be able to:

✔ Create an unbound form to act as a dialog box.

✔ Find a record in a form's recordset.

✔ Filter records in a report using criteria the user selects.

Nearly every business phone number you call these days has some sort of automated answering system. It's becoming rare to talk to an actual person, unless of course you first jump through all the required hoops. But if you're like me, you've chosen to wait for the good old human representative more than a few times!

These systems save companies lots of money and often provide just the information callers need. But even as we become more accustomed to them, it's clear that they're much less flexible than most human beings. Automated answering systems are limited—for now, anyway—by the keypad provided on your telephone. They don't always have the options you need at a given time, and you have to answer several questions to get where you want to be.

Like a telephone answering system, your database applications need to help users get to information. Fortunately, your computer's interface is much more flexible than a telephone, but you'll still consider the same types of challenges and pitfalls. You need to ask users questions about what they want to do—establish a dialogue with them—and respond to their input. Of course, these conversations can exchange quite a bit more information than pressing 0 through 9 on a telephone keypad.

One of the tools you have for conversing with the user is the *dialog box*, a form you can present on the screen to provide information and ask questions. In this chapter, you'll learn to communicate with your application's users by creating dialog boxes and accessing the information the users provide in them.

Ch 08
Subscription
.mdb

This chapter uses the practice file Ch08 Subscription.mdb that you installed from the book's CD-ROM. For details abut installing the practice files, see "Using the Book's CD-ROM" at the beginning of this book.

Getting Started

● Start Microsoft Access, and open the Ch08 Subscription database in the practice files folder.

Creating an Application from Scratch

In Parts 1 and 2 of this book, you enhanced a database that you created with the Database Wizard. But as a Microsoft Access developer, you're likely to need databases that the wizard doesn't create. Your applications may need to store a type of data that the wizard doesn't handle, or you may just want to communicate with users in your own way. In Part 3, you'll create an application user interface on your own.

When you create an application from scratch, you need to plan in advance the features you want it to have. Then you create the tables that will store all the information you need. Next you begin creating forms, reports, and other objects that make up the interface for your application. Finally, you'll tie all the objects together by writing Microsoft Visual Basic code. Along the way, you might use many different wizards and builders to help you—even if you bypass the Database Wizard, you can get help creating parts of your application by relying on other wizards, such as the Table Wizard and the Command Button Wizard.

View the Tables in the Subscription Database

Starting in this chapter, you'll work with an application that stores subscriptions to a publication. The Subscription practice database already has tables full of subscriber data, and even some of the forms and reports you'll need—but you'll create additional objects and the Visual Basic code that makes the application work. First, however, you should take a look at what's already in the Subscription database.

1 In the Database window, click the Tables shortcut.

The Subscription database contains two tables, *Subscribers* and *Payments*. If you'd designed this database from scratch, you would have created these tables and chosen their fields either by running the Table Wizard or by using Table Design view.

Relationships

2 Click the Relationships button on the toolbar.

Access displays the Relationships window, showing the fields in the *Subscribers* and *Payments* tables and the relationship between the two tables.

As you can see, the *Subscribers* table includes fields for name and address information—everything you'll need to send mailings to subscribers. The *Payments* table includes fields that store each payment received from a subscriber. There is a *one-to-many* relationship between the tables, because for each subscriber, there can be many related payment records.

This line indicates that the two tables are related based on values in the Subscriber ID field.

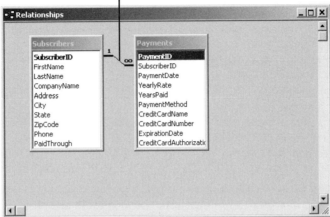

3 Close the Relationships window.

These two tables are all that's required for this database. But for a more complex application, you may need many tables that relate in different ways.

Open the *Subscribers* Form

Most applications have a main form—the place where users spend most of their time viewing and entering data. In the Subscription database, the main form is the *Subscribers* form, which is already provided for you in the practice database.

1 In the Database window, click the Forms shortcut.

2 Double-click the *Subscribers* form.

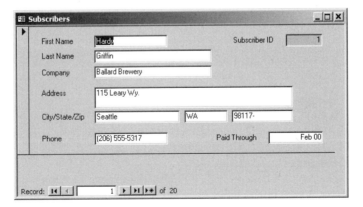

To create a form like this for your own application, you can use the Form Wizard. After you create a form and let the wizard lay out the fields for you, you may want to open the form in Design view to rearrange and resize fields, or perhaps to add formatting or pictures to give the form a custom look. Then you may want to add additional capabilities to the form; for example, in the next section, you'll add a useful command button to the form.

Using Dialog Boxes in Your Applications

So far, the only interaction you've learned to have with the user is through message boxes, which are a simple type of dialog box. You've displayed a message, and the user has responded by clicking a button. But message boxes all look the same and are limited to one, two, or three buttons. By creating a custom dialog box form, you can include any combination of controls and buttons you want. Dialog boxes are especially useful for the following purposes.

Presenting users with a custom message box If you want to display a message that has a custom appearance or special command buttons—with text other than Yes, No, OK, or Cancel—you can't just rely on the *MsgBox* function. For example, you might want a dialog box to allow four or more actions or to include command buttons with icons on them.

Asking questions before opening a form or report When you provide a way for users to open a form or report, you may want to allow them to specify options. For example, you might want to ask users which records they want to view or in which order they want to display them.

Allowing users to specify general options for your application A dialog box can have many controls for entering diverse types of information in one place. For example, you might want to allow users to customize the appearance or behavior of your application by collecting their preferences in a dialog box called Options and then saving them in a table.

Gathering additional information for a menu command If your application uses custom menu bars, you may want one of the commands to open a dialog box to get details on how to proceed. Access, like most Windows-based applications, has several dialog boxes accessible from menus and toolbars. In Chapter 10, you'll learn to create custom menu bars and toolbars that perform actions such as opening a dialog box.

There are as many uses for dialog boxes as there are types of applications. In this chapter, you'll create two common kinds of dialog boxes, and learn all the basic techniques you need to create a dialog box for any purpose.

Creating a Dialog Box to Go to a Specific Record

In this section, you'll create a dialog box that helps users jump to a specific record in the *Subscribers* form. In the dialog box you'll add a list box to display the available records, and you'll write code for a new button to display the record that the user selects.

You've already written code to help users locate a record: in Chapter 3, you created a combo box to do this. But by using a dialog box, you can keep this tool out of the way of users, giving you more room on the form—and more flexibility in how users select the records they're looking for. When a user clicks a button that you will add to the *Subscribers* form, your dialog box will pop up.

Users can select the record they want from a list in the dialog box.

Create the *GoToRecordDialog* Dialog Box Form

A dialog box is a special type of form: instead of displaying data in its controls, it allows the user to set the control values easily so that you can collect information. A form that doesn't display data is called an *unbound* form, because it isn't bound to a table or query—its RecordSource property is blank. You create unbound forms from scratch in Design view, because there's no wizard to create them for you.

Database Window

1 Click the Database Window button on the toolbar.

2 Click the New button.

Access displays the New Form dialog box. Design view is selected by default, so you don't have to choose a design method. And because you want the form to be unbound, you won't select a table or query either.

3 Click OK.

Access creates a blank form and displays it in Design view. As you can see by the Design view rulers, the new form's Detail section is 5 inches wide and 2 inches high.

4 Drag the right side of the form's Detail section to resize it to 4½ by 2 inches.

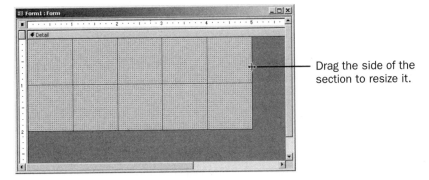

Drag the side of the section to resize it.

Save

5 Click the Save button on the toolbar.

6 Type **GoToRecordDialog**, and then click OK.

Access saves the form in the database.

153

Use a Wizard to Create the Select Subscriber List Box

Now you're ready to add controls to the dialog box to get the user's input. The primary control for the dialog box is a list box from which the user can select a subscriber's record. You'll create this control using the List Box Wizard.

List Box

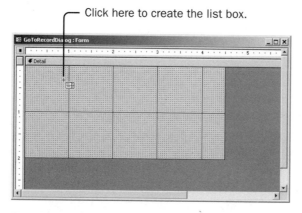

1 In the toolbox, make sure the Control Wizards tool is selected, and then click the List Box tool.

2 Click near the top of the form.

Click here to create the list box.

The List Box Wizard starts, asking how you want the list box to get the values it displays.

3 Select the first option, I Want The List Box To Look Up The Values In A Table Or Query, and then click Next.

The wizard asks which table you want the list box to get values from.

4 Click Table: Subscribers, and then click Next.

The wizard asks which fields you want to include in the list box.

5 Double-click the LastName field to add it to the Selected Fields list, followed by the First-Name, City, and State fields (in that order), and then click Next.

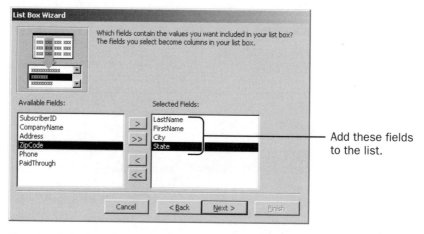

Add these fields to the list.

The wizard displays the list of subscribers as it will appear in the list box.

6 Double-click the right side of the FirstName column selector to have it fit the data and field name, then do the same for the State column selector.

Double-click the column selectors
to resize columns as shown.

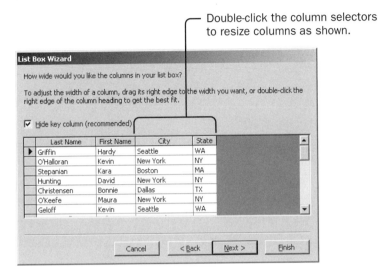

7 Click Next.

The wizard asks which label you want for your list box.

8 Type **Select Subscriber:** and then click Finish.

The wizard creates the list box and places it on your form. Behind the scenes, the wizard sets properties for the list box so that it will display the data you specified. It also includes the SubscriberID field—the primary key field in the *Subscribers* table—as a hidden field in the list box.

Users won't see this field, but the list box will be based on it, and you'll use its value to set the current record in the *Subscribers* form.

Notice that the wizard gave the list box the default name *List0*. You'll use this name in code when referring to the value of the list box.

Position the List Box on the *Dialog Box* Form

The list box isn't quite right yet. Before you test it, you'll want to make a few adjustments.

1 Point to the upper left corner of the list box's label, and then drag it to just above the upper left corner of the list box.

2 If the label isn't large enough to fit the text, double-click the right side of the label to resize it.

3 Drag the list box to move it near the upper left corner of the form.

4 Drag the bottom right corner of the list box to make it slightly wider (increase the width by about ¼ inch) and nearly as high as the Detail section of the form.

Gather Information in a Dialog Box

The form should look like this:

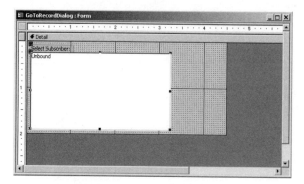

To test your list box, you can switch to Form view.

Form View

5 Click the Form View button on the toolbar.

The list box shows records from the *Subscribers* table.

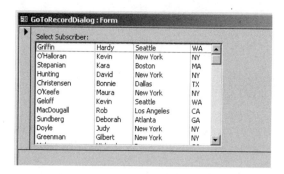

Modify the List Box to Sort by Last Name

You may have noticed that the records in the form aren't sorted alphabetically—unfortunately, the List Box Wizard doesn't do this for you. It would be quite a bit easier for users to find the records they want if the subscribers were in order. To sort the records, you'll need to modify the *RowSource* query that the wizard created for your list box.

Design View

1 Click the Design View button on the toolbar.

2 If the list box isn't selected, click to select it.

Properties

3 If the property sheet isn't open, click the Properties button to display it.

4 Click the Data tab in the property sheet.

5 Click the RowSource property, and then click the Build button.

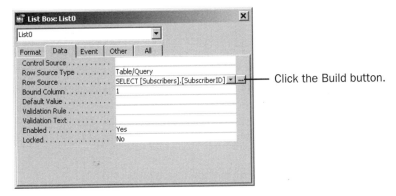

Click the Build button.

Access displays the query for the list box in a Query Builder window.

6 Select the Sort row underneath the LastName field, and then click the down arrow and select Ascending from the list.

Set the sort order of the
LastName field to *Ascending*.

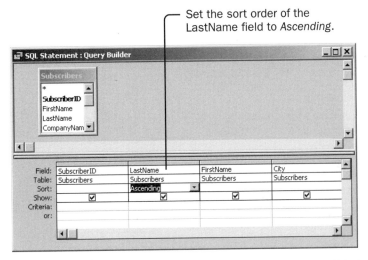

7 Select the Sort row underneath the FirstName field, and then click the down arrow and select Ascending from the list.

8 Close the Query Builder window, clicking Yes when Access asks if you want to save changes to the RowSource property.

Now records in the list box will be sorted by last name, and if there are duplicate last names, by first name as well. The list box is ready to go!

9 Close the property sheet.

Add a Button to Change Records in the *Subscribers* Form

You'll try out the list box soon enough—first, you need to add buttons and Visual Basic code to the dialog box to make it work. The most important item to add is the button that actually finds the selected record in the *Subscribers* form.

Control Wizards

1 In the toolbox, click the Control Wizards tool to deselect it, and then click the Command Button tool.

2 Click near the top of the form, just to the right of the list box.

Click here to create the button.

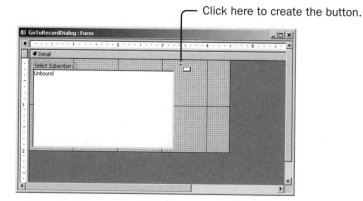

Access creates the button, giving it a default caption such as Command2.

Properties

3 Click the Properties button on the toolbar, and then click the All tab in the property sheet.

4 Click the Name property, and then type **ShowRecord**.

5 Click the Caption property, and then type **&Show Record**.

6 Set the Default property to *Yes*.

With the Default property set to *Yes*, the button will be selected automatically if the user presses the Enter key while in the dialog box.

7 Set the Enabled property to *No*, and then close the property sheet.

Setting the button's Enabled property to *No* disables it, so the user can't click it when the dialog box first opens. You wouldn't normally want to disable a button, but in this case, there's a good reason to do so. When you first open a form that has a list box, the list box doesn't have a value—nothing is selected. Until the user selects a subscriber in this list box, you don't want the Show Record button to be available. Later, you'll add code that enables the button as soon as the user selects something in the list.

8 With the right mouse button, click the ShowRecord button, and then click Build Event.

9 Double-click Code Builder.

Access opens Visual Basic and displays the event procedure for the button's *Click* event.

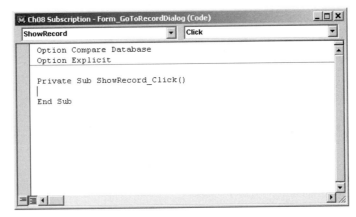

10 Add the following code to the procedure (except the *Sub* and *End Sub* lines, which are already there).

```
Private Sub ShowRecord_Click()
' Find the selected record, then close the dialog box.

    Dim rst As DAO.Recordset

    ' Store the recordset for the Subscribers form.
    Set rst = Forms!Subscribers.RecordsetClone

    ' Locate the record for the selected subscriber.
    rst.FindFirst" "SubscriberID =" " & List0

    ' Set the form's Bookmark property to move to the record.
    Forms!Subscribers.Bookmark = rst.Bookmark

    ' Close the dialog box.
    DoCmd.Close acForm," "GoToRecordDialog"
End Sub
```

This code changes the current record in the *Subscribers* form to the one the user has selected in your list box. Let's look at this code more closely.

■ The *Dim* statement creates a DAO Recordset-type variable called *rst*. You'll use this variable to represent the set of subscriber records in the *Subscribers* form.

■ The second line of code begins with the *Set* statement. This line contains an expression—*Forms!Subscribers.RecordsetClone*—that refers to the records shown in the *Subscribers* form. Every form has a RecordsetClone property that you can use to get a copy of the form's underlying recordset. As you've seen before, you refer to a form other than the current form by preceding the form name with the *Forms* keyword, followed by an exclamation point. And to refer to a property, you separate the object and its property with a period.

■ A recordset-type variable is an *object* variable—it stores an object rather than a simple value—which means you must use the *Set* statement to assign an object to it. In plain English, the whole line says, "Create a copy of the set of records in the *Subscribers* form and assign it to the *rst* variable so that I can refer to it later."

Recordset objects have many methods that help you work with them. In Chapter 7, you learned how to add a record to a recordset by using the *AddNew* method. The third code line uses a new method, *FindFirst*, to move to a specific record in the recordset. To use a method, you follow the object variable with its method, separated by a period, as in *rst.FindFirst*.

The *FindFirst* method takes an argument that specifies the criteria you want to use to find the record. As you recall, when you created the *List0* list box, you specified that its value should be based on the subscriber ID for the selected subscriber. Now you want this argument to specify that the value you're looking for in the recordset is the one that's selected in the list box. Using the ampersand (&) operator, this line combines the string *SubscriberID =* with the list box value.

All put together, this line of code says, "In the recordset stored in the *rst* variable, find the first record where the SubscriberID field contains the same value as the List0 list box."

Normally, your next step would be to check whether Access found the record you were looking for. In this case, however, you know that the record is there because the list box contains the same records as the *Subscribers* form. So the current record in the *rst* recordset is now the one the user selected in the list box.

It's important to note that finding the record doesn't automatically change the record shown in the *Subscribers* form. This is because you're actually working with a *copy* of the recordset, which you stored in the *rst* variable using the RecordsetClone property. To actually move to the record you want, the next line of code sets the Bookmark property of the *Subscribers* form. Forms and recordsets both have a Bookmark property, which is a special value Access uses to keep track of which record is current—just as if the record were the page you had reached in a book. When two recordsets contain the same records, you can synchronize one recordset with another by setting its Bookmark value to the same value as the other's.

At the risk of oversimplification, you can read the Bookmark line as saying, "In the *Subscribers* form's set of records, move to the same record that's current in the *rst* recordset object."

Now that you've moved to the record the user specified, the work of the dialog box is complete. The next line of code uses the *Close* method of the *DoCmd* object to close the dialog box. The arguments for the *Close* method specify which object to close. Using the predefined constant *acForm*, you tell Access that the object to close is a form; with the second argument, you give the name of the form to close, *GoToRecordDialog*.

Add Code to Enable the Show Record Button

As you recall, you made sure the Show Record button is disabled by default, because no item is selected in the list when the dialog box first appears. As soon as the user selects a value in the list, you want to enable the button. You can do this by responding to the list box's *AfterUpdate* event, which occurs whenever the user changes the value of the list box.

View Microsoft
Access

1   Switch back to Access.

2   On the *GoToRecordDialog* form, click the list box control.

Properties

3 Click the Properties button on the toolbar, and then click the Event tab in the property sheet.

4 Click the AfterUpdate property, and then click the Build button.

5 Double-click Code Builder.

Access switches to Visual Basic and displays the *List0_AfterUpdate* event procedure.

6 Add the following code to the procedure:

```
Private Sub List0_AfterUpdate()
' Once a record is chosen in the list, enable the ShowRecord button.

    ShowRecord.Enabled = True

End Sub
```

The line of code in this procedure sets the Enabled property for the ShowRecord button to *True*—just as if you'd set the property to *Yes* in the property sheet—so that the button appears enabled and the user can click it.

Add Code to Respond When the User Double-Clicks an Entry

To make your dialog box easier to use, there's one other event that you can respond to. When the user double-clicks a value in the list box, you want to respond as if the Show Record button had been clicked immediately afterward. This way, a user can avoid the added step of clicking the button after selecting a subscriber.

1 In the Code window's Procedure box, select DblClick.

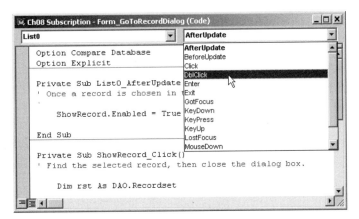

Visual Basic displays the *List0_DblClick* procedure.

2 Add the following code to the procedure.

```
Private Sub List0_DblClick(Cancel As Integer)
' When the user double-clicks, act as though
' the ShowRecord button was chosen.
```

(continued)

continued

```
      If Not IsNull(List0) Then
          ShowRecord_Click
      End If

End Sub
```

The line in the middle of this procedure tells Visual Basic to run the *ShowRecord_Click* event procedure. You can run a procedure in the current module by simply entering the name of the procedure on a line by itself. When Visual Basic encounters this line, it jumps to the *ShowRecord_Click* procedure, running it just as it would have if the Show Record button had actually been clicked.

The *If...Then* statement in this procedure is a safety measure. It checks to make sure the List0 list box has a value; if it doesn't, the button shouldn't be enabled, so you wouldn't want to run its event procedure. Normally, when the user double-clicks the list box, this action sets a value for the list box. However, by double-clicking the list box label, it is possible to make the *DblClick* event occur when the list box has no value. If the *List0* control doesn't have a subscriber selected, the value of the expression *Not IsNull(List0)* is *False*, so the code in the procedure does nothing.

Check your Visual Basic Code for Errors

You've written quite a bit of code for the dialog box! It's a good idea to get in the habit of compiling your code from time to time—this lets Visual Basic catch any errors right away and saves you from being interrupted when you run your code.

1 On the Debug menu, click Compile Ch08 Subscription.

If Visual Basic encounters any errors, it identifies them for you—otherwise, it does nothing (other than preparing your code to run). Of course, if there are errors, you should fix them and compile your code again.

View Microsoft
Access

2 Switch to Access.

3 Close the property sheet.

4 Click the Save button on the toolbar.

Add a Cancel Button to Close the Form

Your dialog box is almost complete! But in addition to a button that performs an action, such as the Show Record button you created, every dialog box should have a Cancel or Close button, in case the user has a change of heart and doesn't really want to do anything. In this case, you just need a button to close the *GoToRecordDialog* form, performing no action at all. The easiest way to create this button is by using the Command Button Wizard.

Control
Wizards

1 In the toolbox, click the Control Wizards tool, and then click the Command Button tool.

2 Click the right side of the form, just underneath the left side of the ShowRecord button as shown on the next page.

Click here to create the command button.

The Command Button Wizard starts, asking what action you want the button to perform.

3 Click Form Operations in the Categories list, click Close Form in the Actions list, and then click Next.

The wizard asks whether you want a picture or text on your button.

4 Click the Close Form text in the Text box, type **Cancel** to replace the text, and then click Next.

The wizard asks what you want to name the button.

5 Type **Cancel**, and then click Finish.

The wizard creates the Cancel button.

6 Drag the bottom right corner of the Cancel button to make it the same size as the ShowRecord button.

Now that the button is complete, there's one more step. With most any Cancel or Close button on a dialog box, you want users to be able to press the Esc key in lieu of clicking the button. To make this possible, you just set the button's Cancel property to Yes—identifying it to Access as the Cancel button for the form.

Properties

7 Click the Properties button on the toolbar, and then click the Other tab in the property sheet.

8 Set the Cancel property to Yes.

The button is finished—and you're ready to put the final touches on your dialog box.

Set Properties for the Dialog Box

Although a dialog box is a form like any other, you want it to look and behave differently in many ways. First you'll take a look at the form as it stands now, with its default property settings. Then you'll change several properties to make it work the way you want.

Form View

1 Click the Form View button on the toolbar. (You may need to move the property sheet down and to the right so that you can see the form.)

The list box shows records in alphabetical order, and everything seems to be in its place. Notice, however, that like any ordinary Access form, this form has several features used for moving around in a set of records—navigation buttons, scroll bars, and a record selector—all things that dialog boxes *don't* customarily have.

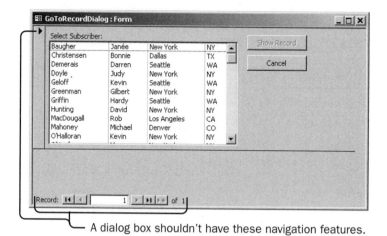

A dialog box shouldn't have these navigation features.

Each of these features has a corresponding form property you can set to remove it from your form. You'll set most of these properties in Form view so that you can see their effect immediately.

2 To select the form so that you can set its properties, click the record selector bar on the left side of the form (the property sheet will show *Form* in its title bar).

3 In the property sheet, click the Format tab.

4 Set the following properties to the values shown here:

Property	Value
Caption	*Go To Record*
ScrollBars	*Neither*
RecordSelectors	*No*
NavigationButtons	*No*
AutoCenter	*Yes*
BorderStyle	*Dialog*

These settings will make your dialog box look much like any other Windows dialog box—a thin border, a simple title, and no extra navigation tools. However, there are three additional properties you'll want to set so that your dialog box works the way a dialog box should. To set these properties, you'll switch back to Design view.

Design View

5 Click the Design View button on the toolbar.

6 On the Edit menu, click Select Form.

7 In the property sheet, click the Other tab.

8 Set the PopUp property to *Yes*.

This setting makes your dialog box into a pop-up form: it will appear on top of all other windows, including Access itself.

9 Set the Modal property to *Yes*.

This setting makes your dialog box *modal*, which means that users won't be able to click outside of the dialog box while it's open. Most dialog boxes are modal: you intend that the user will complete the action—such as locating a record—and then close the dialog box to move on to the next task.

10 Set the AllowDesignChanges property to *Design View Only*.

This setting ensures that the property sheet will no longer show when the dialog box is displayed in Form view.

11 Close the *GoToRecordDialog* form, clicking Yes when Access asks if you want to save changes to the form.

Add a Button to the Subscribers Form to Open the Dialog Box

Your dialog box is complete—the only thing left is to attach it to the *Subscribers* form. To do this, you'll add a button using the Command Button Wizard.

1 Switch to the *Subscribers* form, which is still open behind the Database window.

Design View

2 Click the Design View button on the toolbar.

3 Scroll down in the form to display the Form Footer section.

Command
Button

4 In the toolbox, click the Command Button tool.

5 Click the left side of the form footer.

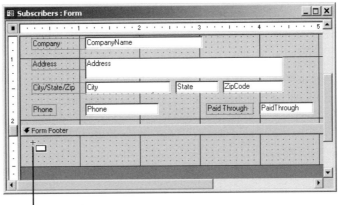

— Click here to create the command button.

The Command Button Wizard starts, asking what action you want the button to perform.

6 Click Form Operations in the Categories list, click Open Form in the Actions list, and then click Next.

The wizard asks which form you want to open. Because the *GoToRecordDialog* form is already selected, you don't have to click it.

7 Click Next.

The wizard asks whether you want a picture or text on your button.

8 Click the Open Form text in the Text box, type **&Go To Record** to replace the text, and then click Next.

The wizard asks what you want to name the button.

9 Type **GoToRecord**, and then click Finish.

The wizard creates the button, including an event procedure that automatically opens your dialog box whenever the button is clicked.

Save

10 Click the Save button on the toolbar.

Try the New Dialog Box

No more waiting—you're ready to click that button and try out the dialog box!

Form View

1 Click the Form View button on the toolbar.

2 Click the Go To Record button.

The Go To Record dialog box appears.

As you can see, the form no longer looks like an ordinary Access form—it has a thin border and no navigation tools. Because the form is modal, if you try to click an Access menu or the *Subscribers* form behind the form, your computer beeps and nothing happens. The only actions you can take are to move or close the dialog box or select a record in the list box and click a button.

And notice that the Show Record button is disabled because you haven't yet selected a subscriber in the dialog box.

3 In the Select Subscriber list box, click the entry for Judy Doyle.

The Show Record button is now enabled—when you set the value of the list box, the *After-Update* event procedure ran, and your code set the Enabled property.

4 Click the Show Record button.

Your event procedure for the button changes the current record in the *Subscribers* form's recordset to the record for Judy Doyle and then closes the dialog box. It works!

5 Click the Go To Record button again.

This time, you can test the double-clicking feature you added.

6 In the Select Subscriber list box, double-click the entry for Gilbert Greenman.

The *Subscribers* form now shows this record—your event procedure for the list box's *DblClick* event took care of it.

Finally, you should test the Cancel button in the dialog box.

7 Click the Go To Record button again, and then click any entry in the list box.

8   Click the Cancel button.

The *Subscribers* form still shows the same record—as expected, the record does not change if you click Cancel.

9   Close the *Subscribers* form.

As you've seen, quite a bit of work goes into creating a custom dialog box. (As you practice, you'll learn ways to make it easier.) It's worthwhile, though, when you consider how polished your applications can look by using custom dialog boxes to meet users' needs.

Tip

To save time when creating a dialog box for your own application, you may want to copy or import an existing dialog box form and start work from there. Because many dialog boxes have similar controls and property settings, you'll be well on your way—and much happier than if you'd started from scratch.

Filtering Data in a Report

Because the task of selecting a subset of data is so important in database applications, one common use for a dialog box is to specify criteria for filtering records. Access provides a powerful interface for filtering records in forms, so your applications can rely on standard filtering tools in many cases. In other cases, however, you'll want to provide a custom method for selecting records. This is especially true for selecting records to include in reports, because filtering records for reports is much less straightforward than it is for forms. In this section, you'll add code to a dialog box that helps users select which records to include in a report.

As you might imagine, the most critical reports in a database of mailing addresses are the reports that print mailing labels. The Subscription database includes two reports called *BigMailingLabels* and *SmallMailingLabels*. These reports were created using the Label Wizard, which helps you lay out and print names and addresses on standard mailing label paper. However, users of the Subscription database don't want to print a label for every subscriber every time. By providing a custom dialog box, you'll help them select the subset of labels they want.

Hiding a Dialog Box and Referring to Its Controls

When you click the ShowRecord button on the *GoToRecordDialog* form, it's the code behind the button that performs an action using the information you enter. After it changes records in the *Subscribers* form, the same event procedure then closes the dialog box.

However, there's another possible strategy that you could use for this dialog box, one that might prove easier to implement for some dialog boxes. Rather than close a dialog box when the user finishes with it, your code can instead simply hide the dialog box, making it look like it's closed. To do this, you set the dialog box's Visible property to *False*. The advantage to this strategy is that you can still refer to values on the dialog box from code you've written in other forms. In this case, for example, you could hide the *GoToRecordDialog* form—set its Visible property to *False*—and then add code to the *Subscribers* form

167

that would move to the specified record. From that code, you could refer to the list box value in the dialog box, even though it would no longer be in view.

The strategy you did use—performing actions from code in the dialog box form itself—usually results in code that's easier to follow. On the other hand, in cases where you want to continue referring to values the user entered long after the dialog box is "gone," it might make more sense to simply hide the dialog box form. However, if you do hide a dialog box and leave it open, you'll usually want to close that form later in your application. What's more, you'll need to watch out for code that assumes the dialog box form is open behind the scenes, unless you make sure that it stays open.

Try the SmallMailingLabels Report

Before working on the dialog box, let's preview one of the mailing label reports by itself.

1 In the Database window, click the Reports shortcut.

2 Double-click the SmallMailingLabels report.

Access displays the report in Print Preview, showing all 20 subscribers' names and addresses. This could be useful if you want to send a mailing to everyone who's ever subscribed—not too many people at this point. But as the database grows and the mailing labels span many pages, users will need a way to print only the labels appropriate for a particular mailing.

3 Close the report window.

Open the *MailingLabelsDialog* Form in Design View

The Subscription database contains a dialog box for filtering records in the report. This form was created for you using many of the same steps you followed to create the *GoToRecordDialog* form. Now you'll add the Visual Basic code to make it work.

1 In the Database window, click the Forms shortcut.

2 Click the *MailingLabelsDialog* form, and then click the Design button.

The first thing you may notice on this form are the two tabs at the top: Mailing Type and Label Type. These are part of a special type of control you may not have tried yet, called a *Tab control*. You can put a Tab control on any form where you want to keep options or fields separate—it's like having several pages on the form, except that users simply click the tabs at the top to move from page to page.

The form uses a Tab control to keep the printing options organized.

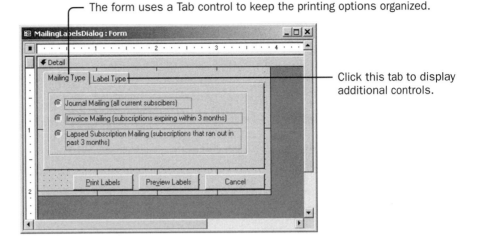

Click this tab to display additional controls.

On the Mailing Type tab, you can see an option group that allows the user to select which group of subscribers to include in a mailing. There are three options: the first includes all subscribers who are paid to the current date, the second includes all subscribers who need to make a payment in the next three months in order to stay current, and the third includes subscribers who recently failed to pay and are no longer receiving issues. You'll use this control to filter the records that print in the mailing label reports.

3 Click the Label Type tab.

This tab contains an option group that allows the user to choose small or large mailing labels. You'll use this control to determine which of the two reports to use, BigMailingLabels or SmallMailingLabels.

Finally, the form has three command buttons, which are outside the Tab control so that they always appear at the bottom of the dialog box: one to print mailing labels, one to preview them, and a third that closes the dialog box without doing anything.

Add Code for the PrintLabels Button

The PrintLabels button doesn't yet have a *Click* event procedure to do the job. When a user clicks this button, you want the code to open one of the two mailing labels reports—that much will be easy using the *OpenReport* method of the *DoCmd* object. But you don't want the report to display all the subscriber records, as it did when you opened it from the Database window. Instead, your code needs to interpret the selected option in the option group, and then filter the subscriber records according to the user's selection.

1 With the right mouse button, click the PrintLabels button, and then click Build Event on the shortcut menu.

2 Double-click Code Builder.

Access switches to Visual Basic and displays the *PrintLabels_Click* event procedure.

3 Add the following code to the procedure:

```
Private Sub PrintLabels_Click()
' Open a mailing labels report with a filter, then close the dialog.
```

(continued)

continued

```
    Dim strFilter As String, strReportName As String

    ' Determine which set of subscribers user wants.
    Select Case MailingType
    Case 1      ' Journal mailing -- all current subscribers.
        strFilter =" "PaidThrough >= Date()"
    Case 2      ' Subscriptions expiring within 3 months.
        strFilter =" "PaidThrough >= Date() And PaidThrough < Date() + 90"
    Case 3      ' Subscriptions that expired in past 3 months.
        strFilter =" "PaidThrough < Date() And PaidThrough > Date() - 90"
    End Select

    ' Determine which mailing labels user wants.
    If LabelType = 1 Then
        strReportName =" "SmallMailingLabels"
    Else
        strReportName =" "BigMailingLabels"
    End If

    DoCmd.OpenReport strReportName, acViewNormal, , strFilter
    DoCmd.Close acForm," "MailingLabelsDialog"

End Sub
```

This code covers mostly familiar territory, but it uses a few new techniques. Here's how it works.

- At the end of this procedure, you specify both the name of the report you want Access to open and filter criteria—a description of the records you want to see in the report. The *Dim* statement at the beginning of the procedure defines two string variables, *strReportName* and *strFilter*, for storing the name and criteria.

- Each criteria string you specify in this procedure refers to a field in the *Subscribers* table called *PaidThrough*. This field stores a date in the last month in which a subscriber should receive an issue (assuming that the subscriber doesn't make another payment). Each time a subscriber makes a payment, the field is updated to reflect the new month.

- Each criteria string also uses the *Date* function, a Visual Basic function that returns the current date stored by the computer system. By comparing the value of this function with the values in the *PaidThrough* field, you can determine whether any given subscriber is" "paid up."

- The *Select Case* statement begins a *Select Case–End Select* block, which allows you to specify three different statements to run, depending on which option the user selected in the option group. The statement uses the expression *MailingType* because that's the name of the option group control on the form.

- The first *Case* block, *Case 1*, runs if the user selected the first option in the group (*MailingType* is 1). For this option, you want to include all subscribers who have paid through the current date—in other words, subscribers whose *PaidThrough* date is the same as or later than the current date. The criteria string is:

```
"PaidThrough >= Date()"
```

- In the second *Case* block, you want to include all subscribers who need to make a payment within three months if they want their subscriptions to continue. To specify this condition, you make two comparisons, combining them with the *And* operator—this way, Access makes sure both comparisons are true for records it includes in the report. This criteria string includes subscribers whose *PaidThrough* date is the same as or later than the current date *and* whose *PaidThrough* date is less than 90 days from the current date.

```
"PaidThrough >= Date() And PaidThrough < Date() + 90"
```

  As this expression demonstrates, adding or subtracting an integer value to a date expression changes the date value by that many days.

- In the third *Case* block, you want to include all subscribers who've let their subscriptions expire—but only those who have done so in the past three months. The criteria string includes subscribers whose *PaidThrough* date is earlier than the current date (they're no longer paid up) *and* whose *PaidThrough* date is within the past 90 days.

```
"PaidThrough < Date() And PaidThrough > Date() - 90"
```

- The *If...Then* block checks the option the user chose in the *LabelType* option group—the one on the second tab of the dialog box—which determines the report to be printed. If the user chose the Small Labels option (number 1 in the option group), the next statement sets the *strReportName* variable to *SmallMailingLabels*. Otherwise, the user must have chosen the Big Labels option, so the statement following the *Else* keyword sets the variable to *BigMailingLabels*.

- After your code sets the *strFilter* variable to the appropriate criteria and the *strReportName* variable to the appropriate report, it's time to use this information to open the report. The line after the *End Select* statement uses the *OpenReport* method of the *DoCmd* object, specifying the *strReportName* variable for the report name argument.

  The second argument to the *OpenReport* method lets you specify whether to open and print the report (specified using the *acViewNormal* constant) or preview the report (specified using the *acViewPreview* constant). The fourth argument—you skip the third argument by including two commas in a row—is the *WhereCondition* argument, with which you specify the criteria string Access will use to filter records in the report. This is where you put your variable, *strFilter*, which contains the filter string you set in the *Select Case* block.

- The last statement in the procedure uses the *Close* method of the *DoCmd* object to close the dialog box form.

  When you click the PrintLabels button, your code will select a filter string, open the report to print the set of labels the user wants, and close the dialog box.

Copy the Code for the PreviewLabels Button

Print Preview is a powerful Access feature that you can easily take advantage of in your applications—and Windows users have come to expect it. Whenever you provide the option to print a report, it's also a good idea to allow previewing. Fortunately, the code you'll use for the PreviewLabels button is nearly identical to the code for printing a report. In fact, you'll just copy the code to the other button's event procedure, and then make a small modification to allow previewing.

1 Select all the code between the *Sub* and *End Sub* lines in the *PrintLabels* event procedure. (Click at the beginning of the second line and drag to just before the last line.)

2 Press the Ctrl+C key combination.

3 In the Code window's Object box (on the left), select PreviewLabels.

   Visual Basic displays the *PreviewLabels_Click* event procedure.

4 Press the Ctrl+V key combination.

5 Edit the line that contains the *OpenReport* method (toward the end of the procedure) to use the *acViewPreview* constant instead of the *acViewNormal* constant, as follows.

```
DoCmd.OpenReport strReportName, acViewPreview, , strFilter
```

   Using this constant for the *View* argument of the *OpenReport* method tells Access to display the form in Print Preview rather than printing it directly.

View Microsoft Access

6 Switch to Access.

7 Close the *MailingLabelsDialog* form, clicking Yes when Access asks if you want to save changes.

Try the Dialog Box

Now that the dialog box is finished, you can use it to open the report.

1 In the Database window, double-click the *MailingLabelsDialog* form.

   The dialog box appears, allowing you to select an option for your mailing labels.

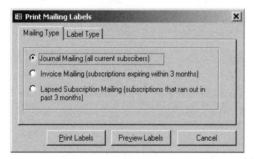

2 Click the second option, Invoice Mailing.

3 Click the Label Type tab.

4 Click the second option, Big Labels.

5 Click Preview Labels.

   Your event procedure runs, opening the *BigMailingLabels* report in Print Preview. Because your code opens the report using the filter string *PaidThrough >= Date() And PaidThrough < Date() + 90* it includes just a few of the subscribers—those whose subscriptions haven't yet expired as of today's date, but that will expire within three months. (Note that depending on the current date setting on your computer, you might see different subscribers in the report or even no subscribers at all. To include subscribers, change their *Paid-Through* date in the table to within three months of the current date.)

Labels for subscriptions that run out
within three months of May 1, 2001

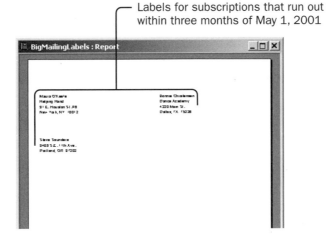

6 Close the report.

If you want to try out the other filters on the report, repeat this procedure, selecting the first and third options in the dialog box.

Other Ways to Change the Records in a Form or Report

The code you wrote uses a straightforward way of filtering the records in a report: specifying an *OpenReport WhereCondition* argument when opening the report. However, there are other ways you can change the records that appear in a report.

Base the report on a query. If you always want to display the same subset of records in a report, or if you want the records to appear in a specific order, create a query that displays records as you want them, and then set the report's RecordSource property to the query. This way, you don't have to write any code to filter records.

Set the report's Filter and FilterOn properties. If you want to change records that are displayed in a report that's already open in Print Preview, you can use Visual Basic code to set the report's Filter property to a criteria string. Then set its FilterOn property to *True* to apply the filter.

Set the report's OrderBy and OrderByOn properties. If you want to change the sort order of a report that's already open in Print Preview, you can set the report's OrderBy property to the name of the field you want to sort, and then set its OrderByOn property to *True* to apply the sort.

All these techniques work for forms as well as reports—in fact, in the next chapter you'll learn how to use the Filter property in forms.

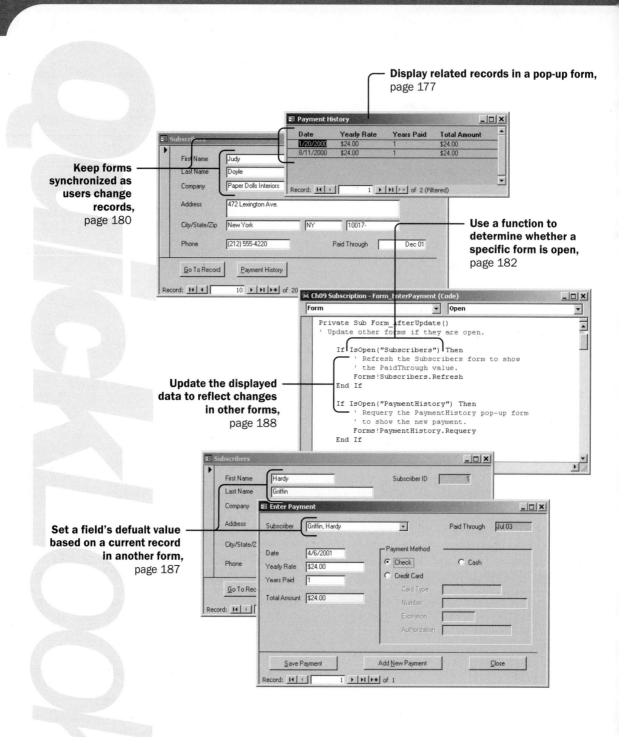

Display related records in a pop-up form,
page 177

Keep forms synchronized as users change records,
page 180

Use a function to determine whether a specific form is open,
page 182

Update the displayed data to reflect changes in other forms,
page 188

Set a field's defualt value based on a current record in another form,
page 187

```
Private Sub Form_AfterUpdate()
' Update other forms if they are open.

    If IsOpen("Subscribers") Then
        ' Refresh the Subscribers form to show
        ' the PaidThrough value.
        Forms!Subscribers.Refresh
    End If

    If IsOpen("PaymentHistory") Then
        ' Requery the PaymentHistory pop-up form
        ' to show the new payment.
        Forms!PaymentHistory.Requery
    End If
```

Chapter 9
Navigate Through Your Application

After completing this chapter, you will be able to:

✔ Display records in a pop-up form.

✔ Synchronize the records in one form with records the user selects in another form.

✔ Requery a form to display current data.

In a relay race, the performance of each individual team member is important, but the transitions are critical. When a runner hands off the baton to a teammate, that's the moment when seconds are gained or lost. Relay teams train extensively to make handoffs as efficient as possible and arrange each of the runners in the position that is most beneficial to the team.

As when planning for a relay race, you'll need to consider the ways the objects in your reports "hand off" from one to another. No matter how well your forms and reports work on their own, it's the way they work together that makes your database applications powerful and easy to use. To make the transitions seamless, you can use Microsoft Visual Basic code to customize the way a new object opens and how it works with other objects. Of course, the structure of an application is much more flexible than the structure of a relay race, so there are even more variables to consider—because of the flexibility of event-driven applications, users can take any number of paths through your application, and you'll need to anticipate all of them.

In this chapter, you'll learn techniques for handing off control from one form or report to another—passing the baton, so to speak. You'll write event procedures that check which other forms are currently open, copy values and set properties from one form or report to another, and update objects at appropriate times. By anticipating how users will run the course, you'll see how to make your application work smoothly.

Ch09 Subscription.mdb

This chapter uses the practice file Ch09 Subscription.mdb that you installed from the book's CD-ROM. For details about installing the practice files, see "Using the Book's CD-ROM" at the beginning of this book.

Getting Started

● Start Microsoft Access, and open the Ch09 Subscription database in the practice files folder.

Making Forms Work Together

In an ideal world, everything computer users need to do their work would be in one place. In a database application, for example, it would be nice if all the data you needed were on a single form. In all but the simplest applications, however, you'll need several objects to handle the different types of information required and the tasks the user needs to complete. For example, you'll have forms for entering information, forms for summarizing information, and still other forms that help users accomplish a specific task. How you organize these objects depends on what information and tasks are most important to users. In planning your application, you'll want to prioritize these items and decide how to best serve everyone's needs.

Most relational database applications store information in separate but related tables. For example, in the Subscription database, the *Subscribers* and *Payments* tables contain related information. In presenting this information on the screen, you can take several different approaches—some approaches work on their own, while others require Visual Basic code to make them work. Here are some of the ways you can organize data in an application, and factors you'll need to consider when using them.

Place subforms on forms to display related records. The subform control provides a powerful way to display related records in a single form without writing any code. For example, you could use a subform to display a list of subscriber payments—on the same form that displays subscriber information. You can set up this type of subform using the Subform Wizard, or create a form and a subform using the Form Wizard. However, in many cases there won't be enough room on the screen to display all the information you need on the main form as well as all the related information contained in a subform. Additionally, subforms can be less intuitive for entering data, especially when space is limited. Still, because Access handles the relationships between forms and subforms automatically, you may want to use this approach when you want all related information to appear in one place.

Build forms and reports based on multiple-table queries. By designing queries that combine information from two or more tables, you can easily present data from several tables on a single form or report. Whenever possible, Access allows users to update all the information in a query, automatically making changes in the underlying tables—but beware: some fields in multiple-table queries aren't updateable, so users can sometimes encounter unintelligible error messages when trying to make changes. And as with subforms, you won't always have room on a single form for all the fields you need to display. For forms and reports in which you summarize information, however, queries are indispensable tools for combining data from multiple tables.

Create a separate form for each table. By making separate forms for data in related tables, you present a very straightforward model to users: "Here is where you view and enter information about this; for other types of information, click these buttons." This approach requires users to switch from one form to another more frequently—between a main form and a pop-up form, for example—but it gives you the most screen space and flexibility for each form. When you do have several forms, however, users will expect them to work together intelligently. For example, if you've chosen a value in one form, you shouldn't have to choose it again in another form. As you'll see, it's important to link objects together using Visual Basic event procedures.

Separate data entry and data display. In some cases, you'll want to provide more than one form for the same information, each of which is used for a different task. Forms that allow you to enter new data often need different controls and features than those for finding or summarizing data. But as you increase the number of forms that make up your user interface, your application becomes much more complex. In some cases, you'll want to limit what users can do in a given form, making some forms or controls read-only and carefully controlling the paths users can take through your application.

In this chapter, we'll focus on the last two techniques, connecting separate forms in the Subscription database to display and enter related information. In the process, you'll learn to write Visual Basic code that links objects together in custom ways. In your own applications, you'll most likely draw from all these approaches—using subforms and queries to combine some of your application's data, while linking together a series of forms when it makes sense to keep information separated into different chunks.

Displaying Related Records in a Pop-Up Form

In any database that contains more than one table, you'll commonly have records in one table that are related to records in another. For example, in the Subscription database, each subscriber has one or more related payment records documenting the payments that the subscriber has made. When users are viewing records in a main form, such as the *Subscribers* form, they'll commonly want to see related records on the screen. One way to show related records is in a *pop-up* form, a special type of form that always remains on top of other windows. In this section, you'll add a pop-up form that displays the payment history for the current subscriber (the subscriber currently selected in the *Subscribers* form).

Open the *PaymentHistory* Form

The practice database already includes the *PaymentHistory* form, which displays payment records. By default, the form shows payments for all subscribers together in one list.

1 In the Database window, click the Forms shortcut.

2 Double-click the *PaymentHistory* form.

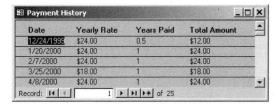

This simple form has the *Payments* table as its record source and has four fields. The TotalAmount field is not actually in the *Payments* table—it's a calculated field, which means that its ControlSource property is set to an expression. The expression multiplies the YearlyRate value by the YearsPaid value to show the total.

Display the *PaymentHistory* Form as a Pop-Up Form

When users view the *PaymentHistory* form, they'll want it to remain on top of other windows so that they can see it while they work in the *Subscribers* form. To make it work this way, you'll set its PopUp property to *Yes*. You'll also set properties to make the form read-only so that users can view payments in the form but not change them.

Design View

1 Click the Design View button on the toolbar.

2 If the property sheet isn't displayed, click the Properties button on the toolbar.

Properties

3 Click the Other tab in the property sheet.

4 Set the PopUp property to *Yes*.

5 Click the Data tab in the property sheet.

6 Set the AllowEdits, AllowDeletions, and AllowAdditions properties to *No*.

7 Close the *PaymentHistory* form, clicking Yes when Access asks if you want to save changes.

Add a Button to the *Subscribers* Form to Open the *PaymentHistory* Form

The *PaymentHistory* form is designed to work hand in hand with the *Subscribers* form. To make the pop-up form accessible, you'll add a button that opens it, displaying the payment records for the current subscriber. You can use the Command Button Wizard to create the button and its event procedure.

1 In the Database window, select the *Subscribers* form, and then click the Design button.

The form opens in Design view. (If the property sheet is in the way, drag it to the lower right corner of the screen.)

Control Wizards

2 Scroll down in the form to display the Form Footer section.

3 In the toolbox, make sure the Control Wizards tool is selected, and then click the Command Button tool.

Command Button

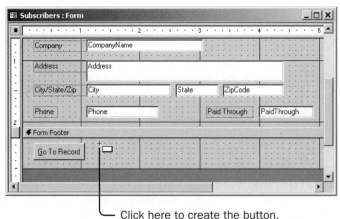

4 Click the form footer just to the right of the Go To Record button.

Click here to create the button.

The Command Button Wizard starts, asking what action you want the button to perform.

5 Click Form Operations in the Categories list, click Open Form in the Actions list, and then click Next.

The wizard asks which form you want to open.

6 Click PaymentHistory, and then click Next.

The wizard asks whether you want to display specific information in the form. This gives you the chance to filter records in the pop-up form to include only the payments for the current subscriber.

7 Click Open The Form And Find Specific Data To Display, and then click Next.

The wizard asks which field in the *Subscribers* form contains matching data in the *PaymentHistory* form. Because the *Subscribers* and *Payments* tables are related based on the SubscriberID values in each record, you'll specify this field.

8 Click SubscriberID in both list boxes, click the button between the lists to create a link between them, and then click Next.

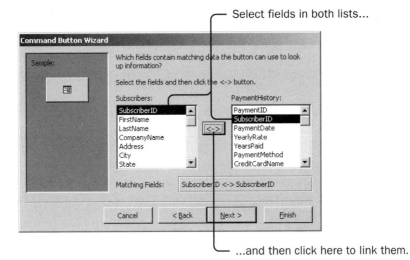

Select fields in both lists...

...and then click here to link them.

The wizard asks whether you want a picture or text on your button.

9 Click the Open Form text in the Text box, type **&Payment History** to replace the text, and then click Next.

The wizard asks what you want to name the button.

10 Type **PaymentHistory**, and then click Finish.

The wizard creates the button.

Try the New Button

Now you can use your new button to open the pop-up form.

Form View

1 Click the Form View button on the toolbar.

2 Click the Payment History button.

The button's *Click* event procedure runs, opening the *Payment History* pop-up form.

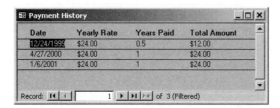

The form shows only three records: the past payments made by Hardy Griffin, whose subscriber record is displayed in the *Subscribers* form.

Change Records in the *Subscribers* Form

When the *PaymentHistory* pop-up form is open, you can still work in the *Subscribers* form—the pop-up form isn't modal like a dialog box. Let's see what happens when you change subscriber records.

1 Click anywhere on the *Subscribers* form. (If necessary, you can first drag the *PaymentHistory* form out of the way so that you can see the name of the current subscriber.)

2 Press the Page Down key several times to change records.

The same three records are displayed in the *PaymentHistory* form, regardless of which subscriber record you're viewing. When the user changes records in the *Subscribers* form, you'd like the *PaymentHistory* form to display payment records for the currently selected subscriber—in other words, you'd like the pop-up form to stay *synchronized* with the main form.

3 Close the *PaymentHistory* pop-up form.

Add Code to Keep the Pop-Up Form Synchronized

To make the pop-up form stay synchronized, you need to update the records it displays each time the user changes records in the main form. To do this, you'll add an event procedure to the *Subscribers* form that makes sure the pop-up form displays related payment records as you move from one subscriber to another.

Design View

1 Click the Design View button on the toolbar.

2 On the Edit menu, click Select Form.

3 In the property sheet, click the Event tab.

4   Click the OnCurrent property, and then click the Build button.

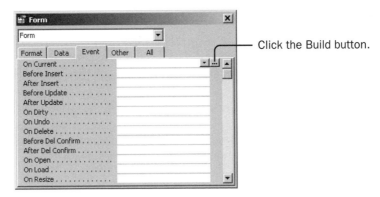

— Click the Build button.

5   Double-click Code Builder.

Access opens Visual Basic and displays the form's *Current* event procedure. The code you add to this procedure will run any time the user changes from one record to another in the *Subscribers* form.

6   Enter the following code for the procedure:

```
Private Sub Form_Current()
' Synchronize the PaymentHistory form if it's open.

    If IsOpen("PaymentHistory") Then
        Forms!PaymentHistory.Filter = "SubscriberID = " & _
            Nz(SubscriberID, 0)
    End If


    End Sub
```

The *If...Then* statement in this code uses a user-defined function called *IsOpen* to check whether the *PaymentHistory* form is open. This is an important step, because unless the user has opened the pop-up form, attempting to change the records it displays would cause an error. The *IsOpen* function returns *True* if the form is open, causing the line of code in the *If...Then* block to run. The *IsOpen* function is included in the practice database in the *Miscellaneous* module; for more information, see the next section, "Looking into the *IsOpen* Function."

If the *PaymentHistory* form is open, the next line synchronizes the form. To do this, it sets the pop-up form's Filter property, referring to the property by using the expression *Forms!PaymentHistory.Filter*. For the property setting, the code combines the text *SubscriberID =* with the actual SubscriberID value currently on the *Subscribers* form. For example, if the current subscriber's ID is 4, it sets the Filter property to *SubscriberID = 4* and the pop-up form displays only the payment records for that subscriber.

The line also uses the *Nz* function ("Nz" stands for Null-zero), which converts the SubscriberID value to *0* in the unlikely event that it is *Null* (has no value). This is necessary because if the value is *Null*—which occurs if the user moves to the new (blank) record in the *Subscribers* form—the Filter would get set to *SubscriberID =* with nothing to the right of the equal sign and an error would occur. This way, if the SubscriberID value is *Null*, the Filter gets set to *SubscriberID* = *0* and the pop-up form displays no records (because no subscriber is number 0).

Looking into the *IsOpen* Function

The Subscription database includes a standard module named *Miscellaneous*, which contains three general procedures provided as part of the practice application. The first two are the procedures you wrote in Chapter 5 to display message boxes. The third is the *IsOpen* function, which you just used in the *Subscribers* form's *Current* event procedure to check whether the *PaymentHistory* form is open. Because it's so useful, you may want to include the *IsOpen* function in other applications you create.

Here's the code, which you can also view by opening the *Miscellaneous* module in the Subscription database:

```
Public Function IsOpen(ByVal strFormName As String) As Boolean
' Returns True if the specified form is open in Form view.

    Const conDesignView = 0
    Const conObjStateClosed = 0

    IsOpen = False
    If SysCmd(acSysCmdGetObjectState, acForm, strFormName) <> _
            conObjStateClosed Then

        If Forms(strFormName).CurrentView <> conDesignView Then
            IsOpen = True
        End If
    End If
End Function
```

As its function declaration states, the *IsOpen* function accepts as an argument the name of a form and returns a *Boolean* value: either *True* or *False*, depending on whether the specified form is open or not. Early in the function, a line of code sets the return value to *False*—assuming the form is *not* open—and then the function goes on to check whether to change this value to *True*.

The procedure uses *If...Then* statements to check two conditions.

Is the form in Access's list of open objects? Access keeps an internal list of all the objects that are open. The *SysCmd* (read as "Sis-command") function is a built-in function that lets you ask for information about the system and its status. By calling this function, you can find out whether a form is open.

You pass three arguments to the *SysCmd* function: a constant that specifies the type of information you want, in this case the state of an object; the type of object you're interested in, in this case a form; and a string containing the name of the object, in this case the string variable that was passed to the *IsOpen* function. The *SysCmd* function returns a number that indicates the status of the form, and this code compares the return value with a constant value indicating that the object is closed. If the return value doesn't equal the value for a closed object, the code continues; otherwise, the *IsOpen* function returns *False*.

Is the form in Design view? If the form is in Design view, you want the *IsOpen* function to return *False*, because most code that refers to a form in Design view would cause errors. Forms have a property called CurrentView, which stores a number representing the current view of the form. This code compares the current view to the constant value that indicates Design view and then sets the function's return value to *True* if the property doesn't equal that value.

The expression that refers to the CurrentView property uses a technique you haven't seen yet. So far, you've used the exclamation point operator to refer to a form in the database, as in *Forms!Subscribers*. An alternative method for referring to a form—and the method you must use when the form name is contained in a variable—is to use *Forms("Subscribers")*. To refer to the form that was passed to the function, this code uses the expression *Forms(strFormName)*.

Because the *IsOpen* function is provided for you in the practice database, you don't need to concern yourself too much with how it works—you can simply call it whenever you want to check whether a form is open. As you've seen, the expression *IsOpen("NameOfForm")* gives you the information you need. To take advantage of the techniques you learn in this chapter, simply copy or import this function into any application that needs to refer to one form from another.

Add Code to Close the Pop-Up Form

The *PaymentHistory* pop-up form only works as an auxiliary tool for the *Subscribers* form. If the user closes the *Subscribers* form while the pop-up form is still open, the application may as well close the pop-up form also. To accomplish this, you can add code to the *Subscribers* form's *Close* event procedure.

1 In the Procedure box at the top of the Code window (on the right), select the *Close* event.

   The Module window shows the blank *Form_Close* event procedure.

2 Enter the following code for the procedure:

```
Private Sub Form_Close()
' Close the PaymentHistory pop-up form if it's open.

    If IsOpen("PaymentHistory") Then
        DoCmd.Close acForm, "PaymentHistory"
    End If

End Sub
```

Like the code you wrote to synchronize the two forms, this procedure uses the *IsOpen* function to check whether the *PaymentHistory* form is open. If it is, the *Close* method of the *DoCmd* object closes the form.

View Microsoft
Access

3 Switch to Access.

4 Click the Save button on the toolbar.

Test the Synchronized Form

The pop-up form should now work properly, even if you change records. When you close the *Subscribers* form, the pop-up form should close as well.

Form View

1 Click the Form View button on the toolbar.

2 Click the Payment History button in the form footer.

The *Payment History* pop-up form appears, again showing the three payments for the current subscriber.

3 Click anywhere on the *Subscribers* form, and then press the Page Down key several times to change subscriber records.

Each time you change records, your event procedure runs, setting the pop-up form's Filter property and causing it to display a different set of payments—those related by the SubscriberID value to the current subscriber. As you can see, most subscribers have made only one or two payments.

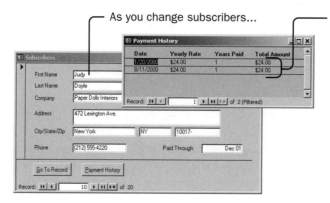

As you change subscribers...

...your code filters the pop-up form to show payments for the current subscriber.

4 Close the *Subscribers* form.

Your *Close* event procedure runs, closing the pop-up form automatically.

Opening a Form to Add Related Records

A pop-up form is useful for showing a small amount of information that you want to keep on top of other forms. However, most forms you present to users won't be pop-up forms, because you'll want users to be able to switch from one form to another, bringing the current form to the front. Any time you provide the user with ways to switch between forms, you'll want to consider how the forms work together. As was the case with the *PaymentHistory* pop-up form, you'll often need to create event procedures to get the results you want.

In this section, you'll work with a form designed for entering new payments into the Subscription database. The form is called *EnterPayment* and is already in the practice database, ready for you to use. Anticipating that users will jump to this form from the *PaymentHistory* form, you'll add code that makes the two forms work together well.

Add a Button to Open the *EnterPayment* Form

Because users will often want to enter a payment for a subscriber while viewing data in the *Subscribers* form, your first step is to add another button to the *Subscribers* form. As before, you'll use the Command Button Wizard.

1 In the Database window, click the *Subscribers* form, and then click the Design button.

The form opens in Design view.

2 Scroll down in the form to display the Form Footer section.

Command Button

3 In the toolbox, click the Command Button tool.

4 Click the form footer just to the right of the Payment History button.

The Command Button Wizard starts, asking what action you want the button to perform.

5 Click Form Operations in the Categories list, click Open Form in the Actions list, and then click Next.

The wizard asks which form you want to open. Because the *EnterPayment* form is already selected, you don't have to select it.

6 Click Next.

The wizard asks whether you want to display specific information in the form. This time, you'll go with the default option, Open The Form And Show All The Records.

7 Click Next again.

The wizard asks whether you want a picture or text on your button.

8 Click the Open Form text in the Text box, type **&Enter Payment** to replace the text, and then click Next.

The wizard asks what you want to name the button.

9 Type **EnterPayment**, and then click Finish.

The wizard creates the button.

Form View

10 Click the Form View button on the toolbar.

11 Click the Enter Payment button.

The button's Click event procedure runs, opening the *EnterPayment* form.

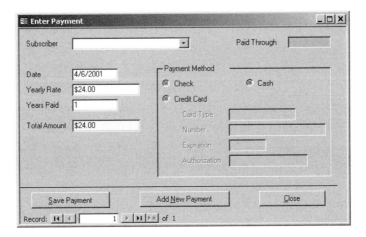

The *EnterPayment* form is designed for entering new payments into the *Payments* table. For example, the form's DataEntry property is set to *Yes*, so it opens without any existing payment records displayed, ready for a new payment. It also has the AllowEdits and AllowDeletions properties set to *No* so that only new payments can be edited in the form.

Note that the Subscriber field on the form is blank, even though you came from the *Subscribers* form where you're viewing a specific subscriber. It would be nice if the subscriber record were automatically set when opening this form so that the user wouldn't have to select one. In the next procedure, you'll add code to make this happen.

Features of the *EnterPayment* Form

The *EnterPayment* form has several features already implemented in the practice file. Although they aren't directly related to the subject you're learning about in this chapter, you may want to take a look at the Visual Basic code for these features to see how the form works. Here's what you'll find behind the form.

- Three command buttons created using the Command Button Wizard: Save Payment, Add New Payment, and Close.

- Code that enables the credit card text boxes in the Payment Method option group when a user selects the Credit Card option. To view this code, open the *AfterUpdate* event procedure for the *PaymentMethod* option group.

- Code that runs when the user tries to save a record, in response to the form's *BeforeUpdate* event. The first half of this procedure checks to make sure the user chose a value for the Payment Method, and cancels the update if its value is *0*. If the record is valid, the second half of the procedure updates the Paid Through field to add the number of months the subscriber paid for. The Paid Through field is actually stored in the *Payments* table, but is included in the underlying query of this form to make it easier to update. Here's the code:

```
Private Sub Form_BeforeUpdate(Cancel As Integer)
' Check to make sure a payment method is selected.
' Then update the PaidThrough field (Subscribers table)
' to reflect additional time due to this payment.

    Dim bytMonths As Byte

    If PaymentMethod = 0 Then
        DisplayMessage "You must select a payment method."
        Cancel = True
        Exit Sub
    End If

    bytMonths = YearsPaid * 12
```

```
    If IsNull(PaidThrough) Or PaidThrough < Date Then
        ' If this is the first payment, set PaidThrough
        ' from current date.
        PaidThrough = DateSerial(Year(Date), Month(Date) + _
            bytMonths, 1)
    Else
        ' Otherwise, add additional months to PaidThrough value.
        PaidThrough = DateSerial(Year(PaidThrough), _
            Month(PaidThrough) + bytMonths, 1)
    End If
End Sub
```

The second part of this procedure uses an *If...Then* statement to check whether the Paid Through field is already set. If it isn't, or if the subscription has expired, it adds additional months to the PaidThrough value beginning at today's date. If the Paid Through field is set and the subscription is current, it adds the additional months to the current Paid Through value.

Both these statements use Visual Basic date functions to calculate the new PaidThrough date value. Date values are stored as numbers by Access, so you can't work with them directly, except to add or subtract days from them. But using date functions as shown in this procedure makes it possible to add months to the date value rather than days, and also makes it easy to set the PaidThrough value to the first day of the month. The *Year* and *Month* functions, as their names suggest, return the year and month for a given date value; the *DateSerial* function lets you build a date value from individual date parts. So the second line that includes these functions in effect says, "Create a date where the year is the same as the PaidThrough date, the month is so many months later than the Paid-Through month, and the day is the first of the month—and set the new *PaidThrough* value to that date."

Add Code to Set the Subscriber ID

When users click the Enter Payment command button on the *Subscribers* form, they most likely want to add a payment record for the subscriber they were looking at. In order to help users enter data more easily, you can set the default value for the *SubscriberID* control on the data entry form.

Design View

1 Click the Design View button on the toolbar.

2 Click the OnOpen property in the property sheet, and then click the Build button.

3 Double-click Code Builder.

Access switches to Visual Basic and displays the *Form_Open* event procedure for the *EnterPayment* form. Whenever a user opens the form, the code in this procedure will run—which makes it a great place to initialize controls on the form such as the *SubscriberID* combo box.

4 Add the following code to the event procedure:

```
Private Sub Form_Open(Cancel As Integer)
    ' Set the default to the current subscriber
    ' on the Subscribers form.
```

(continued)

continued

```
If IsOpen("Subscribers") Then
    SubscriberID.DefaultValue = Forms!Subscribers!SubscriberID
End If

End Sub
```

This code first checks whether the *Subscribers* form is open using the *IsOpen* function, which you used before. Users might open the *EnterPayment* form by itself, in which case trying to match it up with the *Subscribers* form would cause an error.

If the *Subscribers* form is open, the line of code in the middle sets the DefaultValue property of the SubscriberID combo box to the value of the SubscriberID field on the *Subscribers* form. As you've seen before, you can refer to a field on another open form using the Forms keyword. This line of code says, "Set the default value for the Subscriber field (on this form) to the current value of the Subscriber ID field on the form called *Subscribers*."

Form View

5 Switch to Access.

6 Click the Form View button on the toolbar.

Your event procedure runs, using the current subscriber on the *Subscribers* form as the default value for the field. Note that although the combo box displays the name of the subscriber, your code actually set it to the appropriate *SubscriberID* value, because this is the field the combo box is bound to.

The current subscriber...

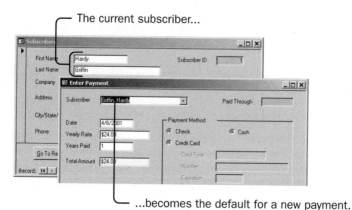

...becomes the default for a new payment.

Add Code to Update Other Open Forms After the User Enters a Payment

When a user enters a payment, the status of that subscriber changes—the Paid Through field gets changed to reflect the new payment, for example. If you open another form to display data after the change is made, that form will reflect the changes, but forms that are already open don't automatically show the new data. If forms that show changed data are open, you should update them. You can do this by adding code to the *AfterUpdate* event procedure for the form, which runs whenever a change gets saved in the form.

Design View

1 Click the Design View button on the toolbar.

2 Click the AfterUpdate property in the property sheet, and then click the Build button.

3 Double-click Code Builder.

Access switches to Visual Basic and displays the *Form_AfterUpdate* event procedure for the *EnterPayment* form. Whenever a user saves a new payment, this event procedure will run.

4 Add the following code to the event procedure:

```
Private Sub Form_AfterUpdate()
' Update other forms if they are open.

    If IsOpen("Subscribers") Then
        ' Refresh the Subscribers form to show
        ' the PaidThrough value.
        Forms!Subscribers.Refresh
    End If

    If IsOpen("PaymentHistory") Then
        ' Requery the PaymentHistory pop-up form
        ' to show the new payment.
        Forms!PaymentHistory.Requery
    End If

End Sub
```

The first *If...Then* statement in this procedure checks whether the *Subscribers* form is open. If it is, the code uses the *Refresh* method for the form, which tells Access to update the data displayed on the form with the current values from the underlying table. Note that using the *Refresh* method doesn't cause the query to run again, so new records aren't added, deleted records aren't removed, and the sort order remains the same. You don't need to make these types of changes now because adding a payment doesn't affect the number of subscribers in the database.

The second part of the procedure checks whether the *PaymentHistory* pop-up form is displayed. If it is, the code uses the *Requery* method of the form, which tells Access to requery records in the form as if you'd closed and reopened it. Unlike refreshing, requerying a form does add new records, which is necessary in this case so that the pop-up form will show the new payment record. Note, however, that this has the sometimes undesirable side effect of resetting the current record—when you requery a form, the first record in the recordset becomes the current one. In an informational pop-up form like this one, you don't mind, because it doesn't matter which record is current.

View Microsoft Access

5 Switch to Access.

6 Close the *EnterPayment* form, clicking Yes when Access asks if you want to save changes.

Try the New Features

If the *Subscribers* form and the *PaymentHistory* form are open, adding a new payment should now be reflected in these two forms. Let's see if it works.

1 On the *Subscribers* form, click the Payment History button.

Code behind the button opens the *Payment History* pop-up form, showing the payments for the current subscriber. Next, you'll enter a new payment for this subscriber.

2 Click the Enter Payment button.

Code behind this button opens the *Enter Payment* form, ready for you to add a payment for the current subscriber. If the *Payment History* form is in the way, you may need to move it out of the way.

3   In the Payment Method option group, select Check.

Changing a field in this form adds a new record to the *Payments* table, and causes it to display the subscriber's current Paid Through date. You could go on to specify values for other fields, but because the other fields all have default values, you don't have to type anything in them (assuming you want the default payment of one year at $24).

4   Click the Save Payment button.

Clicking this button saves the payment record. The date in the Paid Through field is now a year later than before. When the record was saved, your *AfterUpdate* event procedure also updated both the *Subscribers* form and the *Payment History* form. In the pop-up form, you'll notice the new payment is listed—your code requeried that form.

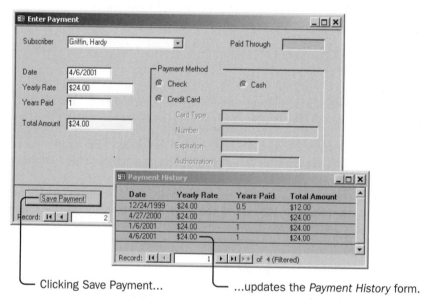

Clicking Save Payment...   ...updates the *Payment History* form.

5   Close the *Payment History* form.

6   In the *Enter Payment* form footer, click the Close button.

The Paid Through field in the *Subscribers* form shows the new date—your code refreshed it.

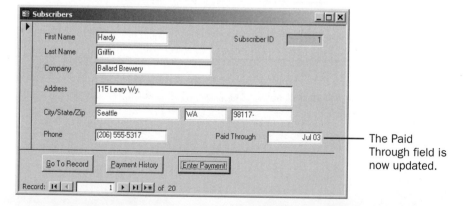

The Paid Through field is now updated.

It's tough to anticipate when you'll need to refresh or requery the data in a form. When you test your application, look out for changes you make that aren't reflected as you expect. If this happens, add a line of code that uses the *Refresh* or *Requery* method.

Tip

You can also use the *Requery* method on a combo box or list box to update the records that are displayed in the list. For example, if you add a new subscriber in the *Subscribers* form, the combo box on the *EnterPayment* form won't include that subscriber (until the next time the form is opened). To take care of this detail, you could requery the list each time a record is saved in the *Subscribers* form.

Chapter Wrap-Up

1   Close the *Subscribers* form, clicking Yes when Access asks if you want to save changes to the form.

2   On the File menu, click Exit.

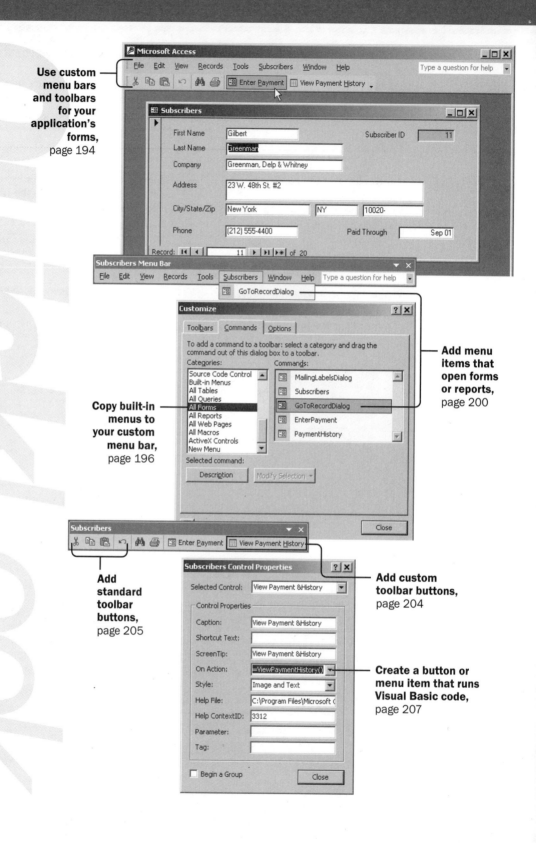

Use custom menu bars and toolbars for your application's forms, page 194

Add menu items that open forms or reports, page 200

Copy built-in menus to your custom menu bar, page 196

Add standard toolbar buttons, page 205

Add custom toolbar buttons, page 204

Create a button or menu item that runs Visual Basic code, page 207

Chapter 10
Display Custom Menus and Toolbars

After completing this chapter, you will be able to:

✔ Create your own menus to run your application's commands.

✔ Create and customize your application's toolbars.

✔ Designate a custom menu bar and toolbar for use with a particular form in your application.

When you work in a well-organized kitchen, cooking can be a joy. The cookware and utensils you need are at hand but not in the way, your ingredients are all within easy reach in the cabinets, and the counter space is clear and ready for action. But if you're like me, you don't always plan ahead for creating your culinary masterpieces—so you end up searching for tools and ingredients, and running out of space. "Next time," you say, "I'll get the kitchen in shape before I start...."

In some ways, using a database application is like working in the kitchen. It's much easier to get your work done if you have all the tools you need within reach—but space on the screen is limited, so you want features to stay hidden away until you're ready to use them. In order to prepare the "data kitchen" for your users, you'll want to organize your application's commands and objects in the cleanest possible way.

In this chapter, you'll learn two important elements of an organized user interface: menus and toolbars. By hiding commands away on menus and using compact toolbar buttons to provide access to forms and reports, you'll keep the Subscription application less cluttered, while at the same time making sure everything users need is easy to find.

Ch10 Subscription.mdb

This chapter uses the practice file Ch10 Subscription.mdb that you installed from the book's CD-ROM. For details about installing the practice files, see "Using the Book's CD-ROM" at the beginning of this book.

Getting Started

● Start Microsoft Access, and open the Ch10 Subscription database in the practice files folder.

Using Menus and Toolbars in Your User Interface

So far, you've used command buttons on forms to make commands available to users—for example, you created three buttons on the *Subscribers* form that allowed users to jump to a specific record, view payment history, and enter payments. Although some common actions are important enough to warrant a command button on a form, most of the commands that users need can be organized on your application's menus and toolbars, where they take less space. Like other Microsoft Windows–based applications, your application can include *both* a menu command and a toolbar button to perform a given action, making it even more accessible. In this chapter, you'll create menus and a toolbar for the *Subscribers* form, replacing the command button strategy you used before.

You can design menus and toolbars to be used with a single form, or to work with several forms. You can even design a global menu or toolbar that's available throughout your application. However, because many commands apply only to certain places in your application, you're likely to need separate menus and toolbars for individual forms. Of course, you can always display the standard Access menu or toolbar for some of the forms and reports in your application if they don't need custom commands.

When creating either menus or toolbars, you also have the option of using existing Access commands. In most cases, you'll want to make most standard commands available to users, especially if they already know how to use Access or other Windows-based applications. On the other hand, if you want to limit the options users have in your application, you can create menus and toolbars that contain only the commands you want to make available. To plan for your menus and toolbars, take a look at the other Windows-based applications you use to see how their interfaces are structured. Then, when you've planned your interface, you'll use the techniques shown in this chapter to put it into place.

Open the *Subscribers* Form

1 In the Database window, click the Forms shortcut.

2 Double-click the *Subscribers* form.

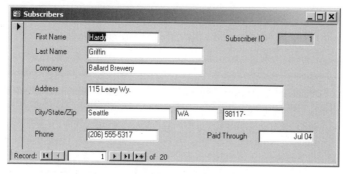

As you can see, the *Subscribers* form in the practice database no longer has command buttons in its footer—you're going to perform their functions with menu commands and toolbar buttons.

Creating a Custom Menu Bar

The menus in Access—File, Edit, View, and so on—are grouped into one object called a *menu bar*. You should think of a menu bar as a type of toolbar (although it looks and behaves differently) because you'll use the same techniques to create and edit both.

Access itself thinks of menu bars and toolbars as the same type of object; in fact, they're both called *command bars* when you refer to them in Microsoft Visual Basic code. Knowing this, you won't be too surprised to hear that the tool you use to create menus is the Customize Toolbars command. Using it, you can add commands and customize the behavior and appearance of both menus and toolbars.

While you can create all the menus for a new menu bar from scratch, you'll often want to place existing Access menus on your menu bar. When a menu's standard set of commands doesn't make sense, you can create a new menu with your own set of commands. On the *Subscribers* form menu bar, for example, you might want to make most of the built-in Access menus available but also include a special menu with custom commands that help users navigate through the application.

To make these menu commands appear with the *Subscribers* form, you'll create a new custom menu bar, copy built-in menus and create your own menus with custom menu commands, and then specify that the *Subscribers* form should use the custom menu bar. Access will take it from there, displaying your additional menu commands whenever the *Subscribers* form is active.

Create a Custom Menu Bar for the *Subscribers* Form

Before you can specify a custom menu bar for a form, you need to create the menu bar and add menus and commands to it. In this section, you'll create a custom menu bar called Subscribers Menu Bar and then add built-in menus to make it look similar to the standard Form View menu bar. Then you'll add your own version of the Tools menu, as well as a new menu designed especially for the *Subscribers* form.

1 On the View menu, point to Toolbars, and then click Customize.

The Customize dialog box appears, displaying the available toolbar options.

2 Click the Toolbars tab.

The dialog box lists all the toolbars and menu bars available to your application. At this point, you could begin making changes to the built-in menu bar or toolbar that's shown; however, your changes would apply for all databases. Since you want your changes to apply to the *Subscribers* form only, you'll begin by creating a new menu bar.

3 Click the New button.

Access asks what you want to name the custom toolbar or menu bar.

4 In the Toolbar Name box, type **Subscribers Menu Bar**, and then click OK.

A blank new toolbar appears near the middle of your screen, and Subscribers Menu Bar appears at the end of the Toolbars list in the Customize dialog box.

5 In the Customize dialog box, click the Properties button.

The Toolbar Properties dialog box appears, where you can set properties that change the behavior of the selected toolbar or menu bar.

6 In the Type box, click Menu Bar.

7 Click the Close button.

8 Move the blank new menu bar up and to the left, out of the way of the Customize dialog box. (As you work through the chapter, you may also need to move the Customize dialog box out of the way of the menu from time to time.)

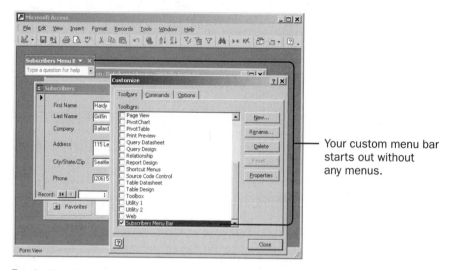

Your custom menu bar starts out without any menus.

For the time being, there are two menu bars. After you add menus to your new menu bar, you'll make sure only one menu bar appears at a time.

Add Built-In Menus to Your Custom Menu Bar

Now that you have a menu bar, you'll add a few built-in Access menus. To add menus or commands to a menu bar or toolbar, you use the Commands tab in the Customize dialog box.

1 In the Customize dialog box, click the Commands tab.

In the Categories list, you can see all the categories of Access commands that you can put on your menu bars and toolbars. As you click each category, such as File, Edit, and so on, the available commands are shown in the Commands list on the right.

Select a category...

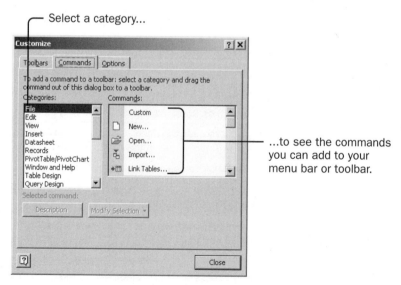

...to see the commands you can add to your menu bar or toolbar.

There are special categories in the list for adding entire built-in menus or creating custom menu commands. You'll use the Built-in Menus category to add several familiar menus.

2 In the Categories list, select Built-in Menus.

3 In the Commands list, drag the File menu entry to your custom menu bar.

Access creates a copy of the built-in File menu, complete with all its commands and sub-menus. (If you want, you can verify that it's all there by clicking the new menu to view its contents.)

Drag from here...

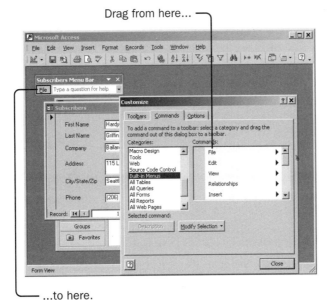

...to here.

4 Drag the Edit menu from the Commands list, placing it just to the right of the new File menu on your custom menu bar.

5 Repeat this procedure for the View, Records, Window, and Help menus, dragging each in turn to the right side of your custom menu bar. (You can skip the Insert, Format, and other menus, because users don't need these menus in Form view, and you'll create your own version of the Tools menu.)

Here's what the menu bar should look like:

Add Your Own Version of the Tools Menu

There are many commands on the Tools menu that are exclusively for power users and developers—you don't want your users to be messing around with them. Rather than including the built-in Tools menu, you'll now create your own version, copying only the commands you want to make available. This way, you'll make the menu much simpler, and you won't have to worry about users getting themselves into trouble.

1 In the Categories list, click New Menu.

2 In the Commands list, drag the New Menu text to your custom menu bar, placing it between the Records and Window menus.

...to here.

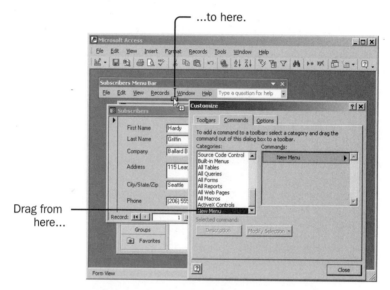

Drag from here...

A menu called New Menu appears on your custom menu bar.

3 With the right mouse button, click New Menu on the menu bar.

A shortcut menu appears showing options for the menu.

4 Click the existing text in the Name box, type **&Tools**, and then press the Enter key.

As with command button captions, you can include an ampersand (&) in a menu name to provide an access key for users who prefer the keyboard. The menu now shows its new name; however, if you click it, you'll see that it has no menu commands yet. Next you'll copy three commands from the built-in Tools menu. To copy a menu or toolbar command, you drag it from one menu bar or toolbar to another while holding down the Ctrl key (if you don't hold the Ctrl key, you move the command rather than copy it).

5 On the built-in menu bar at the top of the Microsoft Access window, click the Tools menu.

Of the commands you see on this menu, you want to include only three on your custom Tools menu: Spelling, AutoCorrect Options, and Options.

6 Holding down the Ctrl key, drag the Spelling command down to the Tools menu on your custom menu bar until the menu drops down, and then (still holding down the Ctrl key) drag it on to the blank menu and place it there.

The Spelling command appears on the menu.

Drag the Spelling command from
the standard Tools menu...

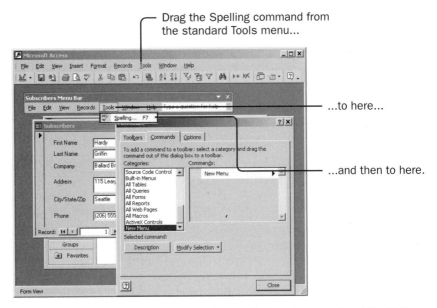

...to here...

...and then to here.

7 Repeat this technique to copy the AutoCorrect Options command and the Options command from the built-in Tools menu, placing them below the Spelling command on your custom menu.

Now your custom Tools menu includes only the three commands that users need. Your last step is to add a dividing line just above the Options menu command—as with standard menu bars, you can group menu commands on your custom menus.

8 With the right mouse button, click the Options command at the bottom of your custom menu bar, and then click Begin A Group on the shortcut menu.

The custom Tools menu is complete.

Tip

If you inadvertently made changes to the built-in menu bar—for example, if you deleted a command from it—it's easy to revert to its standard menus. In the Customize dialog box, select Menu Bar from the list, and then click the Reset button.

Add Another Menu to Your Custom Menu Bar

Next you'll add another new menu to the Subscribers menu bar. Because the menu will contain only commands that are specific to the Subscribers application, you'll name the menu Subscribers.

1 In the Categories list, click New Menu.

2 In the Commands list, drag the New Menu text to your custom menu bar, placing it between the Tools and Window menus.

3 With the right mouse button, click New Menu on the menu bar.

A shortcut menu appears showing options for the menu.

4 Select the existing text in the Name box, type **&Subscribers**, and then press Enter.

The new menu is ready for your custom commands.

Add Custom Commands to Open Forms in Your Application

Users want to perform two primary tasks in the Subscribers application: locating subscribers and printing mailing labels. In Chapter 8, you created the *GoToRecordDialog* form, which provides a better way for users to find records in the *Subscribers* form, and the *MailingLabelsDialog* form, which helps users print a report. Now you'll add custom menu commands that open these forms automatically. There is a special category in the Customize dialog box, called All Forms, that makes it easy to add a command to open an existing form.

1 In the Customize dialog box, click the Commands tab.

2 Click All Forms in the Categories list.

The Commands list displays all the forms in the Subscribers database. To add a command to a menu, drag it from the Commands list to the desired menu.

3 In the Commands list, drag the GoToRecordDialog entry up to the Subscribers menu until the menu drops down, and then drag it down onto the blank menu.

The GoToRecordDialog command appears on the menu.

Your custom menu command will open the *GoToRecordDialog* form.

To match other menu commands, you'll want to change the text shown on this command.

4 With the right mouse button, click the GoToRecordDialog command.

5 Select the existing text in the Name box, type **&Find Record...** and then press Enter.

Once again, you include an ampersand in the name of the menu command to provide an access key. Also, it's customary to include an ellipsis (...) after any menu command that displays a dialog box rather than immediately carrying out an action.

Next you'll copy an appropriate icon—the binoculars icon from the Find command—to the new menu command. The icon is displayed on a button on the current toolbar.

6 With the right mouse button, click the Find button on the toolbar (it's normally the sixth button from the right), and then click Copy Button Image on the shortcut menu.

7 Click the Subscribers menu.

8 With the right mouse button, click the Find Record menu command, and then click Paste Button Image on the shortcut menu.

In two easy steps, you've managed to steal the standard image for your new command—a handy technique that you may want to use with other custom menus and toolbars down the road. Now you're ready to add a second command to the menu.

9 In the Customize dialog box, drag the MailingLabelsDialog entry in the Commands list up to the Subscribers menu until the menu drops down, and then drag it down onto the menu just below the existing menu command.

Another new command, MailingLabelsDialog, appears on the menu.

10 With the right mouse button, click the new menu command.

11 Select the existing text in the Name box, type **&Print Mailing Labels...** and then press Enter.

For this menu command, you'll copy the printer icon from the Print button on the toolbar.

12 With the right mouse button, click the Print button on the toolbar, and then click Copy Button Image on the shortcut menu.

13 Click the Subscribers menu.

14 With the right mouse button, click the Print Mailing Labels menu command, and then click Paste Button Image on the shortcut menu.

Your new menu is complete.

Tell the *Subscribers* Form to Use the Custom Menu Bar

Now that you have a custom menu bar, you can make the *Subscribers* form use this one instead of the standard menu bar by setting the form's MenuBar property.

1 Drag the menu bar up to the top of the Microsoft Access window—between the standard menu bar and the toolbar—to "dock" it there.

(*Docking* a menu bar or toolbar refers to sticking it against the top or side of the screen, rather than letting it float in the middle.)

Dock your custom menu bar just below the standard menu bar.

Next you'll make sure Access displays only one menu bar at a time.

2 In the Customize dialog box, click the Toolbars tab.

3 In the Toolbars list, clear the check box next to Subscribers Menu Bar.

The custom menu bar disappears and will no longer show unless the *Subscribers* form is active. However, you still need to designate it as the menu bar for the *Subscribers* form.

Design View

4 In the Customize dialog box, click the Close button.

5 Click the Design View button on the toolbar.

Properties

6 If the property sheet isn't displayed, click the Properties button on the toolbar.

7 Click the Other tab in the property sheet.

8 Set the MenuBar property to *Subscribers Menu Bar*.

Setting this property tells Access that whenever the *Subscribers* form is active, it should display your custom menu bar instead of the standard one.

Form View

9 Click the Form View button on the toolbar.

Your custom menu bar is shown. You can tell it isn't the standard menu bar, because it has your special Subscribers menu on it.

Try Your Custom Menu Bar

You're ready to test your custom menu bar.

1 On the Subscribers menu, click Find Record.

Your custom command opens the Go To Record dialog box, which you created in Chapter 8.

2 Double-click an entry in the list box.

You jump to the specified record in the *Subscribers* form. Now try out the other command you added.

3 On the Subscribers menu, click Print Mailing Labels.

The Print Mailing Labels dialog box appears.

4 Click Cancel.

Finally you might as well check the Tools menu to make sure your changes are there.

5 Click the Tools menu.

There are only three commands on the menu—the rest of the commands usually found on the Tools menu aren't there. (You may see only two of the three commands when you first click the menu, however, because Access hides less frequently-used menu items. If you leave the menu open a few seconds, all your menu items will appear.)

The extra Tools menu commands are now gone from your custom menu, but they still exist on the built-in menu bar, which you can return to by switching to a window other than the *Subscribers* form.

Database Window

6 Click the Database Window button on the toolbar.

7 Click the Tools menu again.

All the standard commands have returned.

As you can see, your custom menu bar appears only when the *Subscribers* form is active—that's the form you created it for. However, if you create a menu bar that's appropriate for more than one form, the forms can share it: just set the MenuBar property in each form to the same menu name. You can also create a single menu bar that applies to all forms in your application (unless they each have their own menu bar). To specify a "global" menu, you set the Menu Bar option using the Startup command on the Tools menu.

Creating Custom Shortcut Menus

When you click the right mouse button nearly anywhere in Windows or Access, a shortcut menu appears with commands that are appropriate to the current context you're in or the place you've just clicked. For example, when you click a field on a form with the right mouse button, a shortcut menu appears with options for filtering, copying, and pasting. By default, these shortcut menus appear in your application just as any other menu does.

In most cases, the default shortcut menus will work fine for your applications. If you want, however, you can replace shortcut menus with your own—using steps similar to those for regular menu bars. To replace the shortcut menu bar for a form, create a custom menu bar. When the menu bar is finished, set its Type property to *Popup* (rather than *Menu Bar* or *Toolbar*). Then, set the form's ShortcutMenuBar property to the name of the custom menu bar. You can also specify different shortcut menus for individual controls on your forms by setting the ShortcutMenuBar property for each control. (Regular menu bars don't allow this.)

As with a menu bar, you can add commands to a shortcut menu that perform Access menu commands, open existing objects such as forms or reports, or run Visual Basic functions.

Customizing Toolbars

For better or worse, more and more of today's software uses graphical interface elements to interact with users. In your Access applications, one way you can follow this graphical trend is by making use of toolbars. Toolbars are a handy way to make commands available to users. Many buttons can fit on a toolbar, and once users learn what they are, the commands they need are always just a click away. When you want to add new buttons to a toolbar, Access provides many icons to choose from; if you're an aspiring artist, you can create your own.

As with menu bars, there are several basic strategies for creating toolbars. The simplest strategy is to customize an existing toolbar, such as the Form View toolbar, adding and deleting buttons as desired. However, the standard toolbars are stored with your Access installation, so other users who open your databases won't see your toolbar changes.

To make special toolbars available on other computers, you'll want to create your own custom toolbars, either supplementing or replacing the standard ones. Just like custom menu bars, custom toolbars are stored with your application's database, so they're available to all users. When you customize toolbars, you choose which buttons they have and whether the buttons have icons or text on them. You can even customize the ScreenTip text that appears when users hold the mouse pointer over a button.

In this section, you'll create a simple toolbar designed to replace the standard toolbar. Because users won't see the standard toolbar when the *Subscribers* form is active, you'll want to include some of the buttons that users are accustomed to seeing there (such as the Cut, Copy, and Paste buttons) and then add your own selection of buttons in place of those you don't expect users to need.

Creating a Custom Toolbar for the *Subscribers* Form

The toolbar you'll create will help users of the *Subscribers* form to open other forms quickly and easily. Fortunately, as you saw when customizing menus, the easiest type of toolbar button (or menu command) to create is one that opens a form or report in your database. You'll start by creating a new, empty toolbar, and then you'll add several buttons to it.

Create a New Toolbar for the *Subscribers* Form

1 Switch back to the *Subscribers* form.

2 On the View menu, point to Toolbars, and then click Customize.

It's your old friend the Customize dialog box.

3 Click the New button.

Access displays the New Toolbar dialog box.

4 In the Toolbar Name box, type **Subscribers**, and then click OK.

An empty floating toolbar appears near the center of the screen.

5 In the Customize dialog box, click the Close button.

6 Drag the empty toolbar up to the top of the screen—just under the menu bar and to the left of the existing toolbar—to dock it. (Make sure you dock the toolbar at the far left of the window, lined up with the left side of the menu bar.)

Your custom toolbar will soon replace the standard
Form View toolbar for the *Subscribers* form.

7 With the right mouse button, click one of the toolbars, and then click Subscribers on the shortcut menu.

Your custom toolbar disappears for the moment.

Design View

8 Click the Design View button on the toolbar.

9 Set the Toolbar property to *Subscribers*.

Setting this property tells Access that whenever the *Subscribers* form is active, it should display your custom toolbar instead of the standard one.

Form View

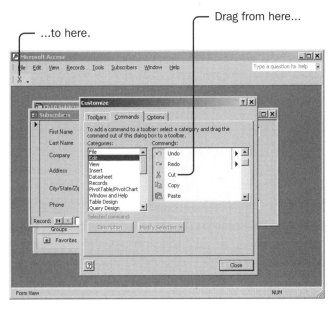

10 Click the Form View button on the toolbar.

Your custom toolbar is shown, although so far it's just a blank box, without any buttons to click.

Add Standard Buttons to the Toolbar

On any toolbar you create, you can add as many standard buttons as you like, and they work just as they do on the built-in Access toolbars. Here you want to include a few of the Edit commands users are accustomed to seeing: Cut, Copy, Paste, and Undo.

1 With the right mouse button, click the empty toolbar, and then click Customize on the shortcut menu.

2 In the Customize dialog box, click the Commands tab.

3 Click Edit in the Categories list.

The standard Edit commands are shown in the Commands list.

4 Select Cut from the Commands list, and then drag the text up to the toolbar.

The Cut button appears on your toolbar.

Drag from here...

...to here.

5 Using the same technique, add the Copy, Paste, and Undo buttons to the right of the Cut button. (When you add the Undo button, you'll notice there are three Undo items in the Commands list. Use the Undo item at the top of the list—this is the Undo Field/Record button.)

Just like standard toolbars, your custom toolbars can include dividing lines for grouping buttons. Because the Cut, Copy, and Paste buttons are a logical group, you want to include a dividing line before the Undo button.

6 With the right mouse button, click the Undo button, and then click Begin A Group on the shortcut menu.

A dividing line appears between the Paste and Undo buttons.

Add Three Custom Buttons

Now you'll add three custom buttons—one to open the *GoToRecordDialog* form, one to open the *MailingLabelsDialog* form, and one to open the *EnterPayment* form. For the GoToRecord and PrintMailingLabels buttons, you'll just copy the commands you created for your custom menu, because this is exactly what you want to show on the toolbar.

1 Click the Subscribers menu to drop it down.

2 Holding down the Ctrl key, drag the Find Record command from the Subscribers menu to the toolbar and place it just to the right of the existing buttons.

The new button appears on the toolbar. As you can see, menus and toolbars are just two different views of the same thing—a place to put commands—and you can therefore share and copy commands between them.

3 With the right mouse button, click the new button, and then click Begin A Group on the shortcut menu.

In this case, you probably don't need to display the text label for the Find Record button.

4 Right-click the Find Record button again, and then click Default Style on the shortcut menu.

Next, you'll copy the Print Mailing Labels menu command to your toolbar.

5 Click the Subscribers menu again.

6 Holding down the Ctrl key, drag the Print Mailing Labels command from the Subscribers menu to the toolbar and place it just to the right of the existing buttons.

7 Right-click the new button, and then click Default Style on the shortcut menu.

Next, you'll add another button to open the *EnterPayment* form.

8 In the Customize dialog box, click All Forms in the Categories list.

9 Click EnterPayment in the Commands list and drag it to the toolbar.

In this case, let's display a text label for the button. To edit the text, set the button's Name property.

10 With the right mouse button, click the new button, select all the text in the Name box, type **Enter &Payment**, and then press Enter.

Your toolbar now has seven buttons ready for action! If you want, you can add other standard buttons, or rearrange buttons by dragging them around on the toolbar.

Each of your custom buttons opens a different form.

11 In the Customize Toolbars dialog box, click Close.

Try Out the New Toolbar

It's time to take your new toolbar for a spin! Try hovering over each of the buttons to view the ScreenTip. Then follow these steps to see the toolbar buttons in action.

1 Click the Find Record button on the toolbar.

  The button opens the Go To Record dialog box.

2 Double-click a subscriber in the list.

3 Click the Print Mailing Labels button on the toolbar.

  The button opens the Print Mailing Labels dialog box.

4 Click Cancel.

5 Click the Enter Payment button on the toolbar.

  The button opens the *EnterPayment* form.

6 Click Close.

Next you'll add one more button to the toolbar before calling it complete—a button that lets users view payment histories. When you're finished, you will have replaced the functionality of all the command buttons that used to be in the *Subscribers* form footer.

Creating Toolbar Buttons to Run Visual Basic Code

The toolbar buttons you've created so far have simply opened forms—they haven't done anything special beyond this. If opening an object is all you want to do, this technique is very straightforward. But you may want a toolbar button to do more—for example, you may want to run a Visual Basic procedure when users click the button. To do this, you set a property of the button to the name of a Visual Basic function you want it to run.

In this section, you'll create a toolbar button that runs a Visual Basic function. In this case, you want the button to open the *PaymentHistory* pop-up form, which shows a subscriber's payment history. However, you don't just want to open the form—you also need to set a filter so that the form displays only payments for the current subscriber. Although a toolbar button can't do this by itself, you can write a simple function that does the job.

Write a Function to Open the *PaymentHistory* Form

1 On the Window menu, click Ch10 Subscription : Database.

2 In the Database window, click the Modules shortcut.

3 Double-click the Miscellaneous module.

Visual Basic opens and shows the module's code.

4 On the Insert menu, click Procedure.

5 In the Name box, type **ViewPaymentHistory**.

6 In the Type group, click Function, and then click OK.

Visual Basic creates the function at the end of the module, entering the *Function* and *End Function* statements for you.

7 Enter the following code for the procedure:

```
' Open the PaymentHistory form and set its filter.

    DoCmd.OpenForm" "PaymentHistory", , ," "SubscriberID =" " _
        & Forms!Subscribers!SubscriberID
```

This code uses the *OpenForm* method of the *DoCmd* object to open the *PaymentHistory* form. It uses the *WhereCondition* argument—a technique you learned in Chapter 8—to specify a filter for the form. When the form opens, it will display only records whose SubscriberID field matches the record currently displayed in the *Subscribers* form.

8 Close Visual Basic.

Add a Toolbar Button That Runs the Function

The last button you'll add to the toolbar will use the *ViewPaymentHistory* function. Of course, you could run a much more complex function when a toolbar button is clicked; in this case, however, all you need to do is open the form.

1 Switch back to the *Subscribers* form.

Your custom menu bar and toolbar appear.

2 With the right mouse button, click the toolbar, and then click Customize on the shortcut menu.

When you plan to provide a Visual Basic function for a button to run, it doesn't matter which command or category you choose—the button will run your code instead of performing its usual action. For this reason, it makes the most sense to select a command with an icon you want the button to have. You'll use the Table icon to represent the View Payment History command.

3 Select View from the Categories list.

4 Select Tables from the Commands list and drag the text up to the new toolbar, placing it just to the right of the Enter Payment button.

As it stands, clicking this button would change views in the Database window. Of course, you have other plans for the button.

5 With the right mouse button, click the new toolbar button, and then click Properties on the shortcut menu.

6 Select the existing text in the Caption box, and then type **View Payment &History**.

7 In the On Action box, type **=ViewPaymentHistory()**.

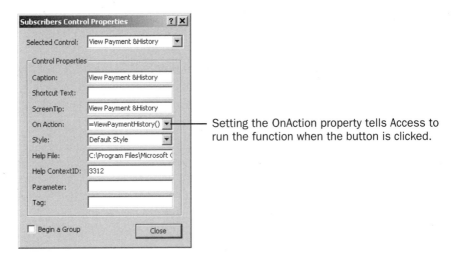

Setting the OnAction property tells Access to run the function when the button is clicked.

When you use a function with the OnAction property, always be sure to precede the function name with an equal sign, and follow it with parentheses (including arguments if the function requires them).

8 In the Subscribers Control Properties dialog box, click Close.

9 Right-click the new button, and then click Image And Text on the shortcut menu.

10 In the Customize Toolbars dialog box, click Close.

Test the Toolbar Once Again

You're ready to try out the final toolbar button.

1 Click the View Payment History button on the toolbar.

The toolbar button runs the *ViewPaymentHistory* function, which in turn opens the *PaymentHistory* pop-up form and sets its filter.

2 Close the *PaymentHistory* form.

Your custom toolbar is complete!

Working with Command Bars in Visual Basic

In this chapter, you've customized menus and toolbars using the tools available in Access. However, if you need additional power—for example, if you want to change menus or toolbars in response to actions users take in your application—you can work directly with menus and toolbars in Visual Basic code. In Visual Basic, menu bars and toolbars are collectively known as *command bars*. They have a complete set of objects, properties, and methods you can use when working with them.

There are many reasons you might want to manipulate command bars, but here are some common possibilities:

- To add or hide menu commands or toolbar buttons in response to events in your application
- To disable custom menu commands or toolbar buttons when they don't apply
- To create and manipulate special command bar controls, such as combo boxes, that aren't available through the standard Access tools

Before you can work with command bars in code, you need to alert Access by choosing the References command (on the Tools menu) and selecting the Microsoft Office 10.0 Object Library. Then you use the *CommandBar* and *CommandBarControl* objects to access menus and toolbars. You'll learn more about using objects in Chapter 12. For information and examples specifically on programming with command bars, search Access Help for "CommandBar object."

Chapter Wrap-Up

1   Close the *Subscribers* form, clicking Yes when Access asks if you want to save changes.

2   On the File menu, click Exit.

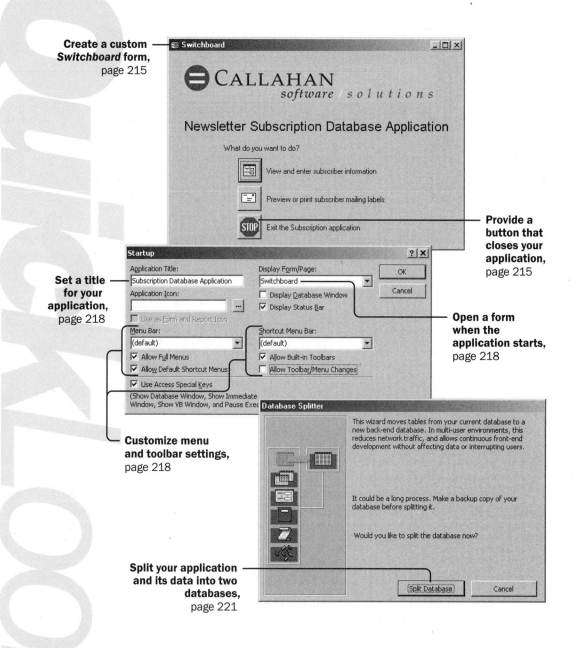

Create a custom
***Switchboard* form,**
page 215

Set a title
for your
application,
page 218

Customize menu
and toolbar settings,
page 218

Provide a
button that
closes your
application,
page 215

Open a form
when the
application starts,
page 218

Split your application
and its data into two
databases,
page 221

Chapter 11
Put Final Touches on an Application

After completing this chapter, you will be able to:

✔ Create an application startup form.

✔ Control how your application starts.

✔ Customize the title bar and appearance of your application.

✔ Separate your application's data from its other objects.

As goes the common wisdom, the first impression is the most important. Of course, it's important that when you order a fancy cake it tastes good, but it's the "icing on the cake" that catches people's attention—and their first look at that delicious cake will affect their overall opinion more than any other factor. As in other areas of life, this maxim holds true for computer software: the appearance and first impression of a product is as important as its capabilities. As Microsoft itself has learned, a polished, graphical product inspires excitement that might cause users to excuse a missing feature or two.

In previous chapters, you've learned how to put most of the substance into your applications, creating and customizing forms, adding menus and toolbars, linking everything together in a logical way. Before your application is ready for public consumption, however, it needs a few final touches—the icing on the cake. After all, the application will represent *you* to the users who start it up, and you want their first experience with your application to be a good one.

In this chapter, you'll learn techniques for making your applications look professional and polished. You'll work with the Subscription application, making it easier for users to get started, and helping the application make a great first impression. Finally, you'll learn tips and tricks for distributing an application to users so that it will be easier to maintain down the road.

Ch11 Subscription.mdb

This chapter uses the practice file Ch11 Subscription.mdb that you installed from the book's CD-ROM. For details about installing the practice files, see "Using the Book's CD-ROM" at the beginning of this book.

Getting Started

● Start Microsoft Access, and open the Ch11 Subscription database in the practice files folder.

213

Controlling How Your Application Starts

After you've created the tables, forms, and reports for your application and added all the code to make them work well together, it's time to prepare your application for delivery. You want to make your application look like a unique, finished product rather than simply an Access database with a few frills. Additionally, if users are to have a good experience with the application, you'll need to make sure it's easy for them to get started.

Here are some of the final preparations you'll want to consider.

Designate a startup form. You can select a form in your database that Access opens automatically each time a user starts the application. For example, you might want to jump directly to your application's main data entry or display form, such as the *Subscribers* form you've been working with. Or, in many applications, you'll want to provide a switchboard-type form—similar to the *Switchboard* form the Database Wizard creates—that acts as a main menu for users' tasks. In either case, you'll most likely want to hide the standard Database window, because your forms will provide users with easy access to all your application's capabilities.

Customize the startup appearance of your application. In addition to providing a startup form, you can customize several other startup details, such as what the title bar displays. And if you create general application menu bars, shortcut menus, and toolbars, you'll want them to be hooked up when your application starts.

Prepare your application for network use and easy maintenance. Before you deliver your application, you should consider how it will be used and maintained. To make things easier down the road, you may want to split your application into two separate files: one for tables, and another for other objects. Additionally, you'll decide whether the application will be located on a network and whether you need to protect your data by setting a password.

Test, test, test! Of course, the final step before you distribute your application is to make sure everything is foolproof. Try all the possible paths through the forms and reports, and make any necessary fixes before you deliver the application. The work you put in up front will pay off in reducing the updates you'll need to provide down the road!

In this chapter, you'll use several of these techniques to customize the Subscription application. When you're finished, the Subscription application will be ready to deliver—making its debut to users as a stand-alone product rather than just another database and helping users get started with their work right away.

Providing a Startup Form for Your Application

Any form in your application can act as the startup form, opening automatically for users. However, the most common strategy for starting an application—and the one you'll use with the Subscription application—is to provide a separate startup form that acts as a main menu for users. The Subscription practice database already includes a preliminary version of such a startup form, designed to introduce the application to users managing an imaginary newsletter subscription database.

In this section, you'll add the final elements to the design of the *Switchboard* form. In the practice database, the form already contains the picture, text in several labels, and two simple buttons created using the Command Button Wizard. You'll add the third button, and then get the form ready for use as the application's startup form. In your own database, you would create a switchboard form from scratch, adding whatever text, pictures, and buttons you'd like. A startup form is a great place to show your creativity and put your personal touch on your application.

Completing the *Switchboard* Form for the Subscription Database

To finish up the *Switchboard* form in the practice database, you'll open it in Design view, add a command button using the Command Button Wizard, and then add a label for the button. You'll also set several form properties that make the form look like a switchboard—similar to properties you set for dialog boxes and pop-up forms in previous chapters.

Add a Command Button

1 In the Database window, click the Forms shortcut.

2 Select the *Switchboard* form, and then click Design.

The *Switchboard* form opens in Design view. The two command buttons on this form open the *Subscribers* form and the *PrintMailingLabelsDialog* form. You'll create one additional button at the bottom of the form, providing an easy way for users to exit the Subscription application when they're finished with their work.

Control Wizards

3 Scroll down a bit in the form to display the blank area underneath the two buttons.

4 In the toolbox, make sure the Control Wizards tool is selected, and then click the Command Button tool.

Command Button

5 Click to create the new button just underneath the left side of the OpenMailingDialog button (the one that has an envelope icon on it).

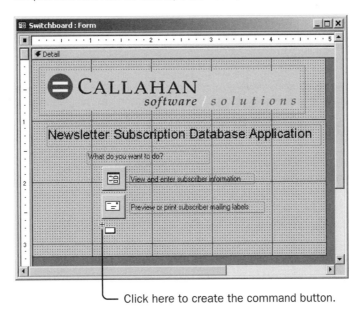

Click here to create the command button.

The Command Button Wizard starts, asking what action you want the button to perform.

6 Click Application in the Categories list.

Quit Application is already selected in the Actions list, so you can continue.

7 Click Next.

The wizard asks whether you want a picture or text on your button. Unlike the command buttons you've created in earlier chapters, for which you typed text, you'll put a picture on this button. The Stop Sign picture, already selected, will do the trick.

8 Click Next.

The wizard asks what you want to name the button.

9 Type **QuitApplication**, and then click Finish.

The wizard creates the button, including an event procedure that closes your application—and Access—whenever the button is clicked.

Label the Command Button

Next you'll add text beside the button to clarify what the button is for.

Label

Aa

1 In the toolbox, click the Label tool.

2 Click just to the right of the new button.

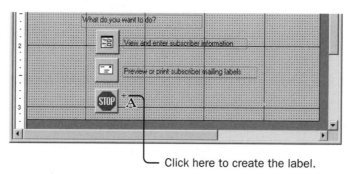

Click here to create the label.

An empty label appears on the form, ready for you to enter the text you want to display. You could use this same technique to add other text to the form, just like the labels that display the title of the application at the top of the form.

3 Type **Exit the Subscription application**.

Set the *Switchboard* Form's Properties

To make the form look and work like a switchboard, all that's left is to set form properties.

1 On the Edit menu, click Select Form.

Properties

2 If the property sheet isn't displayed, click the Properties button on the toolbar.

3 Click the Format tab in the property sheet.

4 Set the following properties to the values shown.

Property	Value
Caption	Switchboard
AllowDatasheetView	No
AllowPivotTableView	No
AllowPivotChartView	No
ScrollBars	Neither
RecordSelectors	No
NavigationButtons	No
AutoCenter	Yes
BorderStyle	Thin
Caption	Switchboard
AllowDatasheetView	No

These settings will make the Switchboard form look much like a dialog box, with a thin border and no extra navigation tools.

5 Close the Switchboard form, clicking Yes when Access asks whether you want to save changes to the form.

Try Out the Switchboard Form

The Switchboard form will act as the control center of your application—users will think of it as their "home base," from which they'll navigate to their various tasks. Let's try it out.

1 In the Database window, double-click the Switchboard form.

The form appears in the center of the screen, announcing your application and showing the three buttons available for navigation.

2 Click the first button, View And Enter Subscriber Information.

The button's event procedure opens the Subscribers form. The toolbar and menus you created in Chapter 10 appear as well, providing a way to navigate through the other parts of your application. When you close the Subscribers form, you'll return to the application's switchboard.

3 Close the Subscribers form.

When users finish working in the Subscription application, they would normally click your new button to exit Access. However, we have some more work to do, so you should just close the form.

4 Close the Switchboard form.

Tip

When you deliver your application to users, you may not want to allow them to close the *Switchboard* form without closing the whole application. To prevent the application from staying open, you could add a simple line of code to the form's *Close* event procedure that either closes the application or exits Access. Use the *CloseCurrentDatabase* method to close the application; to exit Access, use the *Quit* method of the *DoCmd* object.

Make Your *Switchboard* Form Open Automatically

Now that the *Switchboard* form is ready to go, the next step is to tell Access to open the form when users start your application, making it the startup form for the application. You do this with the Startup command.

1 On the Tools menu, click Startup.

Access displays the Startup dialog box, where you can specify options for how your application starts.

2 In the Display Form/Page box, click the down arrow, and then click Switchboard in the list of forms.

Select the form that you want to
open when your application starts.

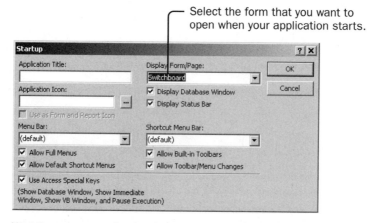

Next time you open the database, the *Switchboard* form will open automatically.

Customizing Your Application's Appearance

While you're in the Startup dialog box, you can set other options for your application. One nice detail to customize is the application's title bar. Instead of "Microsoft Access" you can specify the title of your application. Additionally, now is the time to hide the standard Database window from users, and to make sure users don't change the toolbars you've provided in your application.

Set Startup Options to Control How Your Application Looks

1 In the Startup dialog box, click the Application Title box, and then type **Subscription Database Application**.

This text will appear in the title bar of the application window in place of "Microsoft Access," making your custom application look less like an Access database and more like your own creation.

2   Clear the Display Database Window check box.

Now, when users open the Subscription database, the Database window won't appear. They won't need it—your switchboard form replaces it as the navigation tool for the application.

3   Clear the Allow Toolbar/Menu Changes check box.

Clearing this option ensures that users can't change your custom Subscribers toolbar or menu—or the built-in ones—so they'll always be available.

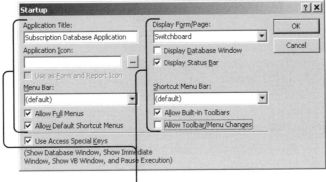

The Startup settings for the Subscription application

4   Click OK.

Although the Subscription database doesn't require any other startup options, you may want to use some of the other options in your own applications. Here are some additional changes you can make by setting options with the Startup command.

Provide your own application icon. By setting the Application Icon option to an icon or bitmap image file, you can change the icon that's displayed in the upper left corner of the title bar (and in the taskbar button when your application is minimized).

Hide the status bar. If you clear the Display Status Bar check box, the status bar won't appear at the bottom of the application window.

Change standard menus. In Chapter 10, you learned how to change menus on a single form. However, you can also specify menu behavior for your entire application by setting startup options. To display a menu bar for forms and reports that don't have their own custom menu bar, set the Menu Bar and Shortcut Menu Bar options. To make built-in menus unavailable, clear the Allow Full Menus and Allow Default Shortcut Menus check boxes.

Hide built-in toolbars. By clearing the Allow Built-In Toolbars check box, you can tell Access not to display the toolbars that are normally available so that only your custom toolbars appear.

Secure your application from tampering. If you click the Advanced button in the Startup dialog box, you'll see the Use Access Special Keys option. By clearing this check box, you can make it impossible for users to break into your application's code. Be careful, though—you'll be locking *yourself* out as well.

Protecting Your Application by Setting a Password

Many databases contain sensitive or confidential information, which you may want to protect by requiring that users enter a password before they begin working in the application. The simplest way to do this is by setting a password for the database. To do this, on the Tools menu point to Security, and then click Set Database Password. Each time the database opens, Access will ask for the password.

Although setting a database password is a simple method of securing your database, it isn't very flexible. For example, what if you want to provide access only to certain objects, or to provide access to data in your application only to specific users and not to others? Or what if you want to provide various levels of access, such as allowing users to view data but not to change it? You can customize access to your application in these ways by setting up user and group security. And if you do create this more advanced type of security, you can protect your application itself from any design changes—making yourself the only user who has permission to view code and change objects.

To set up advanced security, you start by running the User-Level Security Wizard. You then use the other Security commands on the Tools menu to create user and group accounts and to grant permissions to each account for the various objects in your application. Beware, however: advanced security is not for the faint of heart. Although Access provides all the tools you need for setting up security, it is a time-consuming and challenging process. If a single password for your application will suffice, consider sticking with the database password strategy.

Tip

After you've set startup options, they take effect the next time you open your application. Having these options in effect is great for your users. But while your application is still under development, you may not want the startup options to apply. For example, you'll probably want to open the Database window rather than the startup form so that you'll have access to all objects in the application.

To bypass the startup options for an application, hold down the Shift key when you open the database, either as you double-click the database file's icon or as you click the Open button. Access will ignore all options you've set using the Startup command. (To learn about preventing users from doing this, search Help for "AllowBypassKey property.")

Preparing to Distribute Your Application to Users

Your application is ready to go to work—all you need to do is make it available to users. In the simplest case, this just involves copying the database application file to a user's system or to a network location where users can access it. However, before you send out your application, it's a good idea to give some thought to how you'll distribute and maintain it. How will you distribute updates to the application? How will users back up and compact the database? Are there any additional files you need to deliver along with your application?

These questions will become important to you if your application is designed for many users or for users on a network or if it's a large application. Here are some ideas for addressing the challenges of distributing and maintaining an Access application.

Split your application into two database files.   By default, all the data and objects for an application are stored in a single database file. This file can become large and difficult to handle. With a large application, it's a good idea to have one Access file for the queries, forms, and other objects that make your application work, and a separate file for its tables. The main application file is often referred to as the *front-end* database, because this is what users open and use; the data file containing your tables is referred to as the *back-end* database.

Place your application or its data file on a network drive.   Access is a *multiuser* database system, which means that more than one user can view and change data in the same database at the same time. To make your application available to multiple users, you can simply place the file on a network. Or, if you split the application into two separate databases, you can place only the data file on a network drive, while distributing copies of the application file to each user—which may make your application run faster.

Create Windows shortcuts to run your application or perform other tasks.   In Windows, you can provide shortcut icons that make your application easier to run, especially if it's located on a network or stored in a folder along with many other files. You may want to provide other miscellaneous shortcuts for users as well—for example, you might create a shortcut for compacting or backing up a database file. For information on creating shortcuts, see your Windows documentation or search Help for "shortcuts."

Make sure users have all the files they need.   Most everything your application needs is included in your database file or installed with Access. If your application uses more than one file, be sure to distribute all the files users need. For example, if you split your application into two files, users must have access to both. If your application has a splash screen or other external files, these files must be available as well. Finally, if your application uses special features of Access, such as data access drivers or custom controls, users must have installed them with Access.

In this section, you'll implement the first of these strategies for the Subscription application, splitting it into two separate database files for easier maintenance.

Split the Subscription Database into Two Files

As you'll see, splitting an application into two database files is easy: you run the Database Splitter.

1   On the Tools menu, point to Database Utilities, and then click Database Splitter.

The Database Splitter starts.

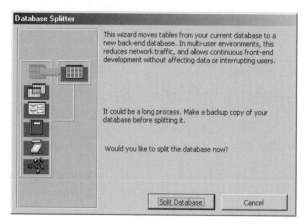

2 Click the Split Database button.

The Database Splitter displays the Create Back-End Database dialog box, where you specify the name and location of the database file that will contain your application's tables.

3 In the dialog box, navigate to the practice files folder on your computer's hard disk.

Note that if you were planning to make this data available to users on a network, you would move instead to a folder on a network drive. That way, the Database Splitter would put the data on the network for you. For your current purpose, however, having both databases on your hard disk is fine.

4 Click the Split button.

The Database Splitter creates a new database file called Ch11 Subscription_be (the "be" stands for "back end"), exports the two tables in the Subscription database to the new file, creates tables linked to them in the current database, and then displays a message saying that the database was successfully split.

5 Click OK.

Even though you've split it into two database files, your application will work exactly as before. Now, however, the database is much more flexible. First, you can back up the data file—a very important task—without backing up the entire application, which doesn't often change. What's more, you can replace the application file (to update forms and reports, for example) without any effect on the existing data. Finally, if users work on a network, they can run your application from their individual systems while accessing the data on a network drive.

Add Code that Checks and Fixes Linked Tables

To access data each time your application opens, the linked tables in your application store the path and file name of the back-end database at the time you performed the split. If you rename or move the data file—for example, if you place it on a network drive— you'll have to refresh the linked tables, or else Access won't be able to find them. Because most users won't know how to do this, it's a good idea to include code in your application

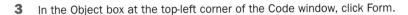

that checks links to the back-end database and fixes them if the back-end data file has been moved or renamed.

1 In the Database window, click the Forms shortcut.

Code Button

2 Click Switchboard in the list of forms, and then click the Code button.

The form's module opens in Microsoft Visual Basic.

3 In the Object box at the top-left corner of the Code window, click Form.

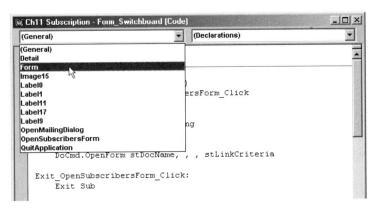

Visual Basic creates the *Form_Load* event procedure—you don't have to select the *Load* event, because it is the default event for the *Form* object.

4 Add the following code:

```
Private Sub Form_Load()
' Check linked tables each time the application opens.

    If CheckLinks() = False Then
        DisplayMessage "You can't use this database without its data."
        Application.Quit
    End If
End Sub
```

The *If...Then* statement in this code uses a user-defined function called *CheckLinks* to check whether the application's linked tables are working properly. If the links are broken and the function can't fix them (it asks the user to specify a new back-end database file), it returns *False*. The code then displays a message and shuts down the application. The *CheckLinks* function is included in the practice database in the Relinker module; for more information, see the next section, "Checking and Fixing Linked Tables."

Before distributing your application, it's a good idea to compile the code one last time to check for errors.

5 On the Debug menu, click Compile Ch11 Subscription.

6 Close Visual Basic.

7 Close Microsoft Access, clicking Yes when Access asks if you want to save changes to the *Switchboard* form.

223

Checking and Fixing Linked Tables

If you try to open a linked table and Access can't find its back-end database, Access displays an error—and doesn't provide an option to fix the problem. You can update broken links in one of three ways: manually delete all linked tables and recreate them, use the Linked Table Manager (on the Database Utilities submenu of the Tools menu) to update tables all at once, or write Visual Basic code that fixes links behind the scenes.

The Subscription database includes a standard module called Relinker, which can help you keep your linked tables working properly. You just used its main procedure—the *CheckLinks* function—in the *Switchboard* form's *Load* event procedure. Because it's so important to maintain linked tables properly, you may want to include the Relinker module in other applications you create.

Here's the code for the *CheckLinks* function, which you can also view by opening the Relinker module in the Subscription database.

```
Public Function CheckLinks() As Boolean
' Check linked tables relink if necessary. Returns true if
' links are okay (or links are successfully refreshed).

    On Error GoTo CheckLinksErr
    Dim tdf As TableDef
    Dim strNewMDB As String
    Dim fd As FileDialog

    ' Loop through each table in the current database.
    For Each tdf In CurrentDb.TableDefs

        ' Check whether this table is linked (connect string not blank)
        ' and whether its link is broken (no fields in the Fields collection).
        If Len(tdf.Connect) > 0 And tdf.Fields.Count = 0 Then

            ' If we don't have an MDB name yet, display a message and
            ' then ask the user to pick a new file.
            If Len(strNewMDB) = 0 Then
                MsgBox "The back-end data file for this database ..."

                ' Create a FileDialog object.
                Set fd = Application.FileDialog(msoFileDialogFilePicker)
                With fd
                    ' Set dialog box properties.
                    .AllowMultiSelect = False
                    .InitialFileName = CurrentDBFolder()
                    .Filters.Add "Access Database File (*.mdb)", "*.mdb", 1
                    .Title = "Select Back-End Data File"
                    .ButtonName = "Link Tables"

                    ' Show the dialog box.
                    If .Show = False Then' User clicked Cancel.
                        Exit Function
```

```
            Else
                ' Selected file is in the SelectedItems collection.
                strNewMDB = .SelectedItems(1)
            End If
        End With
    End If

        ' Refresh the link using the selected back-end database.
        tdf.Connect = ";DATABASE=" & strNewMDB
        tdf.RefreshLink
    End If
Next tdf
CheckLinks = True' Relinking was a success.

CheckLinksDone:
    Exit Function
CheckLinksErr:
    MsgBox "Error #" & Err.Number & ": " & Err.Description, vbCritical
    Resume CheckLinksDone
End Function
```

The procedure does the following:

- **Loops through all tables in the database, checking for broken links** Access keeps an internal list of all tables in the current database in the *TableDefs* collection of the *CurrentDb* object. The *For…Each* statement allows you to loop through the tables in the database, performing the same block of code for each.

   To check whether a table has a broken link, the function tests two things. First it uses the expression *Len(tdf.Connect)* to determine the length of the table's *connection string*—the "address" that each linked table uses to locate the back-end data. If the length of this string is 0, the table isn't a linked table. Then the function checks the Count property of the *Fields* collection to determine whether the table has any fields—because if a linked table has no fields, that's a sure indication that the link is broken.

- **Displays a file dialog box for the user to specify a new database file** The first time the function finds a broken link, it creates a *FileDialog* object, which you use to display a standard file-picker dialog box (like the ones Microsoft Office displays). The code stores the *FileDialog* object in a variable called *fd*, then uses a *With…End* block to set the properties of the dialog box, such as its title and the initial folder it displays. It also adds a *file filter* to the *Filters* collection—a combination of strings that specify a file type—so that the dialog box displays only files that are Microsoft Access databases.

   Once the *FileDialog* object is ready, the function uses the *Show* method to display the dialog box. If the user selects a file, the code then retrieves the file name from the first object in the *SelectedItems* collection, storing it in a variable called *strNewMDB*.

- **Refreshes each broken link using the selected database** Once the function has retrieved the path to a new back-end database file, it's ready to fix the table's link. This involves two steps: first setting the Connect property of the *TableDef* object to a valid connection string (such as *";DATABASE=f:\Subscription_be.mdb")*; then using the *RefreshLink* method to actually update the link to point to the new data.

After looping through all the tables in the database, the function sets its return value to *True*. Of course, if there's any problem along the way—for example, if the user selects a file that doesn't contain the proper tables to be relinked—an error will end the function before its return value is set to *True*.

If some of the advanced concepts used in the *CheckLinks* function aren't clear to you, don't worry. Because it is provided for you in the practice database, you can simply call the *CheckLinks* function whenever you want to verify linked tables—just be sure to import the *Relinker* module into your databases to make the *CheckLinks* function available.

Try Out the Final Subscription Application

Now it's time to test your application's new Startup properties, as well as the linked table code you added.

1 Open the Ch11 Subscription database.

Instead of the Database window, Access automatically displays your startup form: the *Switchboard* form.

Your application name is displayed in the title bar.

Your startup form appears instead of the Database window.

The Subscription database is now a complete, stand-alone application—it has its own title bar and a customized user interface to help users navigate while performing their work. And when they're finished, it even has a customized way for them to quit!

2 On the *Switchboard* form, click the Exit The Subscription Application button.

The button's event procedure runs the *Quit* method of the *DoCmd* object, and Access shuts down.

Finally, it's a good idea to test the code that checks and refreshes linked tables. To do this, you'll rename the back-end data file in the practice files folder.

3 Using Windows Explorer, rename the file Ch11 Subscription_be to **Subscription Data**. (Open the practice files folder, right-click the file, click Rename on the shortcut menu, and then type the new name.)

Now when you open the application, its links to data will be broken. If you hadn't added code to check and fix linked tables, the application would display an error every time you tried to view data. Fortunately, your Visual Basic code can deal with the problem before it comes to this.

4 Open the Ch11 Subscription database file again.

When Access opens the *Subscription* form, it runs the form's *Load* event procedure, where you call the *CheckLinks* function. When that function runs, it discovers that the linked tables aren't where they used to be.

5 Click OK.

Next the *CheckLinks* function displays a file dialog box asking for a new file.

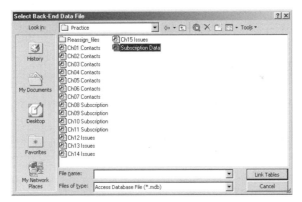

6 Click the Subscription Data file, and then click Link Tables.

The *CheckLinks* function refreshes the linked tables to use the new back-end database file, and the *Switchboard* form appears as before.

Additional Tools in Microsoft Office XP Developer

In order to run your Access application, users must have Access installed on their computers. However, now that you've customized an application so that it looks like it could stand on its own, you may be wondering if there's a way to distribute it to users who *don't* have Access. You can do this—if you have Microsoft Office XP Developer. This product contains several tools for Office developers, including the *run-time* version of Access, a version that runs applications but doesn't allow you to change or create them. You can distribute the run-time version of Access to an unlimited number of users, so they can run your application regardless of whether they have Access.

One other important tool in Office XP Developer is the Package And Deploy Wizard, which allows you to create a full-featured custom Setup program for your application. In addition to installing your application's files on users' systems, the Setup program can install the Access run-time files, create Windows shortcuts, and customize users' systems in other ways.

If you're distributing applications to many different users, you'd probably benefit from purchasing this product. In addition to these tools, Office XP Developer includes a CD with developer tools, samples, and documentation.

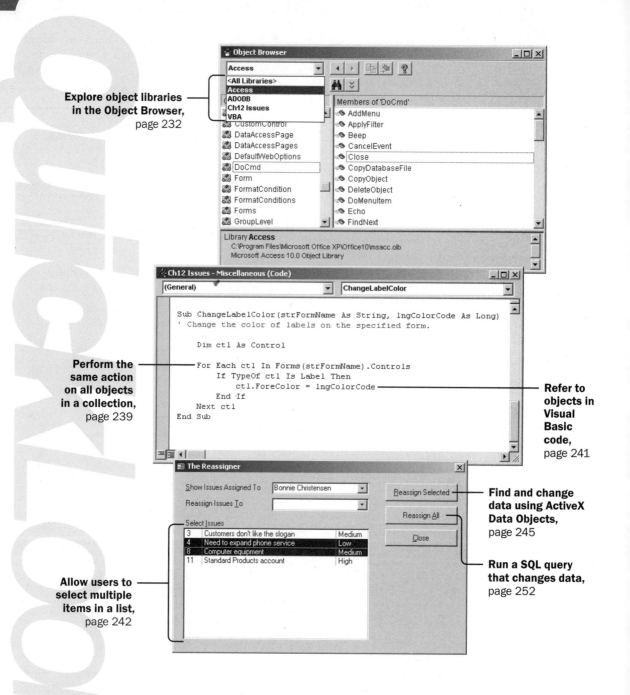

Explore object libraries in the Object Browser, page 232

Perform the same action on all objects in a collection, page 239

Refer to objects in Visual Basic code, page 241

Allow users to select multiple items in a list, page 242

Find and change data using ActiveX Data Objects, page 245

Run a SQL query that changes data, page 252

Chapter 12
Explore Objects and Collections

After completing this chapter, you will be able to:

✔ Understand object references in Microsoft Visual Basic code.

✔ Perform the same action on all objects in a collection.

✔ Create a list box that allows users to select multiple items from the list.

✔ Open a *Recordset* object and change data in selected records.

✔ Use a *Connection* object in code to run a SQL query that changes data.

Looking at the packaging, I see that the noodles I'm planning to cook for dinner tonight are made from semolina flour—the only ingredient. Modern science tells me that this flour is itself made up of many distinct bits called molecules. The molecules, in turn, are composed of atoms, and those, in turn, of still smaller particles. Fortunately, I don't need to understand any of this in order to cook my pasta! On the other hand, if I worked in a food-testing laboratory and wanted to understand precisely how the noodles would behave when cooked, I would need to know what was happening below the surface. I imagine I'd need to consult my chemistry books pretty thoroughly before I could predict how the molecules and atoms would react.

Like chemistry, Microsoft Access admits many different levels of understanding. An Access user editing data, for example, won't usually need to know what's going on behind the scenes. But as an application developer, you'll need a better grasp of the underlying mechanism that makes Access tick. Like a periodic table of chemical elements, the object model of Access is a complex framework of objects that makes it all work—and as you increase your understanding of this foundation, you'll be able to create more powerful applications.

In this chapter, you'll discover the framework of objects and collections underlying every Access application. You'll learn how to use objects to control forms and data in powerful new ways—and along the way, you'll uncover many of the fundamental principles on which Access is built. Although we'll only scratch the surface of the complexities underlying Access, the understanding you'll gain should lay the foundation for any further exploration you do on your own.

This chapter uses the practice file Ch12 Issues.mdb that you installed from the book's CD-ROM. For details about installing the practice files, see "Using the Book's CD-ROM" at the beginning of this book.

Getting Started

● Start Access, and open the Ch12 Issues database in the practice files folder.

   A dialog box appears, introducing the Issues database application, which you'll work with throughout Part 4 of this book.

Introducing the Issues Application

The practice database file you've opened is a useful Access application for tracking issues in a workgroup. The fact that several users can open a database at one time over a network makes Access an ideal environment for creating *workgroup applications*—systems designed to help people work together better in a networked office environment. The Issues application is an example of such a system: it allows users to keep track of open business issues interactively, assigning them to the appropriate employees and querying the database to find out which issues need follow-up.

Sign In to the Issues Application

When you first open the Issues application, a dialog box appears asking you to enter your name. This dialog box is a startup form created using the same technique you used in Chapter 11 for the Subscription application.

The dialog box requires you to "log in" to the Issues application (saving your name for later use) and then opens another form that shows open business issues stored in the database. As the user of the Issues application, your first step is to sign in.

1   In the combo box, click Bonnie Christensen.

   The dialog box has two command buttons, both of which open a form called *Issues*. One of them displays issues for all employees; the other filters issues for employees who want to see only the issues currently assigned to them.

2   Click the Show All Issues button.

   The button's *Click* event procedure opens the *Issues* form, which displays the first issue in the database. Here, you can browse through current issues, assign them to other employees, or make comments concerning them.

The *Issues* form lets users track the status of business issues...

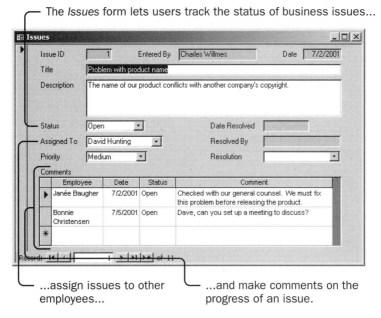

...assign issues to other employees...

...and make comments on the progress of an issue.

The *Issues* form is nearly complete as it stands—you won't have to add much to it. The form already has several event procedures that make it an effective tool for tracking business problems and items that employees need to act on. In this chapter and the remaining chapters of the book, you'll explore some of these features and add some of your own capabilities to this custom application.

Tip

On your own, you may want to browse the Visual Basic code that makes up the application—it uses many of the techniques you've already learned in previous chapters, combining them in new ways. To do this, open the *Issues* form in Design view and then explore its form module.

Open the Miscellaneous Module

Although you'll be seeing more of the *Issues* form, you'll put it aside for now to explore some general principles of Access. Before getting started, you'll need to open a standard module stored in the Issues database.

Database Window

1 Click the Database Window button on the toolbar.

2 Click the Modules shortcut.

3 Double-click the Miscellaneous module.

Visual Basic opens and displays the Declarations section and first procedures of the module.

You'll notice one *Public* statement in the Declarations section of the module—it declares a variable called *lngCurrentEmpID*. Remember the dialog box that asked for your name in the previous procedure? This variable stores the ID number of the employee name entered in the opening dialog box, and because the variable is declared as *Public*, it is available throughout the application, whenever you need to know who the current user is.

Understanding Objects and Collections

Believe it or not, all the Visual Basic code you've written to this point fits into a logical framework called an *object model*. The object model is a hierarchy of all the items you use in an application—forms and their controls, tables and their fields, controls and their properties. Here, for example, is part of the graphical representation of the Access object model provided in online Help.

Many of the objects in Access contain collections of other objects, creating a complex hierarchy.

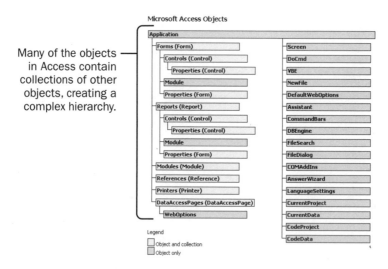

In this section, you'll explore parts of the object model and write some simple Visual Basic code that demonstrates how it works. Then as the chapter continues, you'll explore some practical uses for powerful objects that you haven't yet worked with.

Try Out the Object Browser

So far, you've tried out several of the Visual Basic tools at your disposal. But there's one more handy tool you've yet to try—the Object Browser. The Object Browser is a dialog box that lists all the objects available to your application, shows you how they're related, and allows you to consult online Help about each of them.

Object Browser

1 Click the Object Browser button on the toolbar.

The Object Browser appears.

2 Drag the lower right corner of the Object Browser window to make it a bit larger.

3 Click the down arrow next to the Project/Library combo box (the one that contains the text "<All Libraries>") to display the list.

To shorten the list of objects in the Object Browser,
select the object library you want to browse.

This list includes the object libraries and databases that Visual Basic is aware of. Just about everything you type in code or refer to in an expression—objects, fields, methods, properties, functions, and other items—belongs to one or another of these groups. You'll need to know about the following four object libraries:

- **Access** The Access object library contains the objects, methods, and constants you use to control the user interface of your application, such as forms, reports, and controls. This library also includes the familiar *DoCmd* object and its methods.

- **ADODB** The Microsoft ActiveX Data Objects (ADO) library contains the objects, methods, and constants you use to work directly with database files and the data stored in them.

- **Ch12 Issues** Your application itself is an object library. It contains the forms, reports, and modules of the database, along with their controls, properties, and procedures. Because Visual Basic keeps track of your application's objects in the same way it keeps track of its built-in objects, you can refer to them in code—use a function in a module, for example—just as you would refer to those belonging to the Access or VBA libraries.

- **VBA** The Visual Basic for Applications (VBA) object library contains all the Visual Basic functions and constants you're used to seeing, such as the *MsgBox* function.

Using the Object Browser, you can explore each of these object libraries. In this chapter, you'll learn to work with a few important objects in the Access and ADODB libraries; most of these techniques will apply to other types of objects as well.

Tip

The Projects/Libraries combo box won't always contain the same entries. If you add object libraries to your Visual Basic project using the References command, as described in Chapter 10, Visual Basic will include their objects in the Object Browser. For example, in a project that contains a reference to the Data Access Objects (DAO) library, the Projects/Libraries list would include DAO.

4 In the list, click Ch12 Issues.

In the Classes list on the left, the Object Browser displays the forms, reports, and modules contained in the Issues application. The Classes list also includes an entry for *globals*, items that are available throughout your application.

5 Click Messages in the Classes list.

When you click an entry, the members of that class—its properties, methods (*Sub* and *Function* procedures), and constants—are displayed in the Members list on the right. Each type of member has a different icon so that you can more easily distinguish between them.

Select a class, such as this module in the issues application...

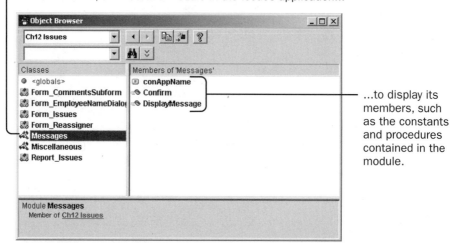

...to display its members, such as the constants and procedures contained in the module.

As you can see, the Messages module has as its members one constant, *conAppName*, and two procedures, *Confirm* and *DisplayMessage*. You may recognize these names as the procedures you created in Chapter 5, which have been copied to the Issues application.

6 Click *Confirm* in the Members list.

The bottom pane of the Object Browser displays information about the *Confirm* function, such as its arguments and the type of data it returns.

Tip

If you see a procedure or constant you're interested in, double-click its name in the Object Browser. Visual Basic jumps directly to the code that defines that object and displays it in a Code window.

Switch to the Access Object Model

If your applications have many modules and procedures, you may find that the Object Browser provides an easy way to take inventory of their contents. But you'll probably find it most useful for exploring the large object models of Access, ADO, and VBA.

1 In the Project/Library combo box, click Access.

The Object Browser displays the object classes that belong to Access. The "<globals>" entry, which is selected by default, is an interesting place to start. Most of the members of this group are constants, some of which you've used in previous chapters to specify arguments in code. However, if you scroll down far enough, near the end you'll begin to see methods, such as *RunCommand* and *SetOption*, and properties, such as MenuBar and Visible.

2   Scroll down in the Classes list and click *DoCmd*.

This part of the Classes list contains more familiar objects in Access. Here you can see *ComboBox*, *CommandButton*, and *Form*, all objects you've used quite a bit. With *DoCmd* selected, the Members list displays all the methods of the *DoCmd* object, many of which you've seen in previous chapters.

3   Click Close in the Members list.

Object classes in the Access hierarchy

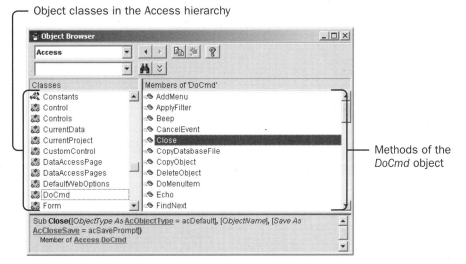

Methods of the *DoCmd* object

Just as when you viewed items in the Issues application, the bottom pane of the Object Browser displays information about the item you select. In this case, the Object Browser displays the arguments you use with the *Close* method.

Use the Object Browser to Get Online Help

Next you'll take a look at the Form class, one of the most fundamental classes in the Access hierarchy. You'll then jump directly from the Object Browser to online Help about the object you're viewing.

1   In the Classes list box, click Form

The Members list on the right displays properties and events belonging to forms—you'll recognize the *AfterUpdate* event and the AllowEdits property, among others. If you scroll down in the list, you'll see some form methods you've used in previous chapters, such as *GoToPage*, *Refresh*, and *Requery*.

2   In the Members list, click Controls.

Controls is the name of a collection of objects. Every form has this collection, and it contains—you guessed it—the controls included on that form.

The Help button in the upper portion of the window (the one with a question mark icon) gives you a handy way to get online Help about the selected item. For Access objects, as you'll see, using online Help is one of the best ways to explore the object model.

3 Click the Help button in the Object Browser (the one with the question mark).

The Help topic for the *Controls* collection appears in a separate window. It provides lots of information about how you can use the collection and includes a jump to a Visual Basic code example. The topic also displays a graphical representation of the portion of the object model that the collection belongs to, which you can use to navigate to other Help topics.

Object model graphic

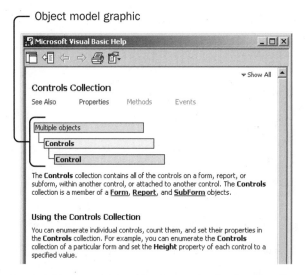

As the object model graphic shows, the *Application* object is at the top of the hierarchy, then further down is the *Controls* collection, which in turn contains individual *Control* objects. The Multiple Objects box indicates that a variety of objects have a *Controls* collection—as the text just under the diagram explains, the *Form* and *Report* objects are among them.

4 Close the Help window.

5 Close the Object Browser window.

Other Handy Features of the Object Browser

In addition to showing you available objects and allowing you to jump to online Help, the Object Browser has the following features you might want to use:

■ If you see text in the Object Browser that you'd like to paste into your Visual Basic code—a method or constant name, for example—you can copy it to the Clipboard using the Object Browser's Copy button. You can even select text that's in the bottom pane of the window, such as the syntax line you see when you select a method in the

Members list. After you copy the text, switch to the Code window and choose the Paste command.

■ You can search for text in an entire object library, or in all available libraries. This is useful if you can't remember where a keyword fits into the object model. Type any part of the name you're looking for in the Search Text box (just underneath the Library/Project box at the top of the Object Browser), and then click the Search button (the one with binoculars).

■ The VBA and Access object libraries have a Constants class, which includes all the built-in constants available in that object library. Other libraries, such as ADODB, include their constants in the Global class. You may also notice that some libraries also have constants grouped into special classes, called *Enum* classes. Because you often use constant values in your code, the Object Browser is a handy place to find out which ones are available, and is especially useful if you can't remember how to spell a constant name.

Referring to Objects and Collections

In earlier chapters, you used plenty of objects—and you learned how to refer to them in your code. For example, you referred to the *Contacts* form in Part 1 using the expression *Forms!Contacts*, and to the *ContactID* control on that form using the expression *Forms!Contacts!ContactID*. In fact, most of the object references you'll use in your code will be fairly simple ones like these. Still, because you use them so often, it's important for you to understand more completely how object references work. And as you'll see later in this chapter, not all expressions that include objects are as simple as those you've used up to this point.

When referring to objects in a collection, such as the *Forms* collection, you can use several alternative forms of reference. One way is to refer to objects by number. Objects in any collection are numbered consecutively starting with 0, so you can refer to an object by placing this number in parentheses. For example, the first form object in the *Forms* collection is *Forms(0)*, the second is *Forms(1)*, and so on. But there are several other ways to refer to a member of a collection—by name, for example, or by using the exclamation point (!) operator. Each of these methods follows slightly different rules.

Rather than reading about them, perhaps the best way to understand these types of references is to try them out. In this section, you'll experiment with several types of object references using the Immediate window.

Try Out Object References in the Immediate Window

1 If the Debug toolbar isn't displayed, point to Toolbars on the View menu and click Debug.

Immediate Window

2 Click the Immediate Window button on the toolbar.

3 Type **?Forms.Count**, and press the Enter key.

The Immediate window displays 1, the number of forms in the *Forms* collection. The one form that's open in Access is the *Issues* form.

The first object in a collection is object number 0, and you can refer to it that way. Let's see what the name of the form is by referring to the Name property.

4   Replace the top line in the Immediate window with **?Forms(0).Name** and press Enter. (You don't have to retype the entire line, just edit the existing line of text.)

The Immediate window displays *Issues*, the name of the first form in the *Forms* collection.

To refer to a member of a collection by name, you can substitute a string value for the object's number—for example, you can use *Forms("Issues")* to refer to the *Issues* form. Let's use the ActiveControl property of the *Forms* collection to see which control on the *Issues* form is currently active.

5   Replace the top line with **?Forms("Issues").ActiveControl.Name**, and press Enter.

The Immediate window displays *Title*, the name of the field that got the focus when you first opened the *Issues* form.

Note that the technique of placing a string in parentheses after a collection has another important use: if you've stored an object's name in a string variable, you can use this same syntax to refer to it. For example, if the name of the form you wanted to use above had been stored in a variable called *strFormName*, you could use the expression *Forms(strFormName).ActiveControl.Name* to refer to the active control on that form.

Of course, if you know the name of a form, you can just put it after the exclamation point operator as you've done in the past. Next, let's try a reference to the *Controls* collection, a collection that every form and report object has. To refer to any collection, follow the object that it belongs to—its *parent* object—with a period, and then type the name of the collection. In the next example, *Forms!Issues* is the parent object, while *Controls* is the collection that belongs to it.

6   Replace the top line with **?Forms!Issues.Controls.Count**, and press Enter.

The Immediate window displays 24, the number of controls on the *Issues* form.

Next, you'll refer to the value of the third object in the *Controls* collection, the *Title* control.

7   Replace the top line with **?Forms!Issues.Controls(2)**, and press Enter.

Because control number 2 on the *Issues* form is the Title text box, the Immediate window displays the title of the issue currently displayed on the *Issues* form. The reference you used is equivalent to saying *Forms!Issues.Controls("Title")*. It's also equivalent to saying *Forms!Issues!Title*, the method of reference you're most familiar with. That's because *Controls* is the default collection for any form object. When you use the exclamation point, Access assumes that what follows is a member of the default *Controls* collection.

Next you'll refer to the subform on the *Issues* form. To do this, you refer to the subform control, *Forms!Issues!Comments*. Because you want to refer to properties of the subform that the *Issues* form is displaying rather than to the subform control itself, you'll follow the control reference with the Form property—and then follow that with the property whose value you want.

8 Replace the top line with **?Forms!Issues!Comments.Form.Name**, and press Enter.

The Immediate window displays *CommentsSubform*, the name of the actual form stored in the Issues database.

There's one exception to the rule that for subforms you must use the Form property to refer to the form. If you want to refer to a control on a subform, you can leave out the *Form* keyword—it makes the reference a bit shorter.

9 Replace the top line with **?Forms!Issues!Comments!Comment**, and press Enter.

The Immediate window displays the text of the first comment shown in the subform. This expression says, "In the *Comments* control on the *Issues* form, what is the value of the Comment field?"

10 Close the Immediate window.

Referring to objects and their properties requires some experimentation. Before you write code that uses a new type of expression, it's a good idea to use the Immediate window to test your syntax. If you don't get the value you want, or if Visual Basic displays an error when you enter the reference, consult online Help for examples of expressions that use the type of object you're interested in.

Now that you've discovered some of the ways you can refer to collections and the objects they contain, you're ready to write some code that uses them. In the next section, you'll see object references in action and learn techniques for storing objects in variables so that you can perform actions using the objects.

Using the *For Each* Statement with a Collection

The objects in a collection share many properties and characteristics, so you'll typically want to perform the same actions on each object in a collection. For example, you might want to change a specific property, such as the color of text, for every control on a form. When you want to run the same block of code for every object in a collection, you surround the block of code with the *For Each* and *Next* statements.

Write a Procedure That Sets Control Properties

To see how the *For Each* statement works, you'll write a procedure that changes the Fore-Color property—the color of the text—for every label on the *Issues* form. You'll create the new procedure, called *ChangeLabelColor*, in the Miscellaneous module. The Code window still shows the Declarations section, which already contains three lines of code. You'll begin entering code for the new procedure underneath the existing *Public* statement.

1 In the Code window, scroll down to the end of the Miscellaneous module, and click underneath the final *End Function* statement to position the insertion point.

2 Type the following code, including the *Sub* header line. (When you type the *Sub* statement, Access enters the *End Sub* line for you automatically.)

```
Sub ChangeLabelColor(strFormName As String, lngColorCode As Long)
' Change the color of labels on the specified form.
```

```
Dim ctl As Control

For Each ctl In Forms(strFormName).Controls
    If TypeOf ctl Is Label Then
        ctl.ForeColor = lngColorCode
    End If
Next ctl
End Sub
```

Here's what this code does:

- The *Sub* procedure head declares two arguments: *strFormName*, which stores the name of the form you want to change labels on, and *lngColorCode*, which stores the code number for the color you want to change labels to. The *lngColorCode* argument uses the long integer data type, because the ForeColor property accepts this type of value.

- The *Dim* line in the procedure declares an object variable. When you want to perform actions on objects, such as tables, forms, or controls, you can store references to them, just as you would store another type of value in a variable. This variable has the data type *Control*, which can store only a control-type object.

- The next statement begins a *loop*, a mechanism for repeating a section of code several times. This loop uses the *For Each* and *Next* statements—one of several types of loops in Visual Basic—which allow the procedure to perform the same set of actions for every control on the form. At the end of any *For Each* statement, after the *In* keyword, is the name of a collection that you want to step through, in this case, the *Controls* collection on the form whose name is stored in the *strFormName* variable. The *In* keyword is always preceded by a variable, in this case *ctl*, that stores each object in the collection as the code steps through it.

- When you use this procedure with the *Issues* form, the block of code between the *For Each* and *Next* statements will run 24 times, once for each control on the form. Each time it runs, the variable *ctl* will represent a different control on the *Issues* form.

- The *If...Then* block inside the loop checks to see whether the current control is a label. To do this, it uses the *TypeOf* keyword, which allows you to check the type of control stored in a variable. If the control isn't a *Label*, the code continues on to the *Next* statement, doing nothing.

- If the current control is a *Label*, the line in the middle runs, setting the ForeColor property of the control to the value you passed to the procedure by the *lngColorCode* argument.

- The *Next* statement includes *ctl*, the variable that gets incremented each time through the loop. You can think of this statement as saying, "We're finished with that control, move on to the next one please." When Visual Basic finishes running the block of code for every control in the collection, the procedure ends.

Save

3 Click the Save button on the toolbar.

4 Close the Miscellaneous module's Code window.

Run the Procedure from the Immediate Window

Now you can change all the label controls on your form in one step by running your procedure from the Immediate window.

1 Click the Immediate Window button on the Debug toolbar.

2 On a new line in the Immediate window, type **ChangeLabelColor "Issues", vbBlue**, and press Enter.

Your procedure runs, changing the foreground color of each label control on the *Issues* form to blue. (The intrinsic constant *vbBlue* provides the correct color code for blue, so you don't have to know it.)

3 Switch to Access.

As you can see, the labels on the *Issues* form are now blue.

4 Switch back to Visual Basic.

5 Replace the second line in the Immediate window with **ChangeLabelColor "Issues", vbBlack**, and press Enter.

6 Switch to Access.

The labels are back in black.

This type of procedure is useful for giving users the capability of customizing forms while your application is running. In the next section, you'll use some of these same tools— object variables and the *For Each* statement—to add powerful features to the Issues application.

Using a Multiple-Selection List Box

So far, you've used list boxes that allow users to select a single item. As you'll see, you can also create a list box that allows more than one item to be selected at a time. The practice database already includes a form that has a multiple-selection list box. The form, called *Reassigner*, is a dialog box form designed to allow users to reassign one or more issues to another employee. Unlike a normal list box, a multiple-selection list box requires you to write some extra code to access the selected items. In the rest of this chapter, you'll add code to the *Reassigner* form to make it work.

To cause a list box to allow multiple selections, you set its MultiSelect property. The property has three settings: *None, Simple,* and *Extended*. If the property is set to *None*, users can select only one item at a time; if it's set to *Simple*, users can select multiple items by clicking them; if it's set to *Extended*, users can select multiple items by holding down the Shift and Ctrl keys while clicking items. The list box you'll work with on the *Reassigner* form has its MultiSelect property set to *Simple*.

Open the *Reassigner* Form

Before you add any code to the *Reassigner* form, let's see how it works so far. To open it, you'll use a menu command located on the *Issues* form's custom menu bar.

1 On the Tools menu, click Reassign Issues.

The *Reassigner* form opens.

2 In the Show Issues Assigned To combo box, click Bonnie Christensen.

The list box on the form shows the four issues currently assigned to that employee.

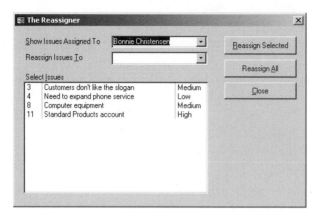

Try Out the Multiple-Selection List Box

With any list box you've used before in this book, each time you click an item, the previous item is deselected—the list box has just one value at a time. In this list box, however, you can select more than one value.

1 Click issue number 4 in the list (the second item), and then click issue number 8 (the third item).

When a list box has just one value, you can just refer to the list box itself to access the value—for example, because the list box control is named *IssueList*, the expression *Forms!Reassigner!IssueList* would return the ID number of the selected issue. When using a multiple-selection list box, by contrast, you find out which items are selected by referring to a collection called *ItemsSelected*. You can see how this works in the Immediate window.

2 Switch to Visual Basic.

To refer to the items in the list, you'll have to use a pretty complex expression. Don't worry, though, it's really quite similar to references you're already accustomed to.

3 On a new line in the Immediate window, type **?Forms!Reassigner!IssueList.ItemsSelected.Count**, and press Enter.

To follow the expression, read it from right to left—it asks for the number of items in the *ItemsSelected* collection of the *IssueList* control on the *Reassigner* form. The Immediate window displays 2, the number of items you selected in the list box.

```
Immediate
   24
Title
Issues
   1
ChangeLabelColor "Issues", vbBlack
?Forms!Reassigner!IssueList.ItemsSelected.Count
   2
```

Next you'll try out expressions that tell you what the selected items are. The *ItemsSelected* collection actually stores numbers corresponding to the position of the selected item in the list. Like items in the collection, the positions in the list are numbered starting with 0, so the first item has position 0, the second position 1, and so on. Therefore, the first item number is stored in *ItemsSelected(0)*, the second item number in *ItemsSelected(1)*, and so on.

4 Replace the line with **?Forms!Reassigner!IssueList.ItemsSelected(0)**, and press Enter.

The Immediate window displays 1, the position of the first item you selected. (You selected the second item in the list, which is position number 1.) You might expect the *ItemsSelected* collection to contain the actual values of the selected items, but it doesn't—it contains only their positions in the list. To find out the value of each selected item, in this case, the *IssueID* for each issue, you have to use the *ItemData* method, supplying the item position number you just found out.

5 Replace the line with **?Forms!Reassigner!IssueList.ItemData(1)**, and press Enter.

The Immediate window displays 4, which is, at long last, the *IssueID* of the first issue you selected.

6 Close the Immediate window.

Although the process of finding out what's selected in a list box is complicated, it's worth the effort to tap into the power of a multiple-selection list box. In the next section, you'll add code that makes this list box work, using the list box concepts you just learned to change data in the issues the user has selected.

Working Directly with Database Objects

When users change data in a form that's bound to a query or table—the *Issues* form, for example—Access automatically makes the changes in the underlying tables. So far, you've allowed Access to do most of this work behind the scenes. However, when you need to take more control over what gets changed in your database, you can work directly with data by writing code that uses one of the two database object libraries provided with Access: the Data Access Objects (DAO) library and the ActiveX Data Objects (ADO) library. In Chapters 7 and 8, you used the DAO *Recordset* object to add and find records in a database. In this section, you'll use ADO code to make the *Reassigner* form do its work. As you'll see, the actual name of the object library file that provides most ADO functionality is "ADODB"—so that's what you will type in your code.

The *Reassigner* form has two command buttons whose event procedures aren't yet complete: Reassign Selected and Reassign All. When a user clicks the Reassign Selected button, you want to open the *Issues* table and update only the records the user has selected in the list box. To do this, you'll use a *Recordset* object. When a user clicks the Reassign All button, you want to update every record in the *Issues* table that has a certain *AssignedTo* value. To do this you'll run an action query. To perform these two operations in code, you'll need to learn new techniques for working with objects.

DAO and ADO: Why Two Database Object Models?

As if database programming weren't already complex enough with one set of standards, Access now provides two standards for working directly with data. The Data Access Objects (DAO) library, inherited from previous versions of Access, was designed specifically for use with the Access database engine (also known as the "Jet" database engine). The ActiveX Data Objects (ADO) library, by contrast, is designed to be more generic in order to support any database that Access can connect to.

It's important to be aware of which object model you're using in your code, because the objects, properties, and methods you use differ between the two models. Which of these object libraries you're using in a database is determined by the object library reference in the Visual Basic project for the database. New databases you create with Access have a reference to the ADO library. On the other hand, if you upgrade a database from a previous version of Access or create a database with the Database Wizard, its project will automatically contain a reference to the DAO object library. In any case, you can specify the libraries you want to use in the References dialog box (as described in Chapter 10). If you include a reference to both object libraries, you can even use both in the same application, defining recordsets in your code with the *DAO.Recordset* and *ADODB.Recordset* object types.

How should you decide which model to use? All other considerations aside, the ADO model is somewhat simpler than DAO. Also, you should use ADO to work with databases stored in Microsoft SQL Server or the Microsoft Data Engine—the additional database engine supplied with Microsoft Office XP and used by Access Data Project (.adp) files. On the other hand, if you want to write code that makes changes to the structure (such as fields and properties) of tables and queries in a Jet (.mdb) database, you should use DAO. Additionally, the recordset that Access uses for forms—the one that is returned by the RecordsetClone property you used in Chapter 8, for example—is a DAO *Recordset* object, so you must use DAO if you want to work with recordsets behind forms.

The following diagram shows the top-level objects in the two database object models. The DAO hierarchy's first layer starts with the *DBEngine* object, which represents the underlying Access database engine. The *DBEngine* object has a *Workspaces* collection, which in turn has a *Databases* collection, which in turn has many other collections, and so on down the line. The ADO hierarchy cuts to the chase a bit more quickly. It starts with the *Connection* object, which is similar to the DAO *Database* object, but can represent a connection to any database engine.

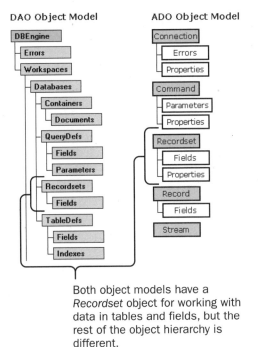

Both object models have a
Recordset object for working with
data in tables and fields, but the
rest of the object hierarchy is
different.

Overwhelming? Start becoming familiar with ADO by completing the steps in the following sections. Then you can use the Object Browser in combination with online Help to learn more about DAO and ADO objects and the capabilities they provide.

Finding and Changing Data in a Recordset

Your first task is to add code for the Reassign Selected button. Whenever a user clicks this button, the application needs to open the *Issues* table, move to each selected record, and change the value of the AssignedTo field for that issue to another employee's ID number: the one the user chooses in the NewAssignee combo box.

When you want to change a record in a table directly using ADO, you first open a *Recordset* object. Next you move to the record you want to change. If the recordset is based on a table in an Access database, such as the *Issues* table, the fastest way to do this is to use the *Seek* method. Then you actually make the change, using the *Update* method after you set the values of the fields you want to change. In this section, you'll add code that will go through this process for each record the user selects in the IssueList list box.

Edit the *Click* Event Procedure for the Reassign Selected Button

The Reassign Selected button already has an event procedure—it's just missing the code that actually reassigns the issues to other employees. Since you're already in Visual Basic, you can use the Project window to open the *Reassigner* form's module.

1 In the Visual Basic Project window (in the upper left corner of the Visual Basic window), double-click Form_Reassigner.

Visual Basic opens the form module for the *Reassigner* form. As you saw before, the *Reassigner* form is nearly complete. It even has code that keeps the *IssuesList* control synchronized with the currently selected employee. Now it's time to add the final touches to the *Click* event procedure for the Reassign Selected button.

2 Click the arrow next to the Code window's Object box—the box is at the upper left of the Code window and should display "(General)"—and then click ReassignSelected.

The Code window jumps to the *ReassignSelected_Click* procedure. As you can see, the procedure already contains several lines of code.

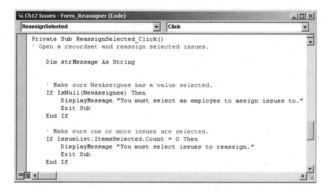

The code that's already present does several things:

- The *Dim* statement declares a variable used later in the procedure to store the text of a message.

- The first block of code checks that the *NewAssignee* combo box has a value in it—otherwise, you wouldn't know which user to reassign issues to. If the combo box is blank, the procedure displays a message and exits.

- The second block of code makes sure that at least one issue is selected in the list—to do this, it checks the Count property of the *ItemsSelected* collection for the list box, just as you did earlier in the chapter.

- Next, the procedure confirms that the user wants to reassign the selected issues. To do this, the procedure calls the *Confirm* function you wrote in Chapter 5—that function is included in this database as well.

- If the user does confirm the operation, the next line of code uses the *Hourglass* method of the *DoCmd* object to display the hourglass cursor while your code changes records. Whenever you run code that might cause a delay, you can use this technique to let the user know your code is working.

■ The last block of code is designed to run after your code finishes reassigning issues, to update what's displayed in the dialog box before the procedure ends. For example, the first line sets the value of the AssignedTo combo box to the ID of the employee you just assigned issues to, and the third line requeries the list box to show the new set of issues. This way, the user can easily see that all changes have taken place.

To complete the procedure, you'll add code in two places: near the top of the procedure you'll declare three variables that your code will use, and near the bottom you'll add the code that changes selected records.

3 Click underneath the *Dim* statement in the procedure, and then enter the following lines of code:

```
Dim cnn As Connection
Dim rstIssues As New ADODB.Recordset
Dim varPosition As Variant
```

These *Dim* statements declare three variables.

■ The *cnn* variable will represent a connection to the current database.

■ The *rstIssues* variable will store a reference to the *Issues* table so that you can change data in it. Using the *New* keyword when declaring this variable tells Visual Basic to actually create the *Recordset* object, not just allocate memory space for it. You should always use the *New* keyword when declaring an ADO recordset, because the *Open* method that you'll use to open a table or query requires that the *Recordset* object already exists.

Note that in the data type declaration, you've preceded the *Recordset* type with the ADODB object library name and a period. Although specifying the object library here isn't strictly necessary (because the Issues project has an object library reference to ADO and not to DAO), it is always a good idea to do so. Otherwise, in a project that uses both the ADO and DAO libraries, you could encounter errors if your code creates the wrong type of recordset.

■ The *varPosition* variable will store the position of each item selected in the list, so you can get hold of the actual ID value for each selected issue. This variable has the Variant data type, because this is the type of value used to store the position number in the *ItemsSelected* collection.

4 Scroll down in the window, click the blank area underneath the *DoCmd.Hourglass True* statement, and then enter the following code:

```
' Open a recordset object in the current database.
Set cnn = CurrentProject.Connection
rstIssues.Open "Issues", cnn, adOpenKeyset, adLockOptimistic, _
    adCmdTableDirect

' Begin a transaction before changing data.
cnn.BeginTrans

' Set the Index property to search on the primary key.
rstIssues.Index = "IssueID"
```

```
' Loop through each selected issue in the list.
For Each varPosition In IssueList.ItemsSelected

    ' Find the record in the Issues table.
    rstIssues.Seek IssueList.ItemData(varPosition)

    ' Change the AssignedTo value in the table.
    rstIssues!AssignedTo = NewAssignee
    rstIssues.Update

Next varPosition

' Save all changes for this transaction.
cnn.CommitTrans
```

Let's walk through this code line by line—it introduces several new concepts.

■ The first line of code uses the Connection property of the *CurrentProject* object to store a reference to the current database, which is required in order to open a table in code. Remember, whenever you set the value of an object variable—as opposed to an ordinary variable, such as a string—you must use the *Set* statement.

■ The second line uses the *Open* method of the *Recordset* object to open the *Issues* table using the recordset you created in the variable *rstIssues*. The first argument to the *Open* method specifies the table or query you want to open. The second argument provides the database connection you want ADO to use, in this case the current database connection which you stored in the *cnn* variable.

■ The next three arguments to the *Open* method use ADO constants to specify the type of recordset you want to open. The third argument, *adOpenKeyset*, causes ADO to request a *dynaset* from Access, a type of recordset that you can make changes to. The fourth argument, *adLockOptimistic*, tells ADO that you want to use *optimistic record locking* if multiple users try to edit data at the same time, which means that records are locked for a minimum amount of time while your code changes them. The final argument, *adCmdTableDirect*, tells ADO that you want a table-type recordset. It's important that you open a table-type recordset, because later code in the procedure uses the *Seek* method, which is allowed only on tables.

■ The next line uses the *BeginTrans* method of the *Connection* object to open a *transaction*. A transaction is a group of changes that you want Access to treat as a single operation. Opening a transaction tells Access to keep track of changes you make, but to wait until you close the transaction to save them on disk. Later, you'll close the transaction using the *CommitTrans* method.

Using a transaction for multiple changes to data has two advantages: first, it can speed up your code, because you access the disk drive or network only once, rather than each time you change a record; second, you'll never end up with partially changed records—if an error occurs before all the changes have been made, you don't have to save the transaction. (To cancel changes made in a transaction, you use the *RollbackTrans* method.)

■ Before you can use the *Seek* method to locate records in a table, you have to set the Index property for the recordset, which tells ADO which field you want to search. The next line sets the Index property to the IssueID field, the primary key of the *Issues* table. The field or fields you designate for searching must either be the primary key of the table or else have an index. Because the field has an index, the search will be very fast.

■ The next line uses the *For Each* statement you learned about in the previous section. In this procedure, you want to update every issue that's selected in the list. Because you'll locate and change records one at a time, you need to run the block of code once for each item in the *ItemsSelected* collection of the list box. This statement says, "Run the following block of code once for each item in the *ItemsSelected* collection of the *IssueList* control, each time storing the position of the selected item in the *varPosition* variable."

■ The four lines of code you'll loop through for each selected issue must locate the issue in the recordset and then change its *AssignedTo* value. The first of these lines uses the *Seek* method to move to the selected record.

■ The *Seek* method takes an argument that tells Access what value to look for. As you saw earlier in this chapter, the way to refer to the value of the selected item in a list is to use the *ItemData* method of the list box control. This argument tells Access to search for the *IssueID* value that's at the current position—stored in the *varPosition* variable—in the *IssueList* control. After this line of code runs, the current record in the *rstIssues* recordset will be the record for one of the issues selected in the list.

■ The next two lines actually reassign the issue by replacing the value in the record's *AssignedTo* field with the value of the *NewAssignee* combo box on the form. After you've finished setting values of one or more fields in the recordset, you complete the change by using the *Update* method.

■ The *Next* statement tells Access to repeat the *For Each* block of code for the next item in the list. After the block of code has run for each selected item, the procedure will continue running from this point.

■ The final line of code you entered uses the *CommitTrans* method of the *Connection* object. This method tells the database engine to save all the changes you made since the beginning of the transaction in this procedure.

5 On the Debug menu, click Compile Ch12 Issues.

If the procedure has any typographical errors, compiling will bring them to light so that you can fix them before trying to run the code.

Try Out the *ReassignSelected_Click* Procedure

Now you're ready to test the procedure by clicking the Reassign Selected button in the dialog box.

View Microsoft Access

1 Switch to Access.

In the dialog box, issue number 4 and issue number 8 are still selected, ready to be reassigned to another employee.

2 In the Reassign Issues To combo box, click Charles Willmes.

3 Click the Reassign Selected button, and then click OK when the procedure asks you to confirm that you want to reassign the selected issues.

Your code runs, opening the *Issues* recordset, cycling through the two records you selected, and changing their *AssignedTo* values in the *Issues* table. When the procedure finishes, the list box displays the issues that changed hands, but now they belong to a different employee, Charles Willmes.

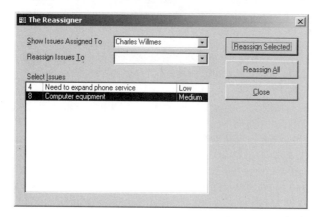

Creating and Running an Action Query

The first command button on the Reassigner dialog box is now complete. The second one, however, still needs some work. This button, labeled Reassign All, is there so that users can reassign all issues, rather than selected issues, from one employee to another. In this section, you'll add the code to do this.

The technique you used to reassign selected issues—opening a recordset, and then locating and changing each record—is perfect for reassigning a few individual issues. On the other hand, when you want to change values in a whole group of records, changing each record individually isn't the most efficient way. To modify a group of records most efficiently, you use an *action query*. With an action query, you can update, add, or delete many records in a single step.

Normally, you use the Access query window to create an action query. However, you can also run queries in your code by using the ADO *Execute* method. To make the Reassign All button do its work, you'll write code that runs a query, changing the values in the *AssignedTo* field for all records in the *Issues* table from one employee's ID to another.

Edit the *Click* Event Procedure for the Reassign All Button

Just like the Reassign Selected button, the Reassign All button already has an event procedure—it's just missing the code that actually reassigns issues. You'll add code that creates and runs an action query to update records.

1 Switch to Visual Basic.

2 In the Code window's Object box, click ReassignAll.

The Code window displays the *ReassignAll_Click* procedure. As you can see, the procedure already contains several lines of code. The code that's there is nearly the same as the code in the *ReassignSelected_Click* procedure: it makes sure the user has selected employees to assign issues to and from, asks the user to confirm the reassignment, and then displays the hourglass cursor.

To complete the procedure, you'll add a line near the top to declare variables, and then you'll add the code that actually runs the query to change data.

3 Click underneath the *Dim* statement in the procedure, and then enter the following line of code:

```
Dim cnn As Connection
```

As before, you'll use the *cnn* variable to represent a connection to the current database.

4 Click the blank area underneath the *DoCmd.Hourglass True* statement and enter the following code:

```
' Execute an UPDATE query to reassign issues.
Set cnn = CurrentProject.Connection
cnn.Execute "UPDATE Issues SET AssignedTo = " & _
    NewAssignee & " WHERE AssignedTo = " & AssignedTo
```

Important

Be sure you put spaces before and after quotation marks, exactly as shown in the code. Otherwise, you may encounter an error when you try to run it.

Here's what this code does:

- The first line you added uses the Connection property of the *CurrentProject* object to store a reference to the current database.

- The second line uses the *Execute* method of the Connection object to create and run a SQL query. When the line runs, ADO will ask Access to execute the query, just as if you were to run an action query from the query window. Using the UPDATE statement tells Access that you want it to change values in existing records. As you can see, this line of code concatenates several items to produce the SQL statement. This code could be typed as one line, but here it's broken up using the underscore (_) character to make it easier to see in the Code window.

The string you create for the SQL property setting combines the SQL text itself with the values of two fields on the *Reassigner* form: the AssignedTo field and the NewAssignee field. When the code runs, Visual Basic will combine all this text to produce a single string that defines the action query. For example, the complete string might look like this:

```
UPDATE Issues SET AssignedTo = 14 WHERE AssignedTo = 20
```

If you ran this particular query, Access would find all records in the *Issues* table that were assigned to employee 20 and reassign them to employee 14.

5 On the Debug menu, click Compile Ch12 Issues.

6 Close Visual Basic.

Handling Errors in ADO Code

For the sake of simplicity, the procedure you worked with in this chapter doesn't contain error-handling code. However, any time you use ADO or DAO to change records, you should definitely include error-handling code in the procedure. Errors can occur for many reasons when your code changes records, and without error-handling code, your application could end abruptly with a run-time error. For example, suppose another user is changing data at the same time your code is running. The records you're trying to update might be locked, causing an error.

To handle these types of errors, you would add an *On Error GoTo* statement at the top of the procedure and then include error-handling code at the end of the procedure; it's similar to the technique you used in Chapter 7. In the error-handling code, you might want to check which error occurred, and if records are locked, give the user the option to resave them. In any case, if you aren't able to update records as expected, your procedure should exit gracefully, displaying a message telling the user about the problem. If you do decide to exit the procedure, you may want to include the *RollbackTrans* method of the *Connection* object, which undoes any changes made since you started the transaction using the *BeginTrans* method—this way, records won't be partially updated, which could confuse the user.

Try Out the *ReassignAll_Click* Procedure

Now you're ready to test the procedure. You're already looking at the two issues you previously assigned to Charles Willmes. You just need to select an employee to reassign them to and click the button.

1 In the Reassign Issues To box, click Bonnie Christensen.

2 Click the Reassign All button, and then click OK when the procedure asks you to confirm the reassignment.

Your code runs, running the action query for the employee values you selected. When it finishes, the list box displays Bonnie Christensen's issues—and as you can see, all four issues belong to her as they did at the beginning of the chapter, which is just what you want.

The *Connection* and *Recordset* objects you've learned to use in this chapter are perhaps the most common ADO objects for working directly with databases. However, they are just the tip of the iceberg. Fortunately, most of the techniques you've learned in this chapter will apply to any work you do with objects and collections. Just remember that by working directly with objects in your code, you can accomplish practically anything Access does on its own—and even more.

Using Structured Query Language

When defining the action query in this section, you'll use the Access query language, called *Structured Query Language*, or SQL. You've probably already noticed examples of SQL statements in the property sheet—SQL is commonly used in the RecordSource and RowSource settings of your forms, combo boxes, and list boxes. When you use wizards to create objects, they frequently set these properties to an appropriate SQL statement. On the *Reassigner* form, for example, the AssignedTo combo box was created using the Combo Box Wizard. The wizard set the RowSource property for the combo box to the following SQL statement:

```
SELECT DISTINCTROW Employees.EmployeeID, Employees.EmployeeName
FROM Employees
ORDER BY Employees.EmployeeName;
```

This statement tells Access to retrieve ("select") the values of two fields—EmployeeID and EmployeeName—from every record in the *Employees* table, sorting the records by name. In your Access applications, you can substitute a SQL statement just about anywhere that the name of a table or query is called for. Additionally, as you'll see in this section, you can build queries in your code using SQL.

To learn SQL, you might want to browse the many SQL topics in online Help. Additionally, there's a handy technique you can use to help you learn SQL. Queries you create using the Query Design window—including action queries—have a SQL view maintained automatically by Access. To see the SQL statement corresponding to any query in Design view, just click SQL on the View menu. You can even copy this SQL text into your ADO code.

Chapter Wrap-Up

1 Click the Close button, clicking Yes when Access asks if you want to save changes.

2 On the File menu, click Exit.

Respond to events as Access formats and prints each section of a report, page 258

Calculate totals while a report is printing, page 264

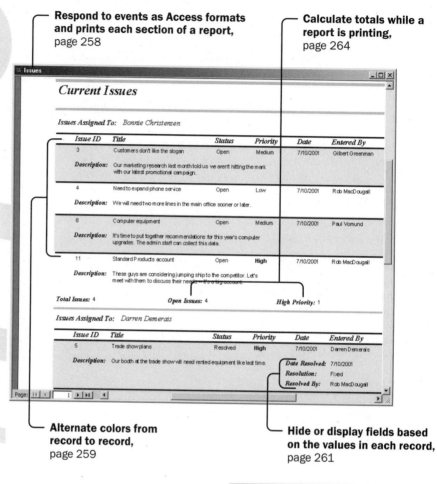

Alternate colors from record to record, page 259

Hide or display fields based on the values in each record, page 261

Add items to a list box, page 270

Chapter 13
Customize Reports with Visual Basic

After completing this chapter, you will be able to:

✔ **Respond to events that occur in reports.**

✔ **Change the formatting of individual fields and records as a report prints.**

✔ **Calculate totals while a report is running.**

✔ **Add items to a list box.**

✔ **Change printer settings before printing a report.**

When you're learning a whole new subject, such as database programming, it's easy to lose the forest for the trees: picking up lots of details but forgetting the main purpose your applications will serve. And as your experience increases, there's still a tendency to spend lots of time adding frills to an application while losing track of its primary purpose. Let's face it—for all the complexities involved in working with databases, the whole endeavor comes down to two basic activities: getting data into the database, and getting data back out.

So far, you've spent lots of energy on ways to get data into forms and work with it easily. In this chapter, you'll turn your attention to one of the primary ways to get data *out* of a Microsoft Access database: by printing it in reports. You'll team up the built-in reporting tools with your own Microsoft Visual Basic procedures to customize and enhance an application's reports—and you'll learn techniques for taking control of exactly what prints on the page.

Ch13
Issues.mdb

This chapter uses the practice file Ch13 Issues.mdb that you installed from the book's CD-ROM. For details about installing the practice files, see "Using the Book's CD-ROM" at the beginning of this book.

Getting Started

● Start Access, and open the Ch13 Issues database in the practice files folder.

Using Standard Reporting Features

Access reports are extremely powerful tools for presenting information, regardless of whether you write any Visual Basic code for them. You can use the Report Wizard to create many complex types of reports for grouping or summarizing information—or, by designing your own custom reports, you can accomplish almost anything you'll need in your applications. Before you write any code, be sure to explore the powerful features built into reports, such as grouping and totaling, automatic growing and shrinking of sections, and flexible page numbering, just to name a few. The Issues report included in the practice database shows off some of these features.

Preview the Issues Report

Before you begin customizing the Issues report, let's take a look at what's already there. As you'll see, the report prints all the open issues in the database, grouped by the employee they're assigned to.

1   In the Database window, click the Reports shortcut.

2   Double-click the Issues report.

    The Issues report appears in Print Preview.

    The Issues report is based on a query called *IssuesForReport*, which combines information from several tables. The report was initially created using the Report Wizard, and then rearranged and polished a bit in Report Design view.

3   Click on the report to zoom in.

4   Using the vertical scroll bar on the report window (not the Microsoft Access scroll bar), scroll down a bit to view additional issues on the page.

    The report groups all the issues assigned to each employee—in this case, the first group of issues belongs to Bonnie Christensen. The report also displays the total number of issues for each group at the bottom of the employee's section.

    The following illustration points out several features of the Issues report.

High-priority value displays in bold text because of conditional formatting applied to field.

Issue records are grouped by employee, with headers repeated for each group of issues.

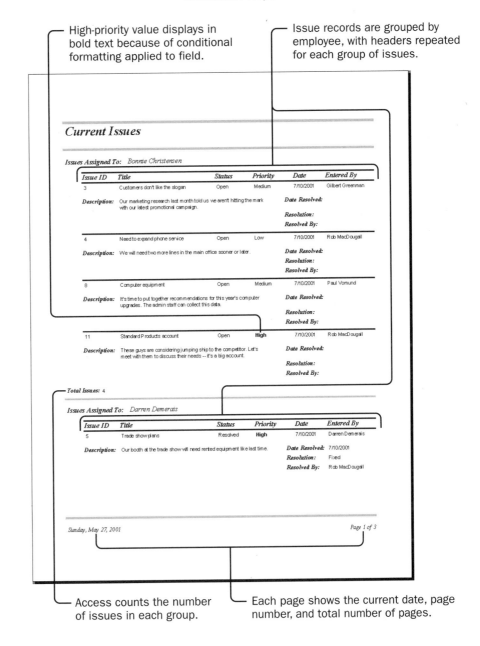

Current Issues

Issues Assigned To: *Bonnie Christensen*

Issue ID	Title	Status	Priority	Date	Entered By
3	Customers don't like the slogan	Open	Medium	7/10/2001	Gilbert Greenman

Description: Our marketing research last month told us we aren't hitting the mark with our latest promotional campaign.

Date Resolved:
Resolution:
Resolved By:

4	Need to expand phone service	Open	Low	7/10/2001	Rob MacDougall

Description: We will need two more lines in the main office sooner or later.

Date Resolved:
Resolution:
Resolved By:

8	Computer equipment	Open	Medium	7/10/2001	Paul Vomund

Description: It's time to put together recommendations for this year's computer upgrades. The admin staff can collect this data.

Date Resolved:
Resolution:
Resolved By:

11	Standard Products account	Open	**High**	7/10/2001	Rob MacDougall

Description: These guys are considering jumping ship to the competitor. Let's meet with them to discuss their needs -- it's a big account.

Date Resolved:
Resolution:
Resolved By:

Total Issues: 4

Issues Assigned To: *Darren Demerais*

Issue ID	Title	Status	Priority	Date	Entered By
5	Trade show plans	Resolved	**High**	7/10/2001	Darren Demerais

Description: Our booth at the trade show will need rented equipment like last time.

Date Resolved: 7/10/2001
Resolution: Fixed
Resolved By: Rob MacDougall

Sunday, May 27, 2001

Page 1 of 3

Access counts the number of issues in each group.

Each page shows the current date, page number, and total number of pages.

All the elements you see on the Issues report as it exists in the practice file—grouping of data, automatic totals, and conditional formatting, for example—are standard features of reports that don't require any code. And this is just the beginning of what you can do in your reports.

In some cases, you won't be able to accomplish what you want using standard reporting features alone. For example, if you want to make changes to the section layout or formatting depending on the data that appears in any given record, no standard mechanism will get the job done—it will take some creative intervention on your part. In the following sections, you'll start adding features to this report that require a bit of Visual Basic code.

Responding to Report Events

When you want to accomplish something in your reports that isn't possible using standard reporting features, you'll be happy to know that you can control nearly everything about your reports by writing Visual Basic code. Programming reports is very similar to programming forms: reports have events you can respond to with Visual Basic event procedures. But the event model for reports is a bit trickier, because users don't actually interact with reports, as they do with forms. Instead, report events occur at certain points during the report printing process—the time between when you tell Access to preview or print a report and when it arrives on the screen or at the printer—and you can write Visual Basic code to change the outcome of this process.

Here are the two types of report events you'll commonly respond to, along with typical reasons for using them.

General report events Several events apply to a report as a whole. Some of these will be familiar to you from programming with forms, such as the *Open* event, which you can use to perform actions when the user first asks to preview or print the report. Two other useful report events are the *NoData* event, which allows you to intervene if the record source of the report turns out to have no records, and the *Page* event, which gives you a chance to run code once for each page. You might use the *Page* event to draw a border around every page, for example.

Events for each report section The most interesting events are those that occur one or more times for each section in the report, including the report header and footer, page header and footer, group headers and footers, and of course the Detail section, where individual records appear. The two most important section events are the *Format* event, which occurs just before Access lays out each section of the report, and the *Print* event, which occurs after page layout is complete but before printing actually occurs. During these events, you have access to the data in the record being formatted or printed—and as you'll see, this gives you the opportunity to make changes based on what's about to print.

In this chapter, you'll write event procedures that respond to the *Format* and *Print* events, customizing the Issues report that's included in the practice database. Although you'll try only a few of the many techniques for controlling report output, you'll learn the fundamental concepts you need for customizing reports.

Customizing Reports by Setting Properties at Run Time

You can determine the look of the formatting on your reports to a great extent by setting properties for controls and sections. And using conditional formatting, you can even make values in your report appear differently from record to record automatically. But what if you want a section to print differently for each record? For example, suppose you want the background color of issues records to alternate so that you can distinguish records more easily. You need a way to change the properties for the Detail section while the report is printing.

This is where event procedures come in. By responding to the *Print* event for the report's Detail section, which occurs just before each record is printed, you can change the section to display the way you want it to. Your code will change the BackColor property of the Detail section before each record prints.

Make the Detail Section Alternate Between White and Gray

When you work with an event procedure in a report, it's important to make sure you associate it with the appropriate section in the report. In this case, you'll select the Detail section of the Issues report, because you want your code to run for every detail record—every single issue printed in the report.

1 On the View menu, click Design View.

The report switches to Design view.

In order to create an event procedure for the Detail section, you'll first view event properties for that section in the property sheet.

2 Double-click the Detail section bar.

Access displays the property sheet for the Detail section.

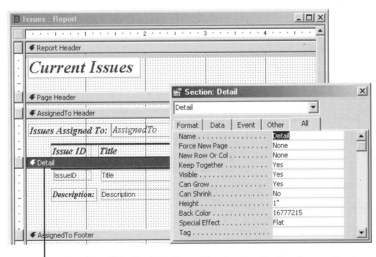

Double-click the Detail section bar to display the section's properties.

3 In the property sheet, click the Event tab, click the OnPrint property, and then click the Build button.

4 Double-click Code Builder.

Visual Basic opens the *Issues* report's module and displays the *Detail_Print* event procedure.

5 Add the following code to the event procedure:

```
Private Sub Detail_Print(Cancel As Integer, PrintCount As Integer)
' Alternate section background between white and light gray.

    Const conLtGray = 15263976

    If Detail.BackColor = conLtGray Then
        Detail.BackColor = vbWhite
    Else
        Detail.BackColor = conLtGray
    End If

End Sub
```

Here's what this code does:

■ At the beginning of the procedure, the *Const* statement declares a constant for the color light gray. You won't need to declare a constant for white because there's a built-in Visual Basic constant *vbWhite*.

■ The *If...Then* statement checks to see if the BackColor property of the Detail section is already gray or not.

■ If the section is gray, the next line sets the BackColor property to the color code for white. Otherwise, the *Else* clause sets the BackColor property to the color code for gray.

This code will run every time Access prepares to print data for an issue in the report. If you print the complete report, which currently contains 11 issues, the procedure will run 11 times.

Preview the Report

View Microsoft Access

Let's preview the report again and see how it works now.

1 Switch to Access.

2 Click the Print Preview button on the toolbar.

Print Preview

Although it happens so quickly you'll doubt it happens at all, Access runs your event procedure once for every single issue record on the page, allowing your code to set the Detail section's BackColor property separately for each one.

3 Scroll down a bit in the Report window to view additional records.

Records alternate gray and white backgrounds.

Changing Report Layout Programmatically

The *Print* event procedure is a good place to perform most types of actions on a report section, because it occurs for every record in the section. Beware, however: when the *Print* event occurs, Access has already laid out all the elements of the section to be printed, so it's too late to make any changes to the layout of the section. For example, if your code performs actions that affect the current section by changing how many records fit on a page, the *Print* event won't work. If you want to perform actions that affect the layout of a section, you should attach the code to the *Format* event instead.

In the Issues report, you probably noticed the three labels at the right side of each issue record. Although most issue records in the report don't have any values for these fields (because the issues themselves aren't resolved), these labels appear in every record of the Detail section. To cause them not to display except when the current issue is resolved, you can write an event procedure. And because the changes you'll make in your code *will* affect the layout of the section, you'll add this code to the *Format* event procedure of the Detail section, rather than to its *Print* event procedure.

Add Code That Hides the Labels of Unresolved Fields

To show or hide controls, you set their Visible property. If you do this for the resolution fields in the *Format* event procedure, Access will take into account whether the controls are to be shown when laying out the section.

1 On the toolbar, click the Close button.

The report returns to Design view.

2 In the property sheet, click the OnFormat property, and then click the Build button.

3 Double-click Code Builder.

Access displays the *Detail_Format* event procedure.

4 Add the following code to the event procedure:

```
Private Sub Detail_Format(Cancel As Integer, FormatCount As Integer)
' When formatting each issue record, display the labels for
' the resolution fields only if the issue is resolved.

    Dim blnResolved As Boolean

    ' Determine whether the DateResolved field has a value.
    blnResolved = Not IsNull(DateResolved)

    ' Set the Visible property for the three labels.
    DateResolvedLabel.Visible = blnResolved
    ResolutionLabel.Visible = blnResolved
    ResolvedByLabel.Visible = blnResolved

End Sub
```

Here's what this code does:

■ The procedure uses a Boolean variable, called *blnResolved*, to record whether the current issue record is resolved. The second statement sets the variable to *True* or *False* based on the expression *Not IsNull(DateResolved)*, which refers to the *DateResolved* field in the Detail section of the report. If the *DateResolved* field contains a date—if it doesn't contain a null value—*blnResolved* gets set to *True*.

■ The next three lines of code use the *blnResolved* value—which is *True* if the resolution fields should appear, *False* if they shouldn't—to set the Visible property for the three labels.

This procedure will run each time Access starts to lay out a record on the page—at least once and potentially several times for each record in the report. Because most issues aren't resolved, it will make these labels invisible in most cases.

Set Properties to Shrink the Detail Section as Appropriate

By default, Access leaves space for fields on a report—even if they're blank—so even when the resolution labels on the *Issues* report are invisible, there will be extra space for them in every record on the report. Fortunately, Access provides the CanShrink property to correct this situation automatically. By setting this property to *True* for the three text boxes and for the Detail section itself, you'll tell Access to "shrink" these fields whenever they're empty, effectively making sure they don't take any space at all.

View Microsoft
Access

1   Switch back to Access.

2   In the property sheet, click the Format tab, and then set the Detail section's CanShrink property to *Yes*.

3   At the right side of the Detail section, select the three text boxes that display resolution information. (Click one of the text boxes, and then hold down the Shift key while clicking the other two. Be sure to select only the text box controls, not their labels.)

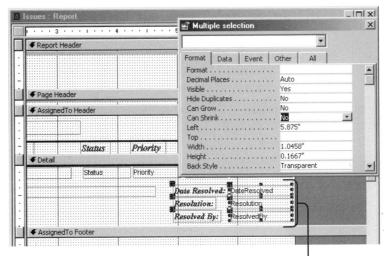

Select these three text boxes so that you can set properties for all of them at once.

4   In the property sheet, set the CanShrink property to *Yes*.

Preview the Report

Print Preview

1   Click the Print Preview button on the toolbar.

Again, your code runs for every issue on the page—first the *Detail_Format* procedure runs several times as Access lays out each record on the page, and then the *Detail_Print* procedure runs as it prints each record. Your newest event procedure makes the three labels invisible in most issue records, because only a few issues have been resolved.

You'll notice that the first page of the report now fits several more issues than before, because it no longer displays empty fields for issues that aren't resolved. By scrolling down in the report, you can verify that the three text boxes do still appear for any issue that is resolved.

2   Scroll down in the window to display the fifth record on the page—the first issue in the second group. (If necessary, scroll to the right a bit to display the resolution fields.)

The three resolution fields appear only once on the page, for the one issue that's currently resolved.

For unresolved issues, the Detail section shrinks to fit only fields that contain data.

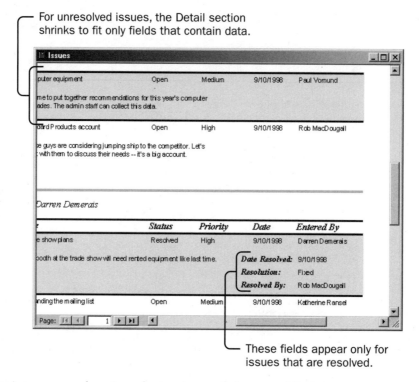

These fields appear only for issues that are resolved.

You've now seen how to make two types of changes while Access prepares your report for printing: changes both before and after the section is formatted. But your changes so far have been limited to setting properties for controls in the section. Although these common types of changes can be very powerful, it's only the beginning—you can also perform calculations, set control values, and even combine various event procedures throughout the report to achieve the results you want. In the next section, you'll use a simple example of these techniques to improve on the Issues report.

Calculating Totals While a Report Is Printing

One standard feature of reports is the ability to calculate totals—the sum or average of values, for example—for all the records in a section or in the entire report. The Report Wizard often sets up such totaling fields for you. You can also add them yourself by placing a text box in a group footer or report footer section and setting its ControlSource property to the appropriate expression. The Issues report has just such a control in the group footer section for each employee: the *TotalIssues* control calculates the "count" or number of issues assigned to that employee.

Although standard totals can perform a wide variety of operations for your reports, you may also want to perform your own calculations using Visual Basic. A common reason for doing this is to include totals for a group of records other than the standard grouping in a report. For example, in addition to the total for each group, you might want to display a running total on the current page of the report. To accomplish this, you would have to keep track of the running total in code while Access prints the report. At the appropriate points, you would put the running total into a text box control on the report.

Another similar reason for calculating totals yourself is to break down the values in a way that the default report grouping cannot. The Issues report, for example, groups issue records by the employee they're assigned to. But suppose you want to display the number of open issues or high-priority issues at the end of each employee's section. In other words, you want the report to summarize by saying, "This employee has four issues, three of which are open and one of which is high priority." There's no simple way to ask for these values in an expression—you have to write Visual Basic code to count the issues yourself. In this section, you'll add code in event procedures that calculates these totals and displays them for each employee in two text boxes in the group footer.

Create Text Boxes to Display Section Totals

To print the results of calculations you perform in a report's event procedures, you need to put unbound controls on the report to contain them. You'll create two text boxes for the group footer section of the Issues report, one to show the number of open issues each employee has, and another to show the number of high-priority issues.

1 On the toolbar, click the Close button.

The report returns to Design view.

2 If you can't see the AssignedTo Footer section of the report, scroll down in the window to display it.

In this group footer section, you'll notice the *TotalIssues* control, which demonstrates the standard method for showing section totals. The control source expression for the control, *=Count([IssueID])*, tells Access to count the number of records in the section that contain an *IssueID* value.

Text Box

ab|

3 In the toolbox, click the Text Box tool.

4 Click the AssignedTo Footer section of the report, to the right of the TotalIssues field and near the center of the report.

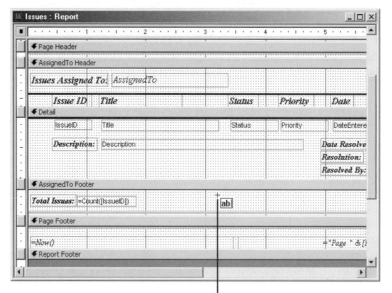

Click here to create the text box.

An unbound text box appears on the report. Its label shows a default name (something like Text55). To make it easier to refer to in code, you'll enter a new name for the control.

5 In the property sheet, click the Other tab, and then set the Name property to **OpenIssues**.

You also need to change the label to the left of the text box.

6 Click the label for the new text box to select it.

7 Change the control's label: double-click the text in the label, and then type **Open Issues** to replace the existing text.

This finishes the OpenIssues text box, which you'll use to display the number of open issues for each employee's section of the report. Next, you'll create a second unbound text box to the right of the one you just finished.

8 In the toolbox, click the Text Box tool, and then click the AssignedTo Footer section between the OpenIssues text box and the right edge of the report.

Another unbound text box appears in the footer section.

9 In the property sheet, set the Name property to **HighPriority**.

10 Change the control's label to **High Priority**.

11 If necessary, drag the two text boxes to position them evenly across the AssignedTo Footer section of the report.

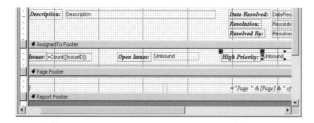

Add Code That Increments the OpenIssues and HighPriority Fields

As an employee's issue records print, you want your code to count the number of open and high-priority issues. You could keep track of the count in either of two ways: by storing the totals in variables you declare, or by placing them in the two unbound text boxes themselves. Here you'll use the latter method (the simpler of the two). Each time the report prints an open or high-priority issue, you'll increment the value of one or both of the text boxes you created. You can do this in response to the *Print* event, which occurs just before each issue is printed.

Additionally, you'll need to reset the values of these fields each time you begin a new employee's section—otherwise, the code would create a cumulative total, adding the new issues onto those of the previous employees. To reset these fields to *0*, you'll add code to the AssignedTo Header section's *Print* event procedure, which occurs just before each employee's section begins printing.

1 Click the AssignedTo Header section bar.

2 In the property sheet, click the Event tab, click the OnPrint property, and then click the Build button.

3 Double-click Code Builder.

Visual Basic displays the report's *GroupHeader0_Print* procedure. Access will run this procedure each time it's about to print the AssignedTo header for another employee.

4 Add the following code to the procedure:

```
' Reset the totals boxes in the footer for each employee.

    OpenIssues = 0
    HighPriority = 0
```

This code sets the values of both of the unbound text boxes you created to *0*, because at the beginning of each section an employee has no issues. As Access progresses through the report, of course, these numbers may change. That will be up to the *Detail_Print* event procedure, your next stop. The *Detail_Print* event procedure already contains the code you added earlier in the chapter.

5 Scroll up in the Code window to show the *Detail_Print* event procedure, click just above the *End Sub* statement, and then enter the following code:

```
' Increment total fields if issue is open or high priority.
If PrintCount = 1 Then
    If Status = "Open" Then
        OpenIssues = OpenIssues + 1
    End If
    If Priority = "High" Then
        HighPriority = HighPriority + 1
    End If
End If
```

This code will keep track of the open and high priority issues while the report is printing. While the code is simple, it illustrates a couple of key concepts. Here's how it works:

- The *Print* event usually occurs only once for each section printed in a report. In certain cases, however, it can occur more than once, such as when the Detail section spans two pages. For this reason, the *Print* event procedure has an argument called *PrintCount*, which can tell you whether the event is occurring for the first time. Because you wouldn't want to count any records twice, the code uses an *If...Then* statement, running the rest of the code in the procedure only if *PrintCount* is 1—in other words, only the first time the procedure runs for a given issue.

- The rest of the code consists of two nearly identical *If...Then* blocks. The first block checks whether the current issue record is open—whether the Status field contains the value *Open*—and increments the value shown in the *OpenIssues* control by 1 if the issue is open. The second block does the same for high-priority issues, incrementing the value of the *HighPriority* control by 1 if the Priority field contains the value *High*.

As you see here, when you want to increment a value in Visual Basic, you follow the control or variable name with an equal sign and then with the expression that calculates the new value. The first of these statements, for example, can be read as: "Set the value of the OpenIssues field to its existing value plus 1."

After this code runs for a given record, the OpenIssues field will contain the number of open issues printed so far, and the HighPriority field will contain the number of high-priority issues printed so far. By the time the group footer section prints, these fields will contain their final values, which are what will appear on the report.

6 On the Debug menu, click Compile 13 Issues.

Preview the Report

View Microsoft Access

Print Preview

You're ready to try the report and see how your totals work.

1 Switch back to Access.

2 Click the Print Preview button on the toolbar.

Now that you've added even more code, all sorts of things are happening when you preview or print the report! When Access gets ready to print the header section for each employee that has open issues, the *GroupHeader0_Print* procedure runs, setting the unbound fields to 0. Then the *Detail_Print* procedure runs for every issue record. By the time the footer section for an employee prints, the text boxes should contain the correct values. Then, when Access moves on to the next employee's section, your code again resets the text boxes to 0.

3 If necessary, scroll down in the window to display the footer section for Bonnie Christensen, and then the one for Darren Demarais.

As you can see, the text boxes you created now display the correct totals.

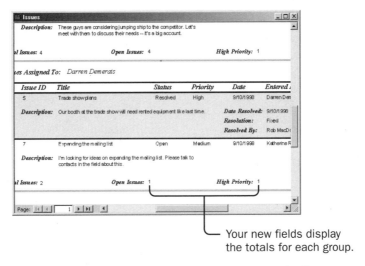

Your new fields display
the totals for each group.

4 Close the report window, clicking Yes when Access asks if you want to save changes.

Advanced Control of Section Printing and Placement

The report changes you made using code in this chapter had a very practical effect on the way the Issues report prints. But even though your code set a few properties and values, it didn't significantly change the course of the report—it more or less assumed that the report would print along to completion, including every record and section in its turn. Because you may want to change which sections print and where, Access provides run-time report properties and event procedure arguments that allow your code to affect the printing process.

The simplest technique for controlling whether a section prints is setting the *Cancel* argument for the *Print* event procedure. If you determine in your code that you don't want to print a given section at all, you can set the *Cancel* argument in the procedure to *True*, and Access won't print the section. For example, in the Issues report, you might want to exclude issues that belong to the employee who's currently logged in. To do this, you'd write code to cancel printing of sections in which the AssignedTo field contains that employee's ID number.

For finer control over which sections print and where, you can use three run-time properties: MoveLayout, NextRecord, and PrintSection. All of these properties are normally set to *True* for every section and record. By setting them to *False* in your code, you can change how the report prints.

Controlling Printer Settings

One of the advantages of Microsoft Windows is the way it manages a great variety of printers so that software developers don't have to. Through the magic of a *printer driver*—system software that tells Windows how to control a given printer—Access and other programs can print to just about any printer. Generally speaking, this means you don't have to concern yourself with printers in your Access application. Windows keeps track of printer settings automatically, and unless users make changes, your Access application prints using default settings.

In some cases, however, you might want to control printer settings directly using Visual Basic code. For example, you might want to select a specific printer, change a report's margins, or print more than one copy. To control print settings, you can set properties of the *Printer* object and the *Printers* collection. Through the *Printers* collection, you can view properties of all the printers installed on the users system; and using the *Printer* object associated with each Access form or report, you can modify print settings for the form or report.

In this section, you'll write event procedures for the *PrintIssues* form, a dialog box form included in the practice application. In this form, users can select a printer for the *Issues* report and specify a number of copies to print. To make the form work, you'll need to write two event procedures—one to fill the list box with printer names, the other to set printer properties and preview the report when users click the OK button.

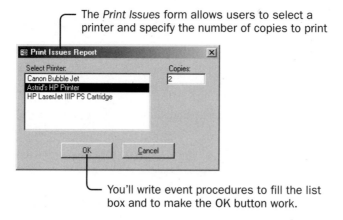

The *Print Issues* form allows users to select a printer and specify the number of copies to print

You'll write event procedures to fill the list box and to make the OK button work.

Add Code That Fills the List Box with Installed Printer Names

Although you've used many list boxes and combo boxes in earlier chapters, they have all derived their contents from tables or queries—because their RowSourceType property has been set to *Table/Query*, Access has filled these lists automatically from the table or query indicated by the RowSource property. In the *PrintIssues* form, you'll use a different strategy: the RowSourceType property of its list box is set to *Value List*, and you'll fill the list one item at a time using the *AddItem* method.

1 In the Database window, click the Forms shortcut.

2 Click the *PrintIssues* form, and then click the Design button.

Each time the form opens, you need to fill the PrinterList list box with currently installed printers; otherwise, the list will be empty. To do this, you'll write a procedure for the form's Open event.

3 In the property sheet, click the Event tab, click the OnOpen property, and then click the Build button.

4 Double-click Code Builder.

Visual Basic opens the *PrintIssues* form's module.

5 Add the following code to the *Form_Open* event procedure:

```
Private Sub Form_Open(Cancel As Integer)
' Add all printer names to the PrinterList list box.

    Dim prn As Printer

    For Each prn In Application.Printers
        PrinterList.AddItem prn.DeviceName
    Next prn
End Sub
```

This code starts by declaring a variable with the *Printer* data type—a special data type for referring to an installed printer. It then uses the *For Each* statement to loop through the *Printers* collection of the *Application* object, temporarily storing each *Printer* object in the variable *prn*.

The one line inside the *For Each...Next* loop runs once for each installed printer. It uses the *AddItem* method of the *PrinterList* control to add the printer's name to the list box. To access the printer's name, it uses the DeviceName property of the *Printer* object. When the event procedure finishes, all installed printer names are shown in the list box.

Add Code That Changes Printer Settings for the Issues Report

When users click the OK button in the *PrintIssues* form, you want to specify a printer, set its properties, and then preview the report so it is ready to print. To do this, you'll write an event procedure for the button's *Click* event.

1 Switch back to Access.

2 On the *PrintIssues* form, right-click the OK button, and then click Build Event on the shortcut menu.

3 Double-click Code Builder.

Visual Basic displays the *OK_Click* event procedure.

4 Enter the following code for the event procedure:

```
Private Sub OK_Click()
' Preview the Issues report using the selected settings.

    Dim prn As Printer

    ' Open the report in Design view to make changes.
    DoCmd.OpenReport "Issues", acViewDesign
    If IsNull(PrinterList) Then
        Reports!Issues.UseDefaultPrinter = True
    Else
        ' Figure out which printer the user selected, then
        ' tell the Issues report to use that printer.
        For Each prn In Application.Printers
            If prn.DeviceName = PrinterList Then
```

271

```
                    Set Reports!Issues.Printer = prn
                    Exit For
            End If
        Next prn
    End If

    ' Set the number of copies.
    Reports!Issues.Printer.Copies = CInt(PrintCopies)

    ' Close this form and preview the report.
    DoCmd.Close acForm, "PrintIssues"
    DoCmd.OpenReport "Issues", acViewPreview
End Sub
```

Here's what the code does:

- The first line declares a variable called *prn* with the Printer data type.

- The *DoCmd* line uses the *OpenReport* method to open the Issues report in Design view so you can change its associated printer.

Important

You might expect to open the report in Print Preview to set its printer properties; unfortunately, this won't work. To change the printer for a form or report, your code should always open the form or report in Design *view*. Then, once the printer settings are ready, you can use the *Open-Form* or *OpenReport* method of the *DoCmd* object to preview or print as in the code shown here.

- The *If…Then* statement checks whether the PrinterList list box has a selection. If the user didn't specifically select a printer, the next line sets the report's UseDefault-Printer property to *True*. This causes the report to print using the Windows default printer, even if it has previously been formatted for another printer.

- If the list box does have a value, the *Else* block sets the printer for the report. To do this, it uses a *For…Each* loop to work its way through the *Printers* collection until it finds a printer with the device name the user selected. When it does, it uses the *Set* statement to change the *Issues* report's associated *Printer* object to the one currently stored in the *prn* variable. Finally, the *Exit For* statement allows the procedure to skip past the *Next* statement after finding the selected printer.

- The next line sets the Copies property of the *Printer* object—the one you just associated with the Issues report. (You can't set properties for printers in the *Printers* collection, only for the *Printer* object associated with a form or report.) Because the Copies property setting must be an integer, while the PrintCopies text box contains a string, the line uses the *CInt* function to convert the text box value to an Integer data type.

- With the printer settings complete, the last two lines close the *PrintIssues* dialog box and then switch the Issues report from Design view into Print Preview. (If you wanted the OK button to actually print the report, you would use the *acViewNormal* constant in place of *acViewPreview*.)

5 On the Debug menu, click Compile Ch13 Issues.

6 Close Visual Basic.

7 Close the form, clicking Yes when Access asks whether you want to save changes.

Try the *PrintIssues* form

The *PrintIssues* form is ready for action.

1 In the Database window, double-click the *PrintIssues* form.

When the form opens, your code fills the list box with all the printers installed on your Windows system.

2 In the Select Printer list box, select a printer (preferably one other than the default system printer, so you can verify that your code changes printers).

3 Type **2** in the Copies box.

4 Click OK.

Your code runs, setting properties for the *Printer* object, then opening the Issues report in Print Preview.

5 On the File menu, click Print.

The settings shown in the Print dialog box confirm that your code did in fact change the printer properties for the report. As you can see, when you change print settings in Visual Basic, Access uses them just as if the user had made them manually in the standard Page Setup or Print dialog boxes.

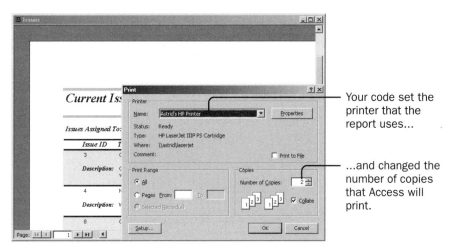

Your code set the printer that the report uses...

...and changed the number of copies that Access will print.

6 Click Cancel. (Or, if you want to test your print settings directly by printing the report, click OK.)

Chapter Wrap-Up

1 Close the report window.

2 On the File menu, click Exit.

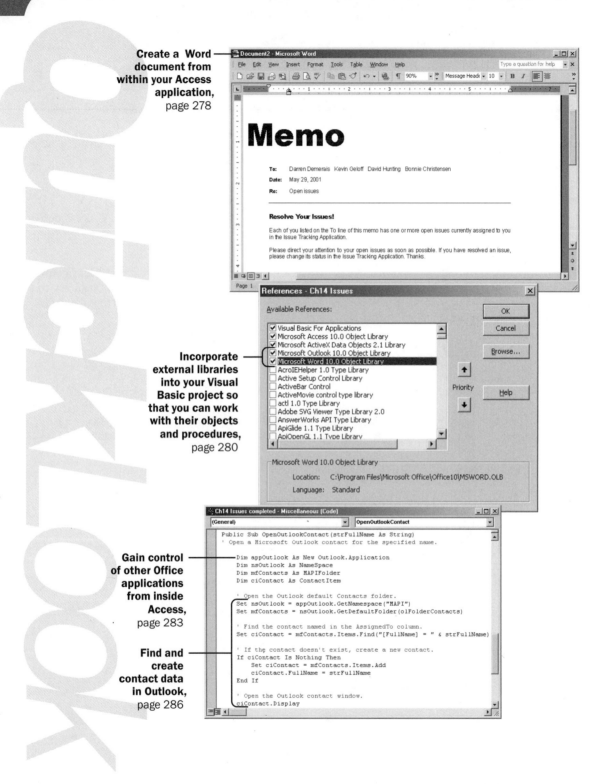

Create a Word document from within your Access application, page 278

Incorporate external libraries into your Visual Basic project so that you can work with their objects and procedures, page 280

Gain control of other Office applications from inside Access, page 283

Find and create contact data in Outlook, page 286

Document2 - Microsoft Word

File Edit View Insert Format Tools Table Window Help

Type a question for help

Memo

To: Darren Demerais   Kevin Geloff   David Hunting   Bonnie Christensen

Date: May 29, 2001

Re: Open issues

_____

Resolve Your Issues!

Each of you listed on the To line of this memo has one or more open issues currently assigned to you in the Issue Tracking Application.

Please direct your attention to your open issues as soon as possible. If you have resolved an issue, please change its status in the Issue Tracking Application. Thanks.

Page 1

References - Ch14 Issues

Available References:

☑ Visual Basic For Applications
☑ Microsoft Access 10.0 Object Library
☑ Microsoft ActiveX Data Objects 2.1 Library
☑ Microsoft Outlook 10.0 Object Library
☑ Microsoft Word 10.0 Object Library
☐ AcroIEHelper 1.0 Type Library
☐ Active Setup Control Library
☐ ActiveBar Control
☐ ActiveMovie control type library
☐ actl 1.0 Type Library
☐ Adobe SVG Viewer Type Library 2.0
☐ AnswerWorks API Type Library
☐ ApiGlide 1.1 Type Library
☐ ApiOpenGL 1.1 Type Library

OK
Cancel
Browse...

Priority

Help

Microsoft Word 10.0 Object Library

Location: C:\Program Files\Microsoft Office\Office10\MSWORD.OLB
Language: Standard

Ch14 Issues completed - Miscellaneous (Code)

(General)   OpenOutlookContact

```
Public Sub OpenOutlookContact(strFullName As String)
' Open a Microsoft Outlook contact for the specified name.

    Dim appOutlook As New Outlook.Application
    Dim nsOutlook As NameSpace
    Dim mfContacts As MAPIFolder
    Dim ciContact As ContactItem

    ' Open the Outlook default Contacts folder.
    Set nsOutlook = appOutlook.GetNamespace("MAPI")
    Set mfContacts = nsOutlook.GetDefaultFolder(olFolderContacts)

    ' Find the contact named in the AssignedTo column.
    Set ciContact = mfContacts.Items.Find("[FullName] = " & strFullName)

    ' If the contact doesn't exist, create a new contact.
    If ciContact Is Nothing Then
        Set ciContact = mfContacts.Items.Add
        ciContact.FullName = strFullName
    End If

    ' Open the Outlook contact window.
    ciContact.Display
```

Chapter 14
Share Data with Other Applications

After completing this chapter, you will be able to:

✔ Use Automation objects to work with other Microsoft Windows–based applications.

✔ Send commands and data to Microsoft Word.

✔ Work with contact information in Microsoft Outlook.

✔ Gather data from another application, such as Microsoft Excel.

When traveling far from home, communicating with strangers can be both challenging and rewarding. Although differing cultures and languages can present obstacles, it seems we humans can usually find a way to communicate our messages to one another, whether by body language, hand signals, or perhaps a broken approximation of a foreign tongue. And as anyone who has traveled much will attest, exposure to other cultures can be very broadening—we seem to absorb a bit of the experience and wisdom of others from such encounters.

As a Microsoft Access programmer, working with other Windows-based applications is a little like communicating with people of different cultures—it's a challenge, but there's a lot to gain in sharing the capabilities of other systems. Fortunately, Microsoft Visual Basic provides a mechanism for talking between two different applications, such as Access and Excel, or Access and Word. It's called *Automation*. Automation gives you a framework for using objects that belong to another application as if those objects were an extension of the application you're working within. But just as with human communication, you'll find that it helps to know a bit about the other party's language. With Automation, you combine the objects, properties, and methods of the other application with the Visual Basic code you write for Access.

In this chapter, you'll learn the general techniques of communicating using Automation. Working with Word and Outlook, you'll find out how to combine the capabilities of two systems to accomplish more in your database applications.

Important

You must have Microsoft Word 2002 and Microsoft Outlook 2002 installed on your computer to complete the steps in this chapter.

This chapter uses the practice files Ch14 Issues.mdb and Ch14 Memo.dot that you installed from the book's CD-ROM. For details about installing the practice files, see "Using the Book's CD-ROM" at the beginning of this book.

Getting Started

● Start Access, and open the Ch14 Issues database in the practice files folder.

Using Automation Objects

Access isn't a very good word processor. Sure, you could create an Access report that would look a lot like a professional letter—but it would take a great deal of work, and would lack the flexibility you take for granted in any word processing application. By the same token, Access isn't a statistical calculator, a project manager, or a presentation graphics program. But it's a great place to store your data!

One way to extend the capabilities of your Access applications is by teaming them up with other applications. Automation is the mechanism that Visual Basic provides for doing this. If the databases you're creating need the capabilities of other Windows-based applications—and if those other applications use Visual Basic—you can write code that combines the power of Access with the strengths of other systems.

In previous chapters, you've learned about several types of objects you can control in Access, such as the *Form*, *Report*, *Database*, and *Recordset* objects. Other applications have objects as well, and your code running in Access can work with them behind the scenes. Excel, for example, has the *Worksheet* and *PivotTable* objects, which you could incorporate seamlessly into an Access application using techniques similar to those you've learned for working with Access objects. And many other Windows-based applications expose their objects for use through Automation.

Although the possible ways you could combine applications are endless, here are some common ways to use Automation with Access.

- **Create or edit documents.** From your Visual Basic code in Access, you can create or open a document in Word or a worksheet in Excel, for example, and control it using the other application's commands. Without any interaction by the user, you can send data from your database to the document or worksheet and even use the other application's commands to print it. You'll use these techniques in this chapter to work with a document in Word.

- **Gather data from another application.** Although you'll usually store your application's data in Access tables (or another format that Access can link to), you might occasionally want to bring in data from another application's files. For example, you might want to incorporate schedule or contact information stored in Outlook. Using Automation in Visual Basic, you can use the objects, properties, and methods of Outlook to access this information.

- **Provide data to other applications.** All the techniques discussed to this point involve writing code in Access to control other applications—alternatively, you can write Automation code in another application to work with data or other objects in

Access databases. This strategy makes the most sense if your application is primarily suited for another programming system. For example, if you create a financial system using Visual Basic in Excel, you might want to store some of the data in Access tables and perhaps even print Access reports from the Excel application.

Although you won't get a chance to try all these techniques in this chapter, you'll discover many Automation concepts that apply to all of them.

Sending Commands to Microsoft Word

Suppose you want your application to create and print a memo, merge names into a mailing list, or print envelopes—tasks you want to perform in Word. Fortunately, Word uses Visual Basic as its programming language, and supports Automation, so you can perform virtually any task from Access that you could perform in Word itself.

One strategy for Automation is to open a document object directly, and then use its methods and properties to control it in Visual Basic. Alternatively, every application that supports Automation has a special object, the *Application* object, through which you can send commands to the application—in this case, Word—just as if you were programming in Word itself. You can open documents, insert text, and control Word in any way you please—all from within a procedure in your Access application. Either way, you declare one or more object variables, use special statements to make the variables refer to objects in Word, and then use Word methods and properties.

In this chapter, you'll write Visual Basic code to perform actions in Word: creating a memo and inserting text into it. The memo your application creates will be a reminder to employees who have open issues stored in the database, and your code will determine which employees to include on the "To" line of the memo.

More Ways to Share Data

Although you won't try them out in this book, there are two additional Windows technologies that, like Automation, help you use other applications with Access. The first is Object Linking and Embedding (OLE). Through OLE, you can insert one application's objects or documents into another. For example, you can place an object frame control on an Access form or report and then insert a worksheet from Excel or a chart from Microsoft Graph into the new frame. Although this strategy doesn't usually involve any programming—OLE objects work automatically based on properties you set—you can use Visual Basic code in Access to control when the object gets updated or to change OLE property settings.

For applications that don't support Automation or OLE, you may be able to write code that uses Dynamic Data Exchange (DDE). With DDE, you can send data and commands from one application to another behind the scenes. For example, some Windows-based communications applications support DDE, and you could use DDE commands in Visual Basic to gather data via modem and store it in an Access database.

For additional information on these techniques, search the Access Help index for "OLE objects" or "DDE."

Open the Word Template That Your Application Will Use

Before you write the Automation code in the Issues application, you'll first open a Word document template, from which you'll create the memo. Using a template is a great way to get a head start on a document you send regularly, such as a form letter. If your template is nearly complete, all your code has to do is fill in any missing information, such as names or addresses stored in your database.

1 Start Word. (On the taskbar, click the Start button, point to Programs, and then click Microsoft Word.)

2 On the File menu, click Open.

3 In the Files Of Type box, select Document Templates.

4 Move to the practice files folder on your hard disk, and open the Ch14 Memo template.

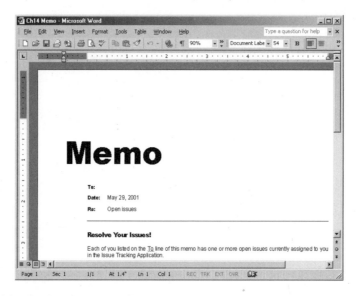

Add a Bookmark to the Template

When your code creates the memo, you'll want to insert employee names into it. The first step is to mark the spot where you'll enter text in the document so that your code can locate it easily. A simple way to do this is to use a *bookmark*, a named Word place marker, because you can jump to any bookmark in a document by using the *GoTo* method in Word.

1 Click the second line of the memo document to the right of the string *To:* to position the insertion point.

This is where you'll type employee names from Access.

2 On the Insert menu, click Bookmark.

Word displays the Bookmark dialog box.

3 Type **MemoToLine** in the Bookmark Name box, and then click Add.

Although you can't actually see the bookmark in the document, it will provide a quick way to jump to this spot from code in Access.

4 On the File menu, click Exit, clicking Yes when Word asks if you want to save changes. Word closes, and Access returns to the front.

Open the *CreateWordMemo* Function in the Miscellaneous Module

The Tools menu on the *Issues* form includes the command Create Word Memo, with which users can run the Automation code you'll write. The menu item runs a function named *CreateWordMemo*, which already exists in the Miscellaneous module. You just need to open this function and then add the Automation code to make it work.

● In the Database window, click the Modules shortcut, and then double-click the Miscellaneous module.

Visual Basic displays the Miscellaneous module. The first procedure in the module is the *CreateWordMemo* function.

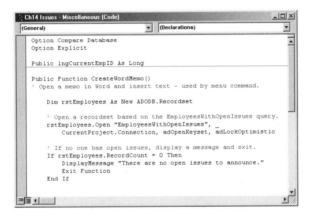

```
Ch14 Issues - Miscellaneous (Code)
(General)                                    (Declarations)

Option Compare Database
Option Explicit

Public lngCurrentEmpID As Long

Public Function CreateWordMemo()
' Open a memo in Word and insert text - used by menu command.

    Dim rstEmployees As New ADODB.Recordset

    ' Open a recordset based on the EmployeesWithOpenIssues query.
    rstEmployees.Open "EmployeesWithOpenIssues", _
        CurrentProject.Connection, adOpenKeyset, adLockOptimistic

    ' If no one has open issues, display a message and exit.
    If rstEmployees.RecordCount = 0 Then
        DisplayMessage "There are no open issues to announce."
        Exit Function
    End If
```

The function already contains some important code—but it's also code you're familiar with from earlier chapters. Here's what it does:

■ The *Dim* statement declares the *rstEmployees* variable and creates an ADO recordset.

■ The next line opens a recordset based on a query named *EmployeesWithOpenIssues*. As its name declares, this query returns a record for each employee who has at least one issue open in the *Issues* table—exactly the list of people you want to send the memo to.

■ The *If...Then* block makes sure there is at least one employee in the recordset—otherwise, there would be no point in sending the memo. The condition that the *If...Then* statement tests refers to a property of the *Recordset* object that you haven't seen yet: the RecordCount property. This property returns the number of records in the recordset that Access has read from disk so far. (Note that this isn't necessarily the total number of records in the recordset, unless you've already moved to the end of the recordset.) If the RecordCount property returns 0, it means that the recordset is empty; in this case the code would display a message and exit the procedure.

Set a Reference to Word's Object Library

Word has its own object library, similar to the Access, VBA, and DAO object libraries you explored in Chapter 12. Before you can use Word's objects in your code, you need to tell Access that you intend to do so by setting a *reference* to the Word object library. And as long as you're setting references, you'll also include one for the Outlook object library, since you'll need it later in the chapter.

1 On the Tools menu, click References.

The References dialog box appears and displays all the object libraries that are registered on your system. The three checked libraries are those you worked with through the object browser in Chapter 12: VBA, Access, and ADODB.

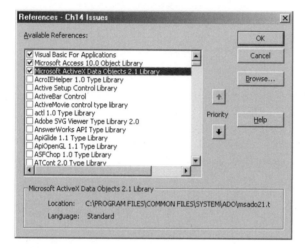

2 Locate Microsoft Outlook 10.0 Object Library and Microsoft Word 10.0 Object Library in the list of available references, and then click the check boxes next to these entries.

3 Click OK.

Tip

In addition to preparing to work with a new object library, you can use the References command to make Visual Basic code in another database available—in order to call procedures from a database, you need only establish a reference to it. In the same way, a reference is often required in order to use add-in products for Access, such as ActiveX controls. To establish a reference to a file that isn't listed in the References dialog box, just click the Browse button and locate the file.

Write Code That Creates a Word Document and Inserts Text

It's time to get your feet wet. First you'll add a line of code to declare a variable for the Word *Application* object; this variable will provide your gateway from Access to Word. Then you'll add a block of Automation code that "talks" to the Word *Application* object, telling it to create the memo document, sending various other commands, and then inserting the employee names from the *rstEmployees* recordset into the document. As you'll see, Automation programming is just like ordinary programming with Access and DAO objects—except that in order to send commands to the other application, you need to learn about a whole new object library, complete with properties, methods, and constants.

1 Add the following code underneath the existing *Dim* statement:

```
Dim appWord As New Word.Application
```

You'll use the object variable *appWord* throughout the procedure to refer to Word and run its commands. Note that the statement declares the variable with the special data type *Word.Application*—this data type is available only because you established a reference to Word's object library. The statement also uses the *New* keyword, which will cause Visual Basic to create an instance of Word, opening it in the background if it isn't already running.

2 Add code at the end of the procedure, just above the *End Function* statement (if Word or the practice files are not in their default folders on your hard disk, be sure to substitute the correct path names in the code).

```
' Open a document based on the memo template, turn off spell check,
' move to the MemoToLine bookmark, and then display Word.
With appWord
    .Documents.Add" "C:\Access VB Practice Files\Ch14 Memo.dot"
    .ActiveDocument.ShowSpellingErrors = False
    .Selection.Goto wdGoToBookmark, Name:=" "MemoToLine"
    .Visible = True
End With

' Loop through the recordset returned by the query, inserting
' the name of each employee into the document.
Do Until rstEmployees.EOF
    appWord.Selection.TypeText rstEmployees!EmployeeName &" " " "
    rstEmployees.MoveNext
Loop
```

Here's how this code does its work:

■ The first six lines of code use something new: a *With* block. The *With* statement simply provides a shortcut in your code for performing several actions using the same object. Access interprets this code as if you'd put the name of the object before each period in the subsequent lines. For example, the first line below the *With* statement is equivalent to *appWord.Documents.Add*, even though the *appWord* variable isn't specified. Note that you can use a *With* block in any object manipulation code—but it's especially useful for Automation, because you often want to perform several commands at a time concerning one object. As you'd expect, the *End With* statement ends the *With* block.

■ The first statement inside the *With* block uses the *Add* method of Word's *Documents* collection. The *Documents* collection in Word contains one *Document* object for each Word document that's currently open, in much the same way that the Access *Forms* collection contains one *Form* object for each form that's open. Using the *Add* method creates a new *Document* object—just as if the user clicked the New command on the File menu. The argument provided for the *Add* method specifies a Word template on which to base the new document, in this case the Ch14 Memo template you just viewed. (Leaving this argument out would create a blank Word document.)

■ The next statement in the block sets a property of the Word document you've just created: the ShowSpellingErrors property. Setting this property to *False* prevents Word from displaying wavy red lines under words it doesn't recognize, such as the employee names your code will enter in the document.

■ The next statement in the block moves the insertion point in Word to the MemoTo-Line bookmark you created. To do this, it refers to an important Word object, the *Selection* object, which represents the insertion point (or currently selected text) in a Word document. The *GoTo* method of the *Selection* object moves the insertion point to a new location. Used with the *wdGoToBookmark* constant as its first argument, the *GoTo* method moves to the bookmark you specify using the *Name* argument.

■ The final statement in the block sets the Visible property of Word to *True*. Until you make Word visible, all this activity in Word takes place behind the scenes. When this line runs, the new Memo document will appear on the screen.

■ Now that the memo is ready and you're in the right spot, the code can go ahead and insert the names from the recordset. To insert every name in the recordset, this code introduces a new method for repeating code, a *Do* loop. The *Do* statement is followed by an *Until* condition: as long as the condition returns *False*, the block of code runs. The *Loop* statement tells it to run again—assuming the condition still isn't *True*—and the loop continues until the condition returns *True*. The condition for the *Do Until* statement refers to the EOF property (EOF stands for End Of File) of the *Recordset* object. The value of a recordset's EOF property is *False* so long as there is a "current" record in the recordset. If you move past the last record in the recordset (or if there aren't any records to begin with), the value of the EOF property will be *True*.

■ The next line uses the *TypeText* method of the Word *Selection* object to actually type a name into the Word document. You can follow the *TypeText* method with any string expression that you want to put into the document—in this case, it's the value of the *EmployeeName* field in the recordset, followed by three spaces (to separate each name from the next).

■ The next statement uses the *MoveNext* method of the *Recordset* object to move to the next record in the *rstEmployees* recordset. Then it's time to loop: if there is another employee, the *TypeText* code runs again; if not, the expression *Not rstEmployees.EOF* returns *False*, and the loop is complete. As is the memo!

3 On the Debug menu, click Compile Ch14 Issues.

4 Click the Save button on the toolbar.

Note that when your procedure finishes, Word will stay open and display the memo for users to edit as they please. If you want Word to exit when you've finished using it in a procedure, you can use the *Quit* method of Word's *Application* object.

Try Out Your Automation Procedure

Let's create a memo! To run the event procedure, you can use the custom menu command on the Tools menu of the *Issues* form's menu bar.

View Microsoft
Access

1 Switch to Access.

2 In the Database window, click the Forms shortcut, and then double-click the *Issues* form.

3 On the Tools menu, click Create Word Memo.

Your code runs—it opens a recordset, creates a Word *Application* object, creates the new memo, and then inserts names from the recordset. When it finishes, you're left in Word looking at the completed memo.

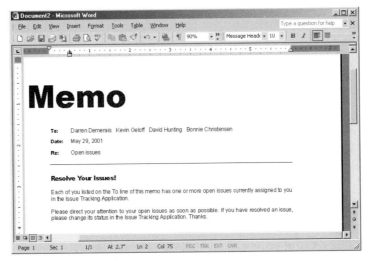

4 Close the memo document, clicking No when Word asks if you want to save changes.

Although this memo involves transferring only a small amount of data, you can easily imagine more powerful uses for this type of Automation. With Word, for example, you could use the same techniques to do easy printing of envelopes, merge data into documents and save them, or even create and print an entire mailing to clients stored in your database. And if you don't want users to have to work in Word themselves, you can do all this work behind the scenes.

Getting Information from Another Application

So far, you've sent commands and data from Access—even set a property in Word—but you haven't gotten anything back from Word. Using Automation, you can also request information from an application's objects, such as the value of a function or property. This allows you to interact with its objects in more powerful ways. For example, suppose you want to run an Excel financial function that doesn't exist in Access. You can create an *Automation* object and then use it to run the Excel function, assigning the answer to a variable in your application's code. Or, if you want to look up phone numbers or e-mail addresses stored in Outlook, you can use Automation to search Outlook folders (as you will later in this chapter), and then access the properties of the Outlook items you find.

Now you'll add a final section to the *CreateWordMemo* procedure that will run the Word *Information* function and use its return value, in this case, the number of pages in the memo. In this code, you'll display a message box that announces the number of pages in the finished memo and asks the user whether to print it.

Display a Message Box in Word That Responds to the User's Choice

Before you add code to the end of the procedure, you'll need to declare a couple of variables at the beginning.

1 Switch to Visual Basic.

The Miscellaneous module still shows the *CreateWordMemo* function.

2 Add the following code below the two existing Dim statements:

```
Dim intPages As Integer, strMessage As String
```

This line declares two variables you'll use with the Word function: *intPages* to store the number of pages that Word tells you are in the memo and *strMessage* to store the message you'll display.

3 Add the following code just before the *End Function* statement, beneath the *Do* loop:

```
' Return to Access.
AppActivate "Issue Tracking Application"

' Get the number of pages in the memo, ask the user whether
' to print it, and then tell Word to print it.
intPages = appWord.Selection.Information(wdNumberOfPagesInDocument)
strMessage = "The memo is complete, and has" & CStr(intPages) & _
    " page(s). Send it to the printer?"
If Confirm(strMessage) Then
    appWord.ActiveDocument.PrintOut
End If
```

Here's what the code does:

- The first statement reactivates Access using the *AppActivate* statement. It specifies the title of the Issues application rather than Access, because *AppActivate* always looks in the title bar to locate the application you want.

- The next line uses the *Information* function, which is a property of the Word *Selection* object you used earlier. This function can return many different bits of information about a document; what information you get back depends on the constant you provide. By specifying the *wdNumberOfPagesInDocument* constant, this statement retrieves the number of pages in the Word document and assigns that number to the *intPages* variable.

- The next line assigns the text of your message to the *strMessage* variable. It uses the *CStr* function to convert the page count value to a string and then concatenates the text with this number to create a message. The code then uses this string to ask the user a question, calling the *Confirm* function you wrote way back in Chapter 5.

■ If the user clicks OK in the message box, the statement in the *If...Then* block runs. The statement sends one final command to Word: it runs the *PrintOut* method of the *Document* object. The document it tells Word to print is the one referred to by the ActiveDocument property—which is, of course, the memo.

4 On the Debug menu, click Compile Ch14 Issues.

Create the Memo Again

Let's try out the procedure with these changes.

View Microsoft Access

1 Switch to Access.

2 On the Tools menu, click Create Word Memo.

This time, when the memo finishes, the focus switches back to the Issues application and a message box appears on top of the document.

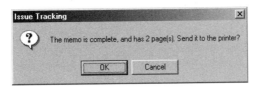

As you can see, your code discovered from Word the number of pages in the document. If you were to click OK, your code would tell Word to print it—but you don't need to test it unless you actually want to print the memo.

3 Click Cancel.

4 Switch to Word.

5 On the File menu, click Exit, clicking No when Word asks if you want to save changes to the memo document.

Access returns to the front.

Working with Folders in Microsoft Outlook

After you've learned to "automate" one application, you're well on your way to working with another. But each application that supports Automation has its own peculiar object model. Suppose you want your application to tap into the data stored in the user's Outlook folders, such as contact information, schedule, or tasks. In this section, you'll write code that searches the user's Outlook contact folder for a person's name and then opens a contact record. In the process, you'll discover a few of the complexities of Outlook's object model.

Important

Before you perform the following steps, you must have used Outlook since installing Office on your machine. (The first time you run Outlook, it asks you questions and creates initialization files.)

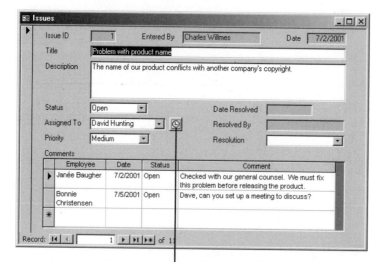

When users click this button, you want the application to look up an assignee in the Outlook contacts folder—or create a new contact item if the employee isn't there.

Add Code to the *OpenOutlookContact* Procedure

The *Issues* form already has a button on it, next to the Assigned To combo box, that runs a *Sub* procedure in the Miscellaneous module called *OpenOutlookContact*. You just need to add code to make the procedure work.

1 Switch to Visual Basic.

The Miscellaneous module is still open.

2 In the Procedure box at the upper right corner of the Code window, click OpenOutlookContact.

As you can see, the *OpenOutlookContact* procedure takes an argument, *strFullName*. This is the contact name you'll look for in Outlook.

3 Enter the following code for the procedure:

```
Public Sub OpenOutlookContact(strFullName As String)
' Open a Microsoft Outlook contact for the specified name.

    Dim appOutlook As New Outlook.Application
    Dim nsOutlook As NameSpace
    Dim mfContacts As MAPIFolder
    Dim ciContact As ContactItem

    ' Open the Outlook default Contacts folder.
    Set nsOutlook = appOutlook.GetNamespace("MAPI")
    Set mfContacts = nsOutlook.GetDefaultFolder(olFolderContacts)
```

```
' Find the contact named in the AssignedTo column.
Set ciContact = mfContacts.Items.Find("[FullName] =" " & strFullName)

' If the contact doesn't exist, create a new contact.
If ciContact Is Nothing Then
    Set ciContact = mfContacts.Items.Add
    ciContact.FullName = strFullName
End If

' Open the Outlook contact window.
ciContact.Display

End Function
```

Here's what the code does:

- There are four variable declarations. The first uses the *New* keyword to open an instance of the Outlook *Application* object to work with in the background. The next line declares an Outlook *NameSpace* object, which you'll use to represent a set of mail folders stored on your hard disk. Next is a *MAPIFolder* object, in which you'll store a reference to the Outlook contacts folder, and finally there is a *ContactItem* object for referring to the contact item you're looking for.

- The next two lines use *Set* statements to assign objects to these variables. The first uses the *GetNamespace* method of the Outlook *Application* object to open the user's personal folder file, which is always identified as *MAPI* in reference to the e-mail standard it follows. The second line uses the *GetDefaultFolder* method along with the *olFolderContacts* constant to open the default Outlook contacts folder. You could use lines similar to these to open any folder in Outlook, such as e-mail, calendar, or task folders.

- The next line uses the *Find* method of the folder's *Items* collection to locate the first contact that matches a filter string. The filter string, enclosed in parentheses, combines the text *[Full Name] =* with the value of the *strFullName* variable, which is the argument passed to the procedure. If you call the *OpenOutlookContact* procedure and specify Bonnie Christensen, for example, this code will ask Outlook to filter the contact items for *[Full Name] = "Bonnie Christensen"*. If the *Find* method succeeds, the code sets the *ciContact* variable to refer to the contact item it found.

- The next line uses the *Is* operator to determine whether or not the *ciContact* object variable points to an object—that is, whether the previous line was able to find the contact with the specified name.

- If the *ciContact* variable is set to *Nothing*, the two lines in the *If...Then* block run. The first line uses the *Add* method to create a new Outlook *ContactItem* object, append it to the *Items* collection, and set the *ciContact* variable to point to it. The second line sets the FullName property of the new contact so that the user won't have to enter it. If you had more employee information stored in Access, such as phone numbers or e-mail names, you could easily set additional properties of the Outlook item.

- The final line uses the *Display* method to open the Outlook contact window and display the *ciContact* item—either the existing contact your code found or the new contact it created.

Share Data with Other Applications

4 On the Debug menu, click Compile Ch14 Issues.

Save

5 Click the Save button on the toolbar.

6 Close Visual Basic.

Try the New Procedure from the *Issues* Form

Let's try automating Outlook by clicking the Open Outlook Contact button on the *Issues* form.

1 Click the Open Outlook Contact button (next to the Assigned To combo box).

Your code starts an instance of Outlook in the background, opens the Contacts folder, and looks for David Hunting. Presumably, it doesn't find him among your contacts, so it creates a new contact item, sets its Full Name property to *David Hunting*, and then displays the Outlook Contact window.

Your code created a contact
and set its Full Name property.

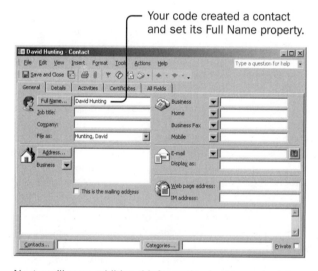

Next you'll save additional information in this contact item, and then use it to make sure your code can find an existing contact.

2 In the Job Title box, type **Partner.**

3 In the Company box, type **Hunting and Associates.**

4 In the Business Phone box, type **212 555 7880.**

5 Click the Save And Close button on the Contact window toolbar.

Now that David Hunting is saved in Outlook, let's see if your code finds him.

6 Click the Open Outlook Contact button.

Sure enough, your code found and displayed the existing Outlook contact record.

7 On the File menu in the Contact window, click Delete.

Outlook deletes the contact record and closes the window.

Using Access Objects from Microsoft Excel

Programming with Automation is a two-way street: just as the procedure you wrote in Access controlled Word, you can write code in another application to control Access. For example, if you write Visual Basic code in Excel, you can open and work directly with Access and ADO or DAO objects.

Here's a Visual Basic procedure that works in Excel—to use it, you would create a new Visual Basic module from Excel and set a reference to the Microsoft Access 10.0 Object Library. The procedure creates an Access *Application* object and then uses it to open the Issues database and print a report.

```
Sub PrintIssuesReport()

    ' Declare and create an Access application object.
    Dim appAccess As New Access.Application

    ' Open the Issues application with Access.
    appAccess.OpenCurrentDatabase_
        "c:\Access VBA Practice Files\Ch14 Issues.mdb"

    ' Print the Issues report.
    appAccess.DoCmd.OpenReport "Issues"

End Sub
```

In declaring the *appAccess* variable used to send commands to Access, the first line of code uses the *New* keyword to create an instance of Access that runs in the background.

The next line in the procedure uses the *OpenCurrentDatabase* method of the *Application* object, which exists specifically to facilitate Automation in Access when it's used from other applications. The last line uses a technique very familiar to you by now—a method of the *DoCmd* object—to open and print the *Issues* report.

Although this example performs only the simplest task, it demonstrates how powerful Automation can be for applications that support Visual Basic, such as Word, Excel, and Microsoft Project. If you write code in these applications, you can control everything from their Visual Basic projects in nearly the same way you can from Access.

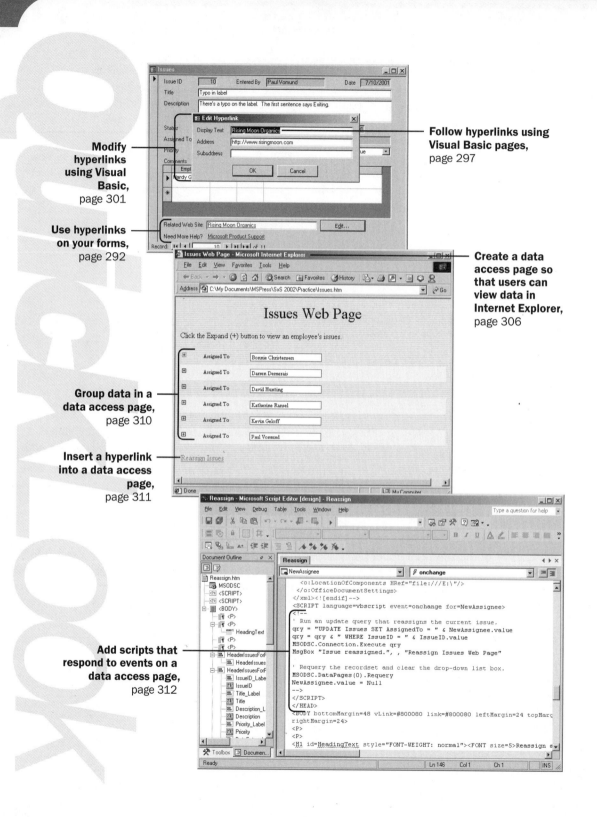

Modify hyperlinks using Visual Basic, page 301

Use hyperlinks on your forms, page 292

Follow hyperlinks using Visual Basic pages, page 297

Create a data access page so that users can view data in Internet Explorer, page 306

Group data in a data access page, page 310

Insert a hyperlink into a data access page, page 311

Add scripts that respond to events on a data access page, page 312

Chapter 15
Connect to the Web

After completing this chapter, you will be able to:

✔ Create and update hyperlinks to Internet data on your Microsoft Access forms.

✔ Create a data access page for viewing data in Microsoft Internet Explorer.

✔ Use the Microsoft Script Editor to write VBScript code for a Web page.

With the increasing popularity of the Internet, the world of information is getting more accessible by the day. Companies large and small have sites on the World Wide Web, making new sources of data available to anyone who's connected. Many workplaces also have an *intranet*, an internal networked Web containing information for employees to use in their work. If you are connected to the Internet or an intranet, your Microsoft Access applications can help users work with data on the network more effectively.

Some of the most exciting innovations in Access are designed to take advantage of the Web. In this chapter, you'll explore two of the features that are likely candidates for your applications. First you'll learn to enhance your Access forms with *hyperlinks*, clickable images and text that are used to navigate through pages in a Web browser. Then you'll learn to create *data access pages*, custom Web pages that display data from your Access applications in Microsoft Internet Explorer.

Important

To complete the steps in this chapter, you must have Internet Explorer 5 or later installed on your computer and be connected to the Internet via a modem or network. Internet Explorer is included with Microsoft Office XP. Also, if you haven't installed the Microsoft Script Editor (it isn't installed with Office by default), Access will need to install it from the Office XP CD-ROM or a network location when you try to use it.

Depending on your system configuration for connecting with the Internet, the steps in this chapter may not work exactly as written. If you can't complete the chapter, you may still be able to learn from your reading and use some of the Web features it covers. Additionally, note that the content of the Web sites may have changed and may no longer match the content shown.

Ch15
Issues.mdb
Reassign.htm
Ressign_files
folder

This chapter uses the practice files Ch15 Issues.mdb and Reassign.htm that you installed from the book's CD-ROM, as well as the supporting files found in the Reassign_files folder. For details about installing the practice files, see "Using the Book's CD-ROM" at the beginning of this book.

Getting Started

● Start Access, and open the Ch15 Issues database in the practice files folder.

Using Hyperlinks

If you've used any Web browser, or even viewed online Help files, you're familiar with hyperlinks. They're often indicated by blue underlined text, but they can also appear with other formatting and in other text colors. (Buttons and images can also be hyperlinks.) Clicking a hyperlink tells the software to jump to another place, either in a file on your computer or network, or to a location on the Internet. If you want to provide this ease of navigation to users of your applications, you can include hyperlinks on your forms. As you'll see, hyperlinks make navigation easier for the application developer as well—while the buttons you've created in previous chapters require Microsoft Visual Basic code to make them work, hyperlinks are automatic. They need only an address, which is the location that they jump to.

Two ways of using hyperlinks are especially suited for forms in your applications. You can create controls on a form and then set properties for the controls to define hyperlinks to Web sites. The addresses associated with the controls are saved with the form and don't change as you move among records. You can also add a field to a table in your database, give the field the Hyperlink data type, and then store hyperlinks there. If you then create a text box on a form that's bound to your Hyperlink field, the hyperlinks appear in the text box. As users navigate among records in the form, the text box displays a hyperlink that changes with every record. With either method, users can simply click any hyperlink to jump to the address it contains.

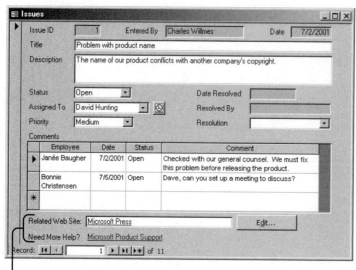

You'll add hyperlinks to the *Issues* form to make it easy for users to jump to Web sites.

In this chapter, you'll use both methods of creating hyperlinks to enhance the Issues application. First you'll add a hyperlink label control to the *Issues* form. The hyperlink will allow users to jump to a Web site that offers help with Access. Next you'll add a new field to the *Issues* form that displays hyperlinks stored in the *Issues* table. These hyperlinks will let users jump to Web sites related to each issue in the database. Finally you'll discover how to work with each type of hyperlink in Visual Basic, writing code that opens hyperlinks automatically and modifies them behind the scenes.

Creating Hyperlink Controls on a Form

To define a hyperlink to a Web site, all you need to do is create a control—a command button, a label, or an image control—and then set properties that tell the hyperlink where to jump. When users click the control, Access jumps directly to the location defined by the hyperlink. If the hyperlink's address points to a Web site, the user's Web browser will open automatically to display the site.

Create a Label with a Hyperlink

To give users an easy way to find help on the World Wide Web, you'll add a new label to the *Issues* form and define the Web address that its hyperlink will jump to. You'll use the Insert Hyperlink command, a shortcut for creating a hyperlink label and setting some of its properties.

1 In the Database window, click the Forms shortcut.

2 Click the *Issues* form, and then click the Design button.

Insert Hyperlink

3 Click the Insert Hyperlink button on the toolbar.

The Insert Hyperlink dialog box appears, asking for the hyperlink address. As you can see, Access makes it easy to create links to Web pages, files on your computer, objects in the current database, or e-mail addresses.

4 In the Address box, type **http://support.microsoft.com/**

By default, Access sets the display text for the hyperlink to the Web address you entered. Instead of the address, you'd like to display the title of the Web page.

5 In the Text To Display box, type **Microsoft Product Support** and then click OK.

Access creates a label that displays the text you entered and refers to the hyperlink address, and then Access inserts it at the top left corner of the form. Next you'll move the label to the bottom of the *Issues* form, a blank area you'll use to display this and other Web-related controls.

6 Drag the label down to the bottom of the form, placing it in the blank area just to the right of the existing label that says "Need More Help?" (If the bottom of the form is not visible, you may need to drag the label down below the form window until Access scrolls down in the window for you.)

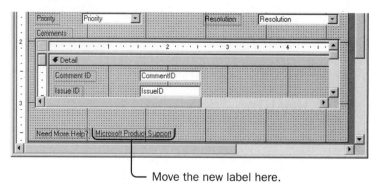

└─ Move the new label here.

Now that the label is where it belongs, you'll rename it in the property sheet to make it easier to refer to in code.

Properties

7 If the property sheet isn't displayed, click the Properties button.

8 Click the All tab in the property sheet.

You'll notice that the label's Caption and HyperlinkAddress properties contain the display text and link location you entered for the hyperlink. But the label has a default name, such as *Label25*.

9 Set the Name property to **HelpLinkLabel**.

10 Close the property sheet.

The text in the label appears in blue and with an underline, showing that it's a hyperlink. Soon you'll use it to jump to the World Wide Web.

Storing Hyperlinks in a Table

If users of your application frequently access Web sites, you may want to let them store hyperlinks for these sites within records in an Access database. The Hyperlink data type can store all the information that might be needed for a hyperlink, including the text the hyperlink displays and the address it jumps to. Using the Hyperlink data type, you can create a table just for the purpose of storing and managing hyperlinks—in a Web site management database, for example. You can also allow users to associate Web sites with other types of records in the database.

The *Issues* table in the practice database contains a new field called WebSite, which already has several useful hyperlinks stored in it. If you open that table, you'll see a new column containing hyperlinks, with their familiar blue clickable text.

The new field in the *Issues* table uses the Hyperlink data to store Web address information related to each record.

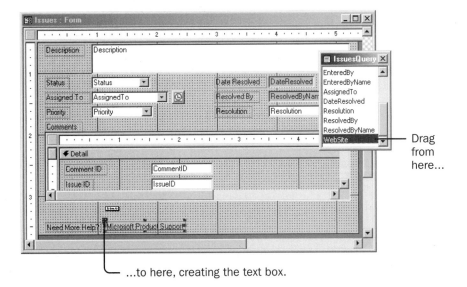

Add the WebSite Field to the *Issues* Form

Your next step is to create a text box control to display the hyperlink that's stored with each issue.

Field List

1 If the field list isn't displayed, click the Field List button on the toolbar.

The field list displays all the fields in the *Issues* table. As you'll see, the new WebSite field is there, ready to display a hyperlink for each issue.

2 Scroll down in the field list to display the WebSite field, and then click the WebSite field and drag it to the blank area of the form, just above the hyperlink label you created earlier.

The text box and its label appear on the form.

Drag from here...

...to here, creating the text box.

Because the field it's bound to has the Hyperlink data type, the text box displays its contents as a blue underlined hyperlink, ready to be clicked.

3 Close the field list.

4 Drag the right side of the new text box to make it twice as wide.

5 Close the *Issues* form, clicking Yes when Access asks if you want to save changes to the form.

Try Out Hyperlinks in the *Issues* Form

1 In the Database window, double-click the *Issues* form.

The form opens and shows the two hyperlinks at the bottom.

2 Press the Page Down key twice to move between records in the form.

As you can see, the Related Web Site field displays a different hyperlink for each issue record. By contrast, the hyperlink label underneath it remains the same; unless you change its properties in Design view, it will always provide a link to the same Web site.

Tip

Although the Web sites included in the practice database aren't actually related to the sample issues in the *Issues* table, they may be of general interest to you. In a real-world situation, users would set these hyperlinks to point to Web sites that other employees could refer to.

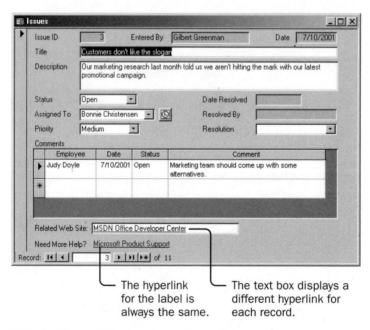

The hyperlink for the label is always the same.

The text box displays a different hyperlink for each record.

3 Click the Microsoft Product Support hyperlink.

Internet Explorer opens (asking you to establish an Internet connection if necessary) and displays the site on the World Wide Web.

If you like, you can browse this Web site or add it to your list of favorite sites by clicking Add To Favorites (on the Favorites menu).

Access passes the correct World Wide Web address to Internet Explorer.

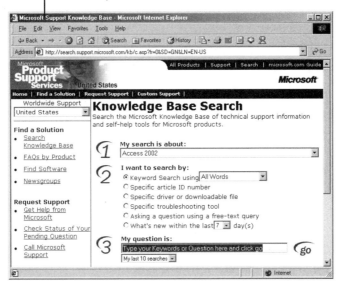

4   Close Internet Explorer, and switch back to Access. (If a message appears asking whether you want to disconnect from the Internet, click No.)

Access returns to the front.

5   Click the blue underlined hyperlink in the Related Web Site field.

The second Web site opens.

6   Close Internet Explorer, and switch back to Access.

As you can see, it's a snap to provide jumps to the Internet on your forms. In your own applications, you'll need to decide which strategy is appropriate: creating hyperlinks directly on forms or storing hyperlinks in a table. Although the former strategy is more straightforward, the latter is more flexible, especially if you have many sites to track or if you want to associate other information with them.

Following Hyperlinks from Visual Basic

The *Issues* form menu bar has two custom menu commands included as alternate ways to jump to Web sites. As you saw in Chapter 10, custom menu commands can run Visual Basic functions; at this point, however, these two menu commands don't have any functions to run. You'll create two functions that jump to the Web sites defined by these hyperlinks.

You'll create functions to make
these menu commands work.

Connecting Hyperlinks to Files or Database Objects

The hyperlinks you'll use in this chapter all point to the World Wide Web. However, your hyperlinks don't all have to jump to Web sites or even to the Internet. As you've seen, the Insert Hyperlink dialog box helps you create many types of links or browse for the object you want to link to. Your hyperlinks can jump to various types of documents, either on the Internet, on your network, or on your own computer.

- **Access database objects** A hyperlink can open any database object, such as a form or report—a task you're accustomed to accomplishing with a command button. In case you are curious about how Access represents this type of link, here's how it works: In addition to its address, each hyperlink has a *subaddress* that points to a specific object or location within a file. To define a hyperlink that opens a database object, Access sets the hyperlink's subaddress to the object's type followed by its name, separated by a space. For example, in a hyperlink to the *Issues* report, the label's HyperlinkSubaddress property would be set to *Report Issues*. When you click the hyperlink, the report opens in Print Preview, just as if you'd used the *OpenReport* method to open it.

- **Microsoft Office documents** A hyperlink can also open any Office document. In this type of hyperlink, the address is the path and filename of the document, such as c:\My Documents\Letter.doc. Using the hyperlink's subaddress, the link can move to a specific location in the file, such as a bookmark in a Word document.

- **Other HTML documents** Web browsers such as Internet Explorer display documents that are formatted using Hypertext Markup Language (HTML). An HTML document doesn't have to be on the Internet—it can be at an intranet address on your company's network or even sitting right there on your computer. For example, if you create your own Web pages using Microsoft FrontPage, you can feature them in your database using a hyperlink.

- **Other Internet addresses** While the addresses you've used with hyperlinks so far have all been for World Wide Web sites (they begin with http://), there are several other types of Internet addresses that Access recognizes. For example, you can set a hyperlink address to transfer a file from an FTP server or to send electronic mail. (These types of Internet addresses begin with ftp:// or mailto:)

As you can see, hyperlinks are extremely flexible. And because the hyperlink display text is independent of the address, users don't necessarily need to be aware of the differences between types. Only you need to know where the documents are located—on the user's computer, a company intranet, or the Internet. Users can just click them.

Create a Procedure That Follows a Hyperlink

To open, or *follow*, the hyperlink defined for a control, you use the *Follow* method of the Hyperlink object.

Database Window

1 Click the Database Window button on the toolbar.

2 Click the Modules shortcut, and then double-click the Miscellaneous module.

Visual Basic displays the module in a Code window.

3 Scroll to the end of the module, and then click in the Code window underneath the final *End Sub* statement.

4 Enter the following code (except the *End Function* statement, which Visual Basic automatically enters for you when you enter the function header).

```
Public Function OpenHelpSite()
' Follow the hyperlink in the HelpLinkLabel control.

    On Error Resume Next
    Forms!Issues!HelpLinkLabel.Hyperlink.Follow
End Function
```

The first line of code in the *OpenHelpSite* function uses the *On Error* statement to tell Visual Basic to suspend error handling. This is important because if there's a problem connecting with the Internet, your system (or Internet Explorer) will display an error message automatically, and you don't want your program to stop running and display an error.

The second line of code specifies a control on the *Issues* form—the *HelpLinkLabel* control—using the expression *Forms!Issues!HyperlinkLabel*. To refer to the hyperlink that this control contains, rather than to the control itself, it uses the Hyperlink property. Finally, it uses the *Follow* method of the hyperlink. If you find it easier, you can read the line from right to left: it tells Access to follow the hyperlink defined in the *HelpLinkLabel* control on the *Issues* form. When a user clicks the Open Help Site menu command to run this line of code, it will have the same effect as clicking the hyperlink.

Create a Procedure That Follows a Hyperlink Stored in a Field

With a hyperlink stored in a field, you can't use the Hyperlink property. Instead, you use a more general method, the *FollowHyperlink* method, specifying the address that you want to jump to.

1 Enter the following code:

```
Public Function OpenRelatedSite()
' Follow the hyperlink stored in the WebSite field.
    Dim Address As String, Subaddress As String

    Address = HyperlinkPart(Forms!Issues!WebSite, acAddress)
    Subaddress = HyperlinkPart(Forms!Issues!WebSite, _
```

(continued)

continued

```
        acSubAddress)

    On Error Resume Next
    FollowHyperlink Address, Subaddress
End Function
```

Here's what this code does:

- The *OpenRelatedSite* function begins by defining two string variables, *Address* and *Subaddress*, to store the address information for a hyperlink.

- A hyperlink has several components: an address, a subaddress, and the text that's displayed for the hyperlink. The next two lines of code use a new function, the *HyperlinkPart* function, to extract the address and subaddress parts of the hyperlink and store them in the two string variables. The first argument for the *HyperlinkPart* function is the hyperlink value itself, in this case the value of the *WebSite* control on the *Issues* form. The second argument to the function is a constant that specifies which part of the hyperlink you want it to return.

- The next line suspends error handling so that your application won't stop running when there's a problem connecting with the Internet.

- The final line uses the *FollowHyperlink* method, specifying the string values you just put into the *Address* and *Subaddress* variables.

When a user clicks the menu item and runs this function, it will have the same effect as clicking the hyperlink in the WebSite text box.

2 On the Debug menu, click Compile Ch15 Issues.

Visual Basic makes sure your code is correct.

Try Out Your Code

The custom menu items are now ready to follow some hyperlinks.

View Microsoft
Access

1 Switch to Access.

2 Switch to the *Issues* form.

3 On the Tools menu, click Open Help Web Site.

Your code uses the *Follow* method for the *HelpLinkLabel* control which causes Access to open the Web site in Internet Explorer.

4 Close Internet Explorer and switch back to Access. (If a message appears asking whether you want to disconnect from the Internet, click No.)

5 On the Tools menu, click Open Related Web Site.

This time, your code gets the address information from the WebSite field and then uses the *FollowHyperlink* method to open the Web site.

6 Close Internet Explorer and switch back to Access. (If you use a dial-up Internet connection, you can disconnect from the Internet now if you like.)

Modifying Hyperlinks Using Visual Basic

When you store hyperlinks in a table, you'll not only want to jump to them, you'll want to work with them, changing the text they display and the address they jump to. The practice application contains a simple dialog box form, called *EditLink*, which is designed to allow users to modify the related Web site hyperlink stored with each record in the *Issues* form. In this section, you'll create the button and add code to open the dialog box and make it work.

You'll create this button
and its event procedure...

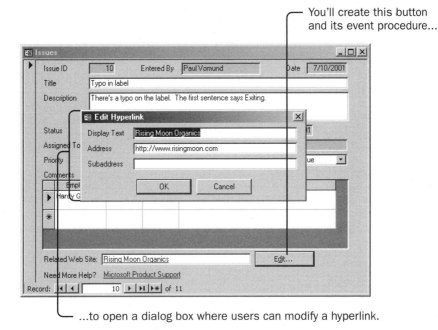

...to open a dialog box where users can modify a hyperlink.

Create a Button That Opens the *EditLink* Form

Your first step is to create a button on the *Issues* form that opens the dialog box. You'll place the button right next to the WebSite field you created so that users will know what it's for.

Design View

Toolbox

Control
Wizards

Command
Button

1 Click the Design View button on the toolbar.

2 Scroll down in the form to display the area below the Comments subform.

3 If the toolbox isn't displayed, click the Toolbox button on the toolbar.

4 In the toolbox, make sure the Control Wizards tool is deselected, and then click the Command Button tool.

5 Click in the form just to the right of the Related Web Site text box.

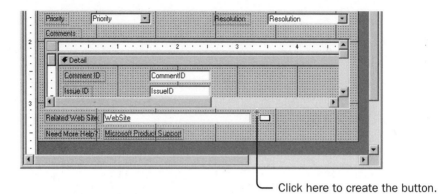

Click here to create the button.

The command button, with a default name such as Command25, appears next to the text box.

Properties

6 Click the Properties button on the toolbar.

7 Set the Name property to **EditHyperlink**.

8 Set the Caption property to **E&dit...**.

9 Close the property sheet.

10 With the right mouse button, click the EditHyperlink button, and then click Build Event.

11 Double-click Code Builder.

Visual Basic displays the *EditHyperlink_Click* event procedure.

12 Add the following code to the procedure (except the *Sub* and *End Sub* lines, which are already there).

```
Private Sub EditHyperlink_Click()
' Open the EditLink form.

    DoCmd.OpenForm "EditLink"

    ' If there is a hyperlink, copy its components
    ' to the text box controls on the form.
    If Len(WebSite) Then
        Forms!EditLink!DisplayText = _
            HyperlinkPart(WebSite, acDisplayText)
        Forms!EditLink!Address = _
            HyperlinkPart(WebSite, acAddress)
        Forms!EditLink!SubAddress = _
            HyperlinkPart(WebSite, acSubAddress)
    End If
End Sub
```

This code opens the *EditLink* form, using the *OpenForm* method of the *DoCmd* object. It then checks to see if the WebSite field for the current record on the form contains a hyperlink. If it does, you want to copy the components of this hyperlink to the dialog box so that users can work with them.

13 On the Debug menu, click Compile Ch15 Issues.

Add Code to Change the Hyperlink

Next it's about time you take a look at the dialog box form we've been talking about. Before you try it out, however, you need to open the form in Design view and add an event procedure—the one that actually modifies the hyperlink stored in the WebSite field.

View Microsoft Access

1 Switch to Access.

2 Close the Issues form, saving changes if you're prompted to do so.

3 In the Database window, click the Forms shortcut.

4 Click the *EditLink* form, and then click the Design button.

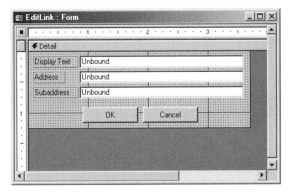

The form has three text boxes where users enter the information for a hyperlink, as well as two command buttons. The Cancel button already contains code that closes the dialog box without doing anything; you'll add code for the OK button.

5 With the right mouse button, click the OK button, and then click Build Event.

6 Double-click Code Builder.

Visual Basic displays the *OK_Click* event procedure. Add the following code to the procedure:

```
Private Sub OK_Click()
' Set the WebSite field on the Issues form.

    Forms!Issues!WebSite = DisplayText & "#" & _
        Address & "#" & Subaddress

    Forms!Issues!WebSite.SetFocus
    DoCmd.Close

End Sub
```

Here's what the code does:

- The first line sets the WebSite field on the *Issues* form. To create the new value, it concatenates the values the user enters in the three text boxes on the form, including the pound sign (#) character between each of the values.

- The next line uses the *SetFocus* method to move back to the WebSite field on the form.

- The final line in the procedure closes the dialog box using the *Close* method of the *DoCmd* object.

7 On the Debug menu, click Compile Ch15 Issues.

8 Close Visual Basic.

9 Close the *EditLink* form, clicking Yes when Access asks if you want to save changes you've made.

Try Out the *EditLink* Form

Let's try out the code you've written by changing one of the hyperlinks stored in the *Issues* form.

1 In the Database window, double-click the *Issues* form.

The form returns to Form view. The first record, currently displayed in the form, has a hyperlink to the Microsoft Press Web site stored with it. Suppose you want to change the hyperlink to a different site.

2 Click the Edit button next to the Related Web Site field.

The *EditHyperlink_Click* event procedure runs, opening the *EditLink* form and filling in the text boxes with the components of the existing hyperlink.

3 Select the existing text in the Display Text box, and then type **The Tax Man**.

4 Select the existing text in the Address box, and then type **http://www.irs.gov/**.

5 Click OK.

The *OK_Click* event procedure runs, setting the hyperlink value in the WebSite field. Back on the *Issues* form, you can see that the hyperlink in the field has changed. (If you like, you can click the hyperlink to try it out, but be sure to close Internet Explorer and return to Access when you're finished browsing.)

6 Close the *Issues* form.

Tip

In this section, you modified a hyperlink stored in a field. Modifying a hyperlink control—such as the Microsoft Product Support label you created earlier in the chapter—is even easier. To modify the hyperlink defined for a control, all you need to do is set the control's properties, and the hyperlink automatically changes. For example, you could change the hyperlink label on the Issues form with the following code.

```
HelpLinkLabel.Caption = "Computer Books Galore"
HelpLinkLabel.HyperlinkAddress = _
   "http://mspress.microsoft.com/"
```

Creating Web Pages for Your Application

So far, you've seen how hyperlinks can put Internet Explorer to work in conjunction with your applications. But what if you want to allow Web users to view or edit data from your Access application? Access provides this capability through *data access pages*, Web pages that are separate from your Access database (.mdb) file but that allow Internet Explorer users to view and edit data in your tables. Like forms and reports, you design data access pages within Access, but you can use them to view and edit data either within Access or in Internet Explorer. And data access pages offer powerful features for grouping, reviewing, and analyzing data in your database, including the *Expand* and *Record Navigation* controls and the Office Spreadsheet, Chart, and PivotTable components.

Data access pages make data available
to Web users in Internet Explorer.

Special controls help users view and analyze data.

In this section, you'll create a data access page to display records from the Issues database. While customizing the page, you'll learn to use some of the tools that Access provides for designing data access pages. Then you'll open another data access page designed to change data in the database. Adding final touches to this page, you'll take a small step into the world of *Web scripting*, using Visual Basic, Scripting Edition (VBScript)—a language similar to Visual Basic in Access, but one that runs in Internet Explorer.

Creating a Data Access Page to Review Data

The Issues application is working just great for users who are accustomed to Access. But nowadays, many users are more comfortable working on the company Web using Internet Explorer. You'd like to provide these users an easy way to view issues—without opening the Issues application at all. You have a spot picked out on the company intranet, now all you have to do is create your Web pages.

As a first step, you'll create a data access page based on an existing query in the Issues database. You'll let the Page Wizard do most of the work, and then you'll open the page in Design view, make formatting changes, and specify grouping. When finished, your page will display issues grouped by the employee they are assigned to, and will feature Expand and Record Navigation controls that make it easy for Web users to browse this information.

Create a Data Access Page for the Issues Application

One of the queries already in the database is the *IssuesForReport* query. Although it is used by the *Issues* report, it just happens to include the fields you want on your Web page.

1 In the Database window, click the Pages shortcut, and then double-click Create A Data Access Page By Using Wizard.

Access displays the Page Wizard.

2 In the Tables/Queries box, click Query: IssuesForReport.

The wizard displays the fields in the query.

3 Click the second button between the Fields boxes (the one that shows >> symbols) to select all fields.

4 Click Finish.

Access creates the HTML code for your new Web page and adds all the objects necessary to display data from the Issues database.

Page View

[icon]

5 Click the Page View button on the toolbar.

In Page view, the page appears as it will in a browser, displaying the first record from the *IssuesForReport* query. The wizard included a navigation bar control at the bottom of the page, which provides buttons you can click to move between records and to filter or sort data.

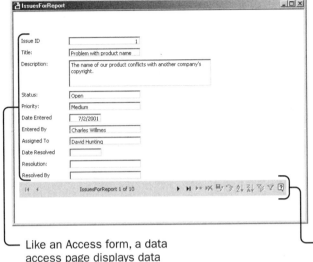

Like an Access form, a data access page displays data from fields in the database...

...and provides tools to navigate, sort, or filter records.

Although the data access page looks a lot like an Access form, there are many differences: controls on the page work somewhat differently, the tools for designing pages are not quite as advanced as those for forms and reports, and unfortunately, you can't use any of the wizards, expressions, or Visual Basic programming tools you've become accustomed to. It's a whole new world!

Format Your Data Access Page

The wizard created your data access page with a default name, a default title, and with no text explaining the purpose of the Web page. It's time to visit Design view and make some changes.

Design View

1 Click the Design View button on the toolbar.

Like the Design view of forms and reports, the Design view of data access pages has a toolbox, a field list, and a property sheet. Because most Web pages have some sort of title text and explanatory body text, data access pages include placeholders for text at the top. To make the data access page friendlier, you'll enter a message to users who find this Web page.

2 Click the title text placeholder at the top of the page (it says "Click here and type title text"), and then type **Issues Web Page**.

3 Click just below your title (above the gray bar), and then type **Click the Expand (+) button to view an employee's issues**.

Next you'll set a *theme* for your page—a set of design attributes such as background and font.

4   On the Format menu, click Theme.

5   Under Choose A Theme, click Bars, and then click OK.

Next you'll set the Title property of the page, which determines what title Internet Explorer will display for this Web page.

Properties

6   Click the Properties button.

7   Click the title bar of the Data Access Page window.

The property sheet displays properties of the page.

8   Click the All tab in the property sheet.

9   Scroll down to find the Title property, and set it to **Issues Web Page**.

10   Close the property sheet.

Save

11   Click the Save button on the toolbar.

Access displays the Save As Data Access Page dialog box. You'll save the Web page along with the other files in the practice files folder.

12   Locate the practice files folder on your hard disk.

13   In the File Name box, type **Issues** and then click Save.

14   If Access displays a warning message about the connection string for your page, click OK. (The message reminds you to specify a network path for the page's connection string before publishing the page to a Web server.)

Access saves Issues.htm on your hard disk, storing a connection to the Issues database in the HTML source code. It also creates several supporting files that are referred to in the HTML code—they define formatting and other elements—and puts them in a new folder called Issues_files.

Important

If you want to make your data access pages available to other users on the Internet or an intranet, you'll need to move the Access database (.mdb) file to a network server and save your pages (and their supporting files) to a Web folder rather than your computer's hard disk. When you do move an existing database or data access page to a Web server, be sure to reopen the database and page in Access—if the references between database and page are incorrect, Access will attempt to repair them, asking you to locate files as necessary.

Group Data in the Issues Web Page

One of the advantages of using data access pages is how easy it is to group data in them. In fact, when you tell Access that you want to *promote* a field to its own grouping level, it automatically adds an Expand control so that users can expand or collapse the records in a group. And the Sorting And Grouping dialog box lets you define exactly how you want your groupings to appear. In the Issues Web page, you'll group data by the AssignedTo field.

1   Scroll down in the Data Access Page window to display the AssignedTo text box.

2   With the right mouse button, click the AssignedTo box, and then click Promote on the shortcut menu.

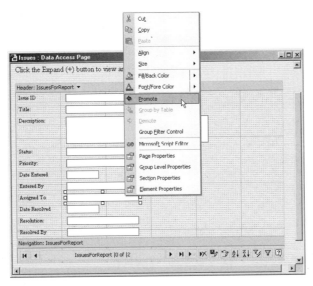

Access creates a group header section above the default section, moves the AssignedTo text box up to the new section, and adds an *Expand* control at the left side of the section. It also creates a new navigation section at the bottom of the form. While the original navigation bar lets users move among issue records, the navigation bar in this new section allows users to move from one employee's issues to the next.

If you anticipate that the page might have many employees to list, you perhaps want this extra navigation bar. But since you know that the list won't be too long, you can simplify the page by getting rid of the group navigation bar and telling Access you want to display all AssignedTo groups when the page opens. You make these changes by setting properties of the report's two group levels.

Group Level Properties **3** Right-click the Issues For Report-Assigned To header bar, and then click Group Level Properties.

You want to set properties for this group header section.

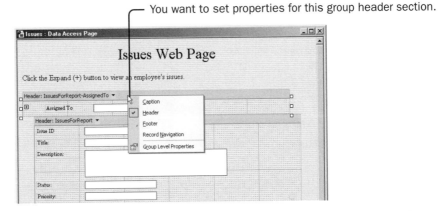

Access displays the property sheet.

4 Set the RecordNavigationSection property to *False*.

Setting this property to *False* causes Access to remove the navigation bar for this grouping level. There will still be a navigation bar for each employee's group of issues.

Next you'll set one property for the second grouping level—the section of the page that displays individual issues.

5 Right-click the Issues For Report header bar, and then click Group Level Properties.

Since each issue record is long, you won't want to display more than one record at a time. Instead, users will click buttons in the navigation bar to move among an employee's assigned issues. To display one record per group, you'll set the DataPageSize property to *1*.

6 Set the DataPageSize property to *1*.

7 Close the property sheet.

How Do Data Access Pages Work?

Web designers commonly want to provide access to data from a database on Web pages. Unfortunately, Web technology has not yet made this task easy to accomplish. Data access pages, while they lack many of the capabilities of Access forms and reports, take a step in this direction. But how do these special Web pages work? If data access pages are just ordinary HTML files, how do they connect to data?

If you open the HTML code in a data access page, you'll see several special HTML tags— <META> and <OBJECT> tags, for example—that Access adds to the page to bind it with your Access database and provide formatting and other capabilities. Like other Web "plug-ins," the objects referred to in these tags are special software libraries that need to be installed and registered with your Web browser and that the Web browser calls whenever it sees the tags. The primary object in a data access page is the Microsoft Office Data Source Control (MSODSC), which acts as the liaison between Internet Explorer and the underlying database engine.

Unfortunately, the objects that support data access pages require an Office 2000 or Office XP license and work only in Internet Explorer 5.0 or later—Web users who haven't installed one of these versions of Office won't be able to view data in your pages. For this reason, and because of their other limitations, data access pages may not be your best bet for putting data on a Web. For a summary of other ways to include Access data on a Web, see "More Ways to Use Access with a Web" later in this chapter.

Try Out the Grouped Page

Let's see how the Issues Web page is working.

Page View

1 Click the Page View button on the toolbar.

Access displays the page, which now shows employees that have issues assigned to them, each with an expand button that allows users to view issues.

2 Click the expand button to the left of Darren Demerais.

Access displays the first issue record assigned to this employee. As you can see in the navigation bar—which says *IssuesForReport 1 of 2*—Darren has two issues currently assigned to him.

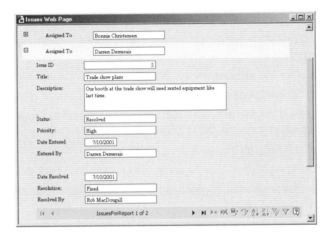

Add a Hyperlink That Links to Another Data Access Page

The Issues page will provide Web users a great way to review the group's issues. But suppose you want to allow Web users to change data—to reassign issues to other employees, for example. The practice files include a data access page already designed to allow users to reassign issues. The final change you'll make to the Issues page is to add a hyperlink that jumps from the Issues page to the Reassign page.

Database Window

1 Click the Database Window button on the toolbar.

2 Click the Pages shortcut, and then double-click the Reassign page.

Access locates the Reassign.htm file on your disk and opens the page in Page view.

Important

Since data access pages are actually stored in files separate from your database, Access needs to find these database files on your hard disk anytime you open a page. If you installed the practice files to a folder other than c:\Access VB Practice Files, Access asks if you want to locate Reassign.htm. Click Locate, find the practice files folder on your computer, and then click OK.

Now that you've verified that the page you want to link to is available, you'll return to the Issues page to insert your hyperlink.

3 Close the Reassign page.

4 Switch to the Issues page.

Design View

5 Click the Design View button on the toolbar.

You'll add the Hyperlink at the bottom of the Web page.

6 Scroll down to the end of the Data Access Page window.

Hyperlink

7 In the toolbox, click the Hyperlink tool.

8 Click at the end of the page (in the blank area underneath the Navigation Section) to create a new hyperlink.

Access displays the Insert Hyperlink dialog box.

9 Under Link To, click Page In This Database.

Access displays the two data access pages that are associated with the Issues database, along with their file paths in parentheses.

10 Under Select A Page In This Database, click Reassign.

11 In the Text To Display box, type **Reassign Issues**, and then click OK.

Access creates a hyperlink on the data access page. Later in the chapter, you'll try this link out in Internet Explorer.

12 Close the Issues data access page, clicking Yes when Access asks whether you want to save changes.

Adding Scripts to Data Access Pages

As you've seen, it's easy to create powerful data access pages—and the features you've tried so far don't even scratch the surface. Data access pages can include many types of controls, including images, option groups, and check boxes. In addition to grouping and navigating through records, you can provide rich data analysis tools using the Office Spreadsheet, Chart, and PivotTable components. And none of these features require any programming.

If you want to enhance your data access pages—for example, to provide special behavior in a data entry form—you can't use the type of Visual Basic code you've learned so far. Data access pages are designed to run in your Web browser, and Internet Explorer doesn't use the same language or event model as Access.

In this section, you'll get a small taste of programming (or *scripting*) for Web pages. You'll write a simple script to make the Reassign Issues data access page work—when users select an employee name in the drop-down list control, Internet Explorer will run your script, reassigning the currently displayed issue to another employee.

You'll write a script in the HTML code of this Web page...

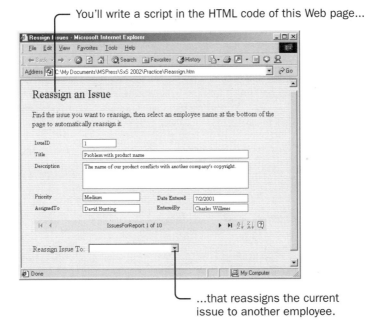

...that reassigns the current issue to another employee.

To become proficient at Web scripting, however, you'll need to read more on your own and get plenty of practice. If you do go on to learn about Web scripting, you'll find that many of the Visual Basic concepts you learned in this book will apply. That's because one of the languages you can use to write scripts is VBScript (another is JavaScript). The event and object models for Internet Explorer are quite different from those of Access, but they work in the same way. As you'll see, you can use ActiveX Data Objects (ADO) in nearly the same way you do in Access.

Add VBScript Code to the Reassign Data Access Page

The drop-down list box control you want to write a script for is called *NewAssignee*. In Internet Explorer, drop-down list boxes have an event called onchange that occurs whenever a user selects a new value in the list—that's the event your script will respond to. Your VBScript code will use a combination of the Internet Explorer object model and ADO, running an UPDATE query to change data in the *Issues* table.

1 In the Database window, click the Reassign page, and then click Design.

The Reassign page is mostly complete, except for the script you'll write. In order to write your script, you'll need to dive into the HTML code behind the Reassign page. Because HTML files are text files, you could open this file in any text editor. However, Office XP includes the Script Editor which, like Visual Basic, includes many additional tools that make it easier to write and debug scripts for Web pages.

2 With the right mouse button, click anywhere on the page, and then click Microsoft Script Editor on the shortcut menu.

The Script Editor opens and displays the HTML source file for the Reassign Web page. The Script Editor includes many familiar tools you've used in Visual Basic for Access, including a Project Explorer, Properties pane, and Toolbox, and some new ones, such as the Document Outline pane.

The Script Editor's code pane displays the HTML code for the Reassign data access page.

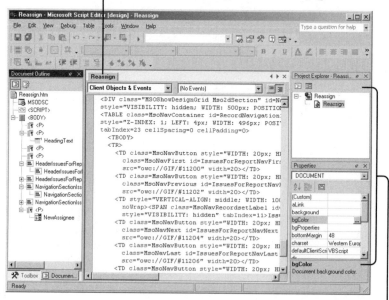

Like the Visual Basic Editor, the Script Editor has tools to help you write and debug scripts.

Don't worry if you don't know how to read or edit HTML; you won't have to create any tags or HTML code to complete these steps. Besides, the HTML for a data access page is complex, due to all the extra information Access adds to make all the special controls and objects work.

3 To make more room for editing, close the Project Explorer and Properties panes at the right side of the Script Editor window. (Click the "X" in the corner of each pane.)

The Script Editor knows all the events associated with each Web page object and can help you insert a blank script to respond to an event.

4 In the Object box at the top of the Reassign code pane (the one named Client Objects & Events), click NewAssignee.

5 In the Event box (the one that now shows "onafterupdate"), click the onchange event.

The Script Editor adds an HTML <SCRIPT> tag to the file, setting its attributes so that the script code you enter will run when the combo box value changes.

6 Type the following VBScript code:

```
' Run an update query that reassigns the current issue.
qry = "UPDATE Issues SET AssignedTo = " & NewAssignee.value
qry = qry & " WHERE IssueID = " & IssueID.value
MSODSC.Connection.Execute qry
MsgBox "Issue reassigned.", , "Reassign Issues Web Page"

' Requery the recordset and clear the drop-down list box.
MSODSC.DataPages(0).Requery
NewAssignee.value = Null
```

The HTML file should look something like this:

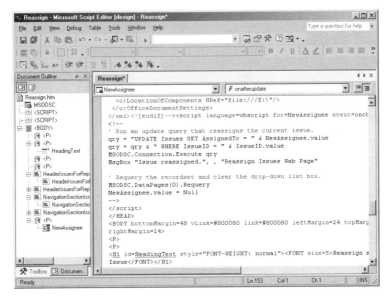

As you can see, VBScript for Internet Explorer is not that much different from Visual Basic for Access. Here's what the script code does:

■ The first two lines build a SQL query to update the *Issues* table. They store the query string in the *qry* variable. The first line combines the value stored in the NewAssignee box with the first half of the SQL statement. One difference you'll notice when using controls in scripts is that you must specify the value property in order to refer to the data in a control. (The value property is not required in Visual Basic because it is the default property.)

■ The second line adds the WHERE clause of the SQL statement, specifying the record you want to change. It refers to the IssueID text box on the page, which contains the ID number of the current issue being reassigned. After these two statements run, the *qry* variable will contain a string something like this:

```
UPDATE Issues SET AssignedTo = 3 WHERE IssueID = 1
```

- The third line runs the query to reassign the issue. The object it refers to is the *MSODSC* object, which you'll find in every data access page.

- Since this object is the liaison between Internet Explorer and Access data, you can use it to access the recordset being used on the page. In this code, you've just used the Connection property of the *MSODSC* object, which you will recognize from ADO programming; it returns the current connection this data access page is using.

- To actually run the query, the line uses the *Execute* method of the *Connection* object, specifying the *qry* variable as the query string to run. The line says, "Using the same connection that the data access page's *MSODSC* object is using, execute the action query stored in the *qry* variable."

- The fourth line displays a message box declaring that the reassignment is complete. Note that this line is exactly as it would be in Visual Basic code for Access—but this message will be displayed by Internet Explorer.

- The fifth line again uses the *MSODSC* object, this time referring to its *DataPages* collection. More specifically, it refers to element 0 of the collection, which in a page with one set of data is the only element in the collection. The line uses the *Requery* method of the *DataPage* object to requery the data in the page. The reason to do this is that the Web page doesn't automatically update to reflect the changed data—your code has to requery the data manually.

- The final line uses the Value property to clear the NewAssignee box by setting it to *Null*.

7 Close the Script Editor window, clicking Yes when the editor asks whether you want to save changes.

8 Close the Reassign page.

Test Your Pages in Internet Explorer

Your pages are ready to roll. Before you call it quits, however, you should test them in Internet Explorer—after all, that's the environment they're intended for. From the Database window, you can open a data access page directly in Internet Explorer using the Web Page Preview command.

1 With the right mouse button, click the Issues page, and then click Web Page Preview on the shortcut menu.

Internet Explorer displays the Issues Web page. You might notice a slight delay as the *MSODSC* object "binds" to the underlying Access data. If you like, you can expand an employee's group and browse issues.

2   At the bottom of the Web page, click Reassign Issues.

Your hyperlink opens the Reassign Issues page. Internet Explorer also loads the script you wrote, attaching it to the onchange event of the drop-down box.

3   In the Reassign Issue To drop-down box, click Rob McDougall.

Your script runs. It builds the query string based on the current issue and the new assignee you selected, runs the query using the page's database connection, and then displays the message box.

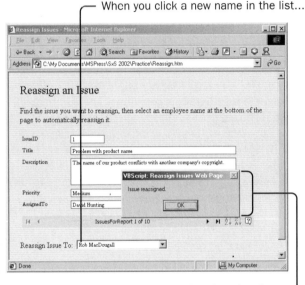

— When you click a new name in the list...

...Internet Explorer runs your script, changing data — in the Access database that the page is bound to.

4   Click OK.

Your code requeries the data in the page, so that Rob MacDougall now appears in the Assigned To field.

5   Close Internet Explorer.

While this introduction to Web scripting was brief, it may help you appreciate the relationship between Access programming and Web programming. Most of all, you now know that if your data access page doesn't do everything you hope, you have the option to write scripts to help it along.

More Ways to Use Access with a Web

In addition to hyperlinks and data access pages, Access includes many other Web-related features. We haven't covered these features in this book, either because they don't involve any Visual Basic programming, or because they aren't likely to apply to most Access applications. However, you may want to explore these features using online Help.

Getting data from a Web To incorporate data from the Internet or an intranet into your databases, you can import it from HTML or XML files into Access tables. Alternatively, you can create links to HTML tables or lists so that the most current Web data is always displayed in your application. To import or link data, use the Get External Data command (on the File menu). Then, in the Import Or Link Tables dialog box, select HTML Documents or XML Documents in the Files Of Type box.

Putting data onto a Web By making data from your databases available on a Web site instead of printing it, you can save a lot of paper! You can export your tables, queries, forms, or reports to a Web-ready format using the Export command (on the File menu). In the Export dialog box, select from four Web formats in the Save As Type box. The HTML Documents format, which works with any Web, saves a static table containing current data. The XML Documents format also saves static data, but in the increasingly popular XML format that other applications may be able to interpret. The Active Server Pages and Microsoft IIS 1-2 formats, which work with Web servers running Microsoft Internet Information Server (IIS), save a dynamic table that updates automatically when users open the page. Finally, if you are exporting a report, you can select Snapshot Format, which saves a picture of the report that users can view, browse, and print from within their Web browser using the Snapshot ActiveX control.

None of these features requires Visual Basic programming—they're all available through standard Access commands. If you want to perform these tasks in Visual Basic, however, use the *TransferDatabase* method of the *DoCmd* object. Additionally, if you export Access documents to HTML, XML, or Active Server Pages formats, you may want to use the Script Editor or FrontPage 2002 to modify them or add your own scripts.

Programming with ActiveX controls Office XP includes the Microsoft Web Browser ActiveX control. The Web Browser control can display HTML pages in your forms, allowing you to create a custom Web browser in your application. To use the control, insert it on a form using the ActiveX Control command (on the Insert menu), set its properties, and then write Visual Basic event procedures using its object model.

Using FrontPage with Access If you design Web pages using Microsoft FrontPage, you'll be happy to know it can help you connect to data in your Access databases. After you import a database into your FrontPage Web, you can use the Database Results Wizard to create pages that display data, or design Web forms that insert data into an Access database.

For more detailed information on these and other Web-related features, search for them in online Help.

What's Next

Congratulations—you've covered a great deal of ground concerning Microsoft Access and Microsoft Visual Basic in these chapters. Access application development is an enormous subject, and as you continue working with Access, you'll find many new frontiers to explore. Here are a few places where you may want to start.

Microsoft Office XP Developer This version of Office allows you to distribute your applications to users who don't have Office or Access—and it includes additional programming information about Office, Internet Explorer, Visual Basic, ActiveX Data Objects (ADO), and Data Access Objects (DAO).

Web resources The Microsoft Web site offers many additional resources for Office and Access, including late-breaking information, online documentation, sample applications, and software downloads. To visit the main Office Web site, click Office On The Web (Help menu). Or, for information on programming Access with Visual Basic, visit the MSDN Office Developer Center at

`http://msdn.microsoft.com/office/`

Your own applications Your database needs are different from anyone else's—for this reason, you'll probably learn more by creating your own Access applications than you'll ever pick up in a book. So jump right in! Just as you did in the first chapters of this book, start by automating tasks on forms in an existing database. After you're comfortable writing and debugging Visual Basic code, try creating a custom application of your own. Then as you discover complex tasks that you want to accomplish in your procedures, delve into new areas of the Access and ADO or DAO object models.

Index

Note: Italicized page references indicate figures, tables, or code listings.

Special Characters

E

error messages, custom, 132–36
  causing error for, 133–34, *134*
  determining error code number, 132–33, *133*
  displaying, 135–36, *136*
errors. *See also* **debugging; error handling**
  anticipating, 146
  causing, 133–34, *134*
  combo box, 136–41
  event procedure, 36
  Form and Design view, 105
  help on, 125
  messages (*see* error messages, custom)
  setting up run-time, 142–43, *143, 144*
  types of, 123–24
event procedures. *See* **general procedures**
  AfterUpdate (*see* AfterUpdate event procedures)
  changing report layout, 261–64, *263, 264*
  changing report printer settings, 271–72
  Click (*see Click* event procedures)
  combo box, 136–41
  command buttons and, 17
  comments, 36, *37*
  converting Access macros to, 17–18
  data entry (*see* data entry)
  debugging of (*see* debugging)
  Error, 132–36
  error handling, 141–47 (*see also* error handling event procedures)
  filtering, 53–55, *54*
  form, 38–40, *39, 40*
  general procedures, using in, 100–101
  incrementing report fields, 267–68
  keyboard, 75–78
  modules and, 89
  opening, 22–23, *23*
  Reset command to stop, 117
  setting report properties at run time, 259–61, *259, 261*
  as *Sub* procedures, 90
  synchronizing pop-up forms, 180–82, *181*
  viewing, 24–27, *25*
event properties, 39, *39*

events
  Click, 17
  command buttons and, 17
  data entry, 67–69, *68* (*see also* data entry)
  Error, 132
  filtering, 53–54, *54*
  form and control, 38–40, *39, 40*, 67–69, *68*
  keyboard, 75
  procedures (*see* event procedures)
  report, 258
Excel. (*See* Microsoft Excel)
exclamation point (!), 140, 159, 237
***Execute* method, 250, 316**
***Exit* event procedure, 69, 71–72, 71**
Expand control, 308–9
***Explicit* option, 92**
exporting data, 318
expressions
  general procedures and, 90
  Immediate Window and values of, 56–57, *56*
  using *Function* procedures in, 102–3
  watch, 119

F

F1 key, 41
fields
  checking for blank, 74–75
  data validation properties, 78–81, *79, 80*
  following hyperlinks in, 299–300
  hiding labels of report, 262
  for hyperlinks, 295–96, *295*
  incrementing report, 267–68
  names of, 79
  relationships between, 150–51, *151*
  setting values for, 72–74, *73, 74*, 121–22, *121, 122*
***FileDialog* object, 225**
files. *See* **databases**
Fill/Back Color button, 48
Filter By Form command, 52–53
  checking for, 55
  displaying message for, 54, *54*
Filter By Selection command, 52
Filter event, 53–54, *54*

filtering events, 53–54, *54*
filtering properties, 55–56
  for reports, 173
  setting, in Immediate Window, 57–58, *57, 58*
filtering records, 52–65
  checking conditions with *If...Then* statement, 54–55
  Click event procedure for, 169–73, *173, 174*
  controls in hidden dialog boxes, using, 167–68
  displaying messages for Filter By Form, 54, *54*
  with Filter By Form, 53, *53*
  filtering commands, 52
  filtering event procedures, 53–54, *54*
  filtering properties, 55–56
  opening dialog box for, 168–69
  option groups for, 58–65, *59, 60, 61, 63*
  for reports, 167–73
  viewing and setting properties with Immediate Window, 56–58, *56, 57, 58*
FilterOn property, 55–56, 57–58, *57, 58*, 173
Filter property, 55–56, 57–58, *57, 58*, 173, 181
***FilterType* argument, 54–55**
Find command, 46
***FindFirst* method, 160**
finding records, 45–52, *46*
  changing combo box appearance, 47–48
  creating combo box, 46–48, *46*
  modifying combo box list, 48–50, *49*
  synchronizing combo box, 50–52, *50, 51*
fixing linked tables, 221–26, *223*
focus, command button, 28–29, *28, 29, 30*
folders, Outlook, 285–88, *286, 288*
***FollowHyperlink* method, 299–300**
following hyperlinks, 297–300, *298*
***Follow* method, 299**
***For Each* statement, collections and, 239–41**
foreground color, 239–41

W

Watch window and watch expressions, 119
Web pages. *See* **data access pages**
Web programming, 291–319
  Access features, 318
  data access pages (*see* data access pages)
  hyperlinks (*see* hyperlinks)
  Internet and, 291
  resources for, 319
Web scripting, 306, 312–17
  data access pages and, 313–16, *314, 315*

testing, in Internet Explorer, 316–17, *317*
Windows shortcuts, 221
***With* statement, 281**
wizards
  application development and, 1, 2
  Combo Box Wizard, 2, 46–47, *46, 47*
  Command Button Wizard, 13–17
  Database Results Wizard, 318
  Database Splitter Wizard, 2, 221–22, *222*
  Database Wizard, 2–6 (*see also* Database Wizard)
  Form Wizard, 152, 176
  Import Text Wizard, 2, 8–9, *8, 9*
  installing, 60
  Label Wizard, 167
  List Box Wizard, 154–55, *154, 155*

  Option Group Wizard, 2, 59–61, *60*
wizards (*continued*)
  Package and Deploy Wizard, 227
  Page Wizard, 306–7, *307*
  Report Wizard, 10–13, *11, 12, 13*
  SQL and, 252–53
  Subform Wizard, 176
  Table Wizard, 150
  User-Level Security Wizard, 220
Word. *See* **Microsoft Word**
workgroup applications, 230

XYZ

XML documents, 318
***Year* function, 187**

About the Author

Evan Callahan owns Callahan Software Solutions, a database consulting firm specializing in Microsoft Access. He worked for Microsoft Corporation from 1989 to 1995, where he created documentation, online Help, and sample applications for Microsoft Access and Microsoft Visual Basic. He received a B.A. degree in philosophy and comparative literature from the University of Washington.

Evan was born and raised in Seattle, Washington, where he lives with his wife, Margaret, and daughters, Fiona and Grace. In his spare time, he enjoys sailing, making music, and being close to family and friends.

Evan's other books published by Microsoft Press include *Microsoft Access 2000, Visual Basic for Applications Fundamentals*, *The Power of Intranets*, and *Troubleshooting Your Web Page*.

Work smarter
as you experience
Office XP
inside out!

You know your way around the Office suite. Now dig into Microsoft Office XP applications and *really* put your PC to work! These supremely organized references pack hundreds of timesaving solutions, troubleshooting tips and tricks, and handy workarounds in concise, fast-answer format. All of this comprehensive information goes deep into the nooks and crannies of each Office application and accessory. Discover the best and fastest ways to perform everyday tasks, and challenge yourself to new levels of Office mastery with INSIDE OUT titles!

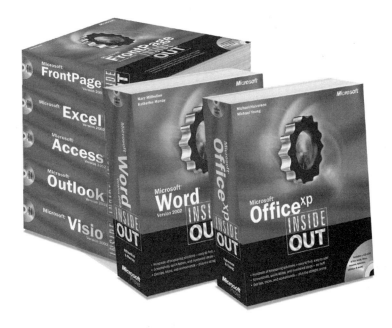

- MICROSOFT® OFFICE XP INSIDE OUT
- MICROSOFT WORD VERSION 2002 INSIDE OUT
- MICROSOFT EXCEL VERSION 2002 INSIDE OUT
- MICROSOFT OUTLOOK® VERSION 2002 INSIDE OUT
- MICROSOFT ACCESS VERSION 2002 INSIDE OUT
- MICROSOFT FRONTPAGE® VERSION 2002 INSIDE OUT
- MICROSOFT VISIO® VERSION 2002 INSIDE OUT

mspress.microsoft.com

Get developer-to-developer *insights* for building and customizing Office XP solutions!

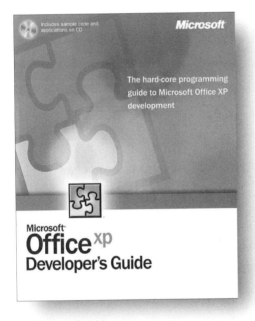

U.S.A. $49.99
Canada $72.99
ISBN: 0-7356-1242-0

Exploit the powerful programmability in Microsoft® Office XP with authoritative information straight from the Office XP development team. This hard-core programming reference comes packed with practical resources to help you maximize your productivity with Microsoft Office Developer. You get both design and coding examples that take advantage of the COM interfaces exposed by Office XP. Use this incisive coverage to build on what you know and to accomplish everything from automating simple tasks to creating complex vertical-market applications. And the companion CD-ROM contains procedure code you can use right now—helping you to focus your creativity on designing solutions, rather than on building rudimentary code. It's everything you need to create better business solutions, faster!

mspress.microsoft.com

Target your
solution *and fix it*
yourself—*fast!*

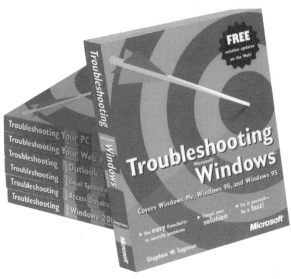

When you're stuck with a computer problem, you need answers right now. *Troubleshooting* books can help. They'll guide you to the source of the problem and show you how to solve it right away. Use easy diagnostic flowcharts to identify problems. Get ready solutions with clear, step-by-step instructions. Go to quick-access charts with *Top 20 Problems* and *Prevention Tips*. Find even more solutions with handy *Tips* and *Quick Fixes*. Walk through the remedy with plenty of screen shots to keep you on track. Find what you need fast with the extensive, easy-reference index. And keep trouble at bay with the Troubleshooting Web site—updated every month with new FREE problem-solving information. Get the answers you need to get back to business fast with *Troubleshooting* books.

Troubleshooting Microsoft® Access Databases
(Covers Access 97 and Access 2000)
ISBN 0-7356-1160-2
U.S.A.	$19.99
U.K.	£14.99
Canada	$28.99

Troubleshooting Microsoft Excel Spreadsheets
(Covers Excel 97 and Excel 2000)
ISBN 0-7356-1161-0
U.S.A.	$19.99
U.K.	£14.99
Canada	$28.99

Troubleshooting Microsoft® Outlook®
(Covers Microsoft Outlook 2000 and Outlook Express)
ISBN 0-7356-1162-9
U.S.A.	$19.99
U.K.	£14.99
Canada	$28.99

Troubleshooting Microsoft Windows®
(Covers Windows Me, Windows 98, and Windows 95)
ISBN 0-7356-1166-1
U.S.A.	$19.99
U.K.	£14.99
Canada	$28.99

Troubleshooting Microsoft Windows 2000 Professional
ISBN 0-7356-1165-3
U.S.A.	$19.99
U.K.	£14.99
Canada	$28.99

Troubleshooting Your Web Page
(Covers Microsoft FrontPage® 2000)
ISBN 0-7356-1164-5
U.S.A.	$19.99
U.K.	£14.99
Canada	$28.99

Troubleshooting Your PC
ISBN 0-7356-1163-7
U.S.A.	$19.99
U.K.	£14.99
Canada	$28.99

Microsoft Press® products are available worldwide wherever quality computer books are sold. For more information, contact your book or computer retailer, software reseller, or local Microsoft Sales Office, or visit our Web site at mspress.microsoft.com. To locate your nearest source for Microsoft Press products, or to order directly, call 1-800-MSPRESS in the U.S. (in Canada, call 1-800-268-2222).

Prices and availability dates are subject to change.

mspress.microsoft.com

Self-paced training that works as hard as you do!

Information-packed STEP BY STEP courses are the most effective way to teach yourself how to complete tasks with Microsoft® Office XP. Numbered steps and scenario-based lessons with practice files on CD-ROM make it easy to find your way while learning tasks and procedures. Work through every lesson or choose your own starting point—with STEP BY STEP modular design and straightforward writing style, *you* drive the instruction. And the books are constructed with lay-flat binding so you can follow the text with both hands at the keyboard. Select STEP BY STEP titles also provide complete, cost-effective preparation for the Microsoft Office User Specialist (MOUS) credential. It's an excellent way for you or your organization to take a giant step toward workplace productivity.

- **Microsoft Office XP Step by Step**
  ISBN 0-7356-1294-3

- **Microsoft Word Version 2002 Step by Step**
  ISBN 0-7356-1295-1

- **Microsoft Excel Version 2002 Step by Step**
  ISBN 0-7356-1296-X

- **Microsoft PowerPoint® Version 2002 Step by Step**
  ISBN 0-7356-1297-8

- **Microsoft Outlook® Version 2002 Step by Step**
  ISBN 0-7356-1298-6

- **Microsoft FrontPage® Version 2002 Step by Step**
  ISBN 0-7356-1300-1

- **Microsoft Access Version 2002 Step by Step**
  ISBN 0-7356-1299-4

- **Microsoft Project Version 2002 Step by Step**
  ISBN 0-7356-1301-X

- **Microsoft Visio® Version 2002 Step by Step**
  ISBN 0-7356-1302-8

Microsoft®

mspress.microsoft.com

Get a **Free**
e-mail newsletter, updates,
special offers, links to related books,
and more when you

register on line!

Register your Microsoft Press® title on our Web site and you'll get
a FREE subscription to our e-mail newsletter, *Microsoft Press
Book Connections.* You'll find out about newly released and upcoming
books and learning tools, online events, software downloads, special
offers and coupons for Microsoft Press customers, and information
about major Microsoft® product releases. You can also read useful
additional information about all the titles we publish, such as detailed book descriptions, tables of contents and indexes, sample
chapters, links to related books and book series, author biographies,
and reviews by other customers.

Registration is easy. Just visit this Web page and fill in your information:

http://www.microsoft.com/mspress/register

Microsoft®

Proof of Purchase

Use this page as proof of purchase if participating in a promotion or rebate offer on
this title. Proof of purchase must be used in conjunction with other proof(s) of
payment such as your dated sales receipt—see offer details.

Microsoft® Access 2002 Visual Basic® for Applications
Step by Step
0-7356-1358-3

CUSTOMER NAME

Microsoft Press, PO Box 97017, Redmond, WA 98073-9830

MICROSOFT LICENSE AGREEMENT
Book Companion CD

IMPORTANT—READ CAREFULLY: This Microsoft End-User License Agreement ("EULA") is a legal agreement between you (either an individual or an entity) and Microsoft Corporation for the Microsoft product identified above, which includes computer software and may include associated media, printed materials, and "online" or electronic documentation ("SOFTWARE PRODUCT"). Any component included within the SOFTWARE PRODUCT that is accompanied by a separate End-User License Agreement shall be governed by such agreement and not the terms set forth below. By installing, copying, or otherwise using the SOFTWARE PRODUCT, you agree to be bound by the terms of this EULA. If you do not agree to the terms of this EULA, you are not authorized to install, copy, or otherwise use the SOFTWARE PRODUCT; you may, however, return the SOFTWARE PRODUCT, along with all printed materials and other items that form a part of the Microsoft product that includes the SOFTWARE PRODUCT, to the place you obtained them for a full refund.

SOFTWARE PRODUCT LICENSE

The SOFTWARE PRODUCT is protected by United States copyright laws and international copyright treaties, as well as other intellectual property laws and treaties. The SOFTWARE PRODUCT is licensed, not sold.

1. **GRANT OF LICENSE.** This EULA grants you the following rights:

   a. **Software Product.** You may install and use one copy of the SOFTWARE PRODUCT on a single computer. The primary user of the computer on which the SOFTWARE PRODUCT is installed may make a second copy for his or her exclusive use on a portable computer.

   b. **Storage/Network Use.** You may also store or install a copy of the SOFTWARE PRODUCT on a storage device, such as a network server, used only to install or run the SOFTWARE PRODUCT on your other computers over an internal network; however, you must acquire and dedicate a license for each separate computer on which the SOFTWARE PRODUCT is installed or run from the storage device. A license for the SOFTWARE PRODUCT may not be shared or used concurrently on different computers.

   c. **License Pak.** If you have acquired this EULA in a Microsoft License Pak, you may make the number of additional copies of the computer software portion of the SOFTWARE PRODUCT authorized on the printed copy of this EULA, and you may use each copy in the manner specified above. You are also entitled to make a corresponding number of secondary copies for portable computer use as specified above.

   d. **Sample Code.** Solely with respect to portions, if any, of the SOFTWARE PRODUCT that are identified within the SOFTWARE PRODUCT as sample code (the "SAMPLE CODE"):

      i. **Use and Modification.** Microsoft grants you the right to use and modify the source code version of the SAMPLE CODE, *provided* you comply with subsection (d)(iii) below. You may not distribute the SAMPLE CODE, or any modified version of the SAMPLE CODE, in source code form.

      ii. **Redistributable Files.** Provided you comply with subsection (d)(iii) below, Microsoft grants you a nonexclusive, royalty-free right to reproduce and distribute the object code version of the SAMPLE CODE and of any modified SAMPLE CODE, other than SAMPLE CODE, or any modified version thereof, designated as not redistributable in the Readme file that forms a part of the SOFTWARE PRODUCT (the "Non-Redistributable Sample Code"). All SAMPLE CODE other than the Non-Redistributable Sample Code is collectively referred to as the "REDISTRIBUTABLES."

      iii. **Redistribution Requirements.** If you redistribute the REDISTRIBUTABLES, you agree to: (i) distribute the REDISTRIBUTABLES in object code form only in conjunction with and as a part of your software application product; (ii) not use Microsoft's name, logo, or trademarks to market your software application product; (iii) include a valid copyright notice on your software application product; (iv) indemnify, hold harmless, and defend Microsoft from and against any claims or lawsuits, including attorney's fees, that arise or result from the use or distribution of your software application product; and (v) not permit further distribution of the REDISTRIBUTABLES by your end user. Contact Microsoft for the applicable royalties due and other licensing terms for all other uses and/or distribution of the REDISTRIBUTABLES.

2. **DESCRIPTION OF OTHER RIGHTS AND LIMITATIONS.**

   - **Limitations on Reverse Engineering, Decompilation, and Disassembly.** You may not reverse engineer, decompile, or disassemble the SOFTWARE PRODUCT, except and only to the extent that such activity is expressly permitted by applicable law notwithstanding this limitation.

   - **Separation of Components.** The SOFTWARE PRODUCT is licensed as a single product. Its component parts may not be separated for use on more than one computer.

   - **Rental.** You may not rent, lease, or lend the SOFTWARE PRODUCT.

   - **Support Services.** Microsoft may, but is not obligated to, provide you with support services related to the SOFTWARE PRODUCT ("Support Services"). Use of Support Services is governed by the Microsoft policies and programs described in the user manual, in "online" documentation, and/or in other Microsoft-provided materials. Any supplemental software code provided to you as part of the Support Services shall be considered part of the SOFTWARE PRODUCT and subject to the terms and conditions of this EULA. With respect to technical information you provide to Microsoft as part of the Support Services, Microsoft may use such information for its business purposes, including for product support and development. Microsoft will not utilize such technical information in a form that personally identifies you.

- **Software Transfer.** You may permanently transfer all of your rights under this EULA, provided you retain no copies, you transfer all of the SOFTWARE PRODUCT (including all component parts, the media and printed materials, any upgrades, this EULA, and, if applicable, the Certificate of Authenticity), **and** the recipient agrees to the terms of this EULA.

- **Termination.** Without prejudice to any other rights, Microsoft may terminate this EULA if you fail to comply with the terms and conditions of this EULA. In such event, you must destroy all copies of the SOFTWARE PRODUCT and all of its component parts.

3. **COPYRIGHT.** All title and copyrights in and to the SOFTWARE PRODUCT (including but not limited to any images, photographs, animations, video, audio, music, text, SAMPLE CODE, REDISTRIBUTABLES, and "applets" incorporated into the SOFTWARE PRODUCT) and any copies of the SOFTWARE PRODUCT are owned by Microsoft or its suppliers. The SOFTWARE PRODUCT is protected by copyright laws and international treaty provisions. Therefore, you must treat the SOFTWARE PRODUCT like any other copyrighted material **except** that you may install the SOFTWARE PRODUCT on a single computer provided you keep the original solely for backup or archival purposes. You may not copy the printed materials accompanying the SOFTWARE PRODUCT.

4. **U.S. GOVERNMENT RESTRICTED RIGHTS.** The SOFTWARE PRODUCT and documentation are provided with RESTRICTED RIGHTS. Use, duplication, or disclosure by the Government is subject to restrictions as set forth in subparagraph (c)(1)(ii) of the Rights in Technical Data and Computer Software clause at DFARS 252.227-7013 or subparagraphs (c)(1) and (2) of the Commercial Computer Software—Restricted Rights at 48 CFR 52.227-19, as applicable. Manufacturer is Microsoft Corporation/One Microsoft Way/Redmond, WA 98052-6399.

5. **EXPORT RESTRICTIONS.** You agree that you will not export or re-export the SOFTWARE PRODUCT, any part thereof, or any process or service that is the direct product of the SOFTWARE PRODUCT (the foregoing collectively referred to as the "Restricted Components"), to any country, person, entity, or end user subject to U.S. export restrictions. You specifically agree not to export or re-export any of the Restricted Components (i) to any country to which the U.S. has embargoed or restricted the export of goods or services, which currently include, but are not necessarily limited to, Cuba, Iran, Iraq, Libya, North Korea, Sudan, and Syria, or to any national of any such country, wherever located, who intends to transmit or transport the Restricted Components back to such country; (ii) to any end user who you know or have reason to know will utilize the Restricted Components in the design, development, or production of nuclear, chemical, or biological weapons; or (iii) to any end user who has been prohibited from participating in U.S. export transactions by any federal agency of the U.S. government. You warrant and represent that neither the BXA nor any other U.S. federal agency has suspended, revoked, or denied your export privileges.

DISCLAIMER OF WARRANTY

NO WARRANTIES OR CONDITIONS. MICROSOFT EXPRESSLY DISCLAIMS ANY WARRANTY OR CONDITION FOR THE SOFTWARE PRODUCT. THE SOFTWARE PRODUCT AND ANY RELATED DOCUMENTATION ARE PROVIDED "AS IS" WITHOUT WARRANTY OR CONDITION OF ANY KIND, EITHER EXPRESS OR IMPLIED, INCLUDING, WITHOUT LIMITATION, THE IMPLIED WARRANTIES OF MERCHANTABILITY, FITNESS FOR A PARTICULAR PURPOSE, OR NONINFRINGEMENT. THE ENTIRE RISK ARISING OUT OF USE OR PERFORMANCE OF THE SOFTWARE PRODUCT REMAINS WITH YOU.

LIMITATION OF LIABILITY. TO THE MAXIMUM EXTENT PERMITTED BY APPLICABLE LAW, IN NO EVENT SHALL MICROSOFT OR ITS SUPPLIERS BE LIABLE FOR ANY SPECIAL, INCIDENTAL, INDIRECT, OR CONSEQUENTIAL DAMAGES WHATSOEVER (INCLUDING, WITHOUT LIMITATION, DAMAGES FOR LOSS OF BUSINESS PROFITS, BUSINESS INTERRUPTION, LOSS OF BUSINESS INFORMATION, OR ANY OTHER PECUNIARY LOSS) ARISING OUT OF THE USE OF OR INABILITY TO USE THE SOFTWARE PRODUCT OR THE PROVISION OF OR FAILURE TO PROVIDE SUPPORT SERVICES, EVEN IF MICROSOFT HAS BEEN ADVISED OF THE POSSIBILITY OF SUCH DAMAGES. IN ANY CASE, MICROSOFT'S ENTIRE LIABILITY UNDER ANY PROVISION OF THIS EULA SHALL BE LIMITED TO THE GREATER OF THE AMOUNT ACTUALLY PAID BY YOU FOR THE SOFTWARE PRODUCT OR US$5.00; PROVIDED, HOWEVER, IF YOU HAVE ENTERED INTO A MICROSOFT SUPPORT SERVICES AGREEMENT, MICROSOFT'S ENTIRE LIABILITY REGARDING SUPPORT SERVICES SHALL BE GOVERNED BY THE TERMS OF THAT AGREEMENT. BECAUSE SOME STATES AND JURISDICTIONS DO NOT ALLOW THE EXCLUSION OR LIMITATION OF LIABILITY, THE ABOVE LIMITATION MAY NOT APPLY TO YOU.

MISCELLANEOUS

This EULA is governed by the laws of the State of Washington USA, except and only to the extent that applicable law mandates governing law of a different jurisdiction.

Should you have any questions concerning this EULA, or if you desire to contact Microsoft for any reason, please contact the Microsoft subsidiary serving your country, or write: Microsoft Sales Information Center/One Microsoft Way/Redmond, WA 98052-6399.